Committing the Future to Memo

Committing the Future to Memory

HISTORY, EXPERIENCE, TRAUMA

Sarah Clift

FORDHAM UNIVERSITY PRESS *New York* 2014

THIS BOOK IS MADE POSSIBLE BY A COLLABORATIVE GRANT
FROM THE ANDREW W. MELLON FOUNDATION.

Library of Congress Cataloging-in-Publication Data

Clift, Sarah.
    Committing the future to memory : history,
experience, trauma / Sarah Clift. — First edition.
        pages cm
    Includes bibliographical references and index.
    ISBN 978-0-8232-5420-0 (cloth : alk. paper)
    ISBN 978-0-8232-5421-7 (pbk. : alk. paper)
    1. Historiography—Philosophy. 2. Civilization,
Modern—Philosophy. 3. Benjamin, Walter, 1892–
1940. 4. Arendt, Hannah, 1906–1975. 5. Hegel,
Georg Wilhelm Friedrich, 1770–1831. 6. Locke,
John, 1632–1704. 7. Blanchot, Maurice. I. Title.
D13.C5838 2014
907.2—dc23
                                        2013015192

Printed in the United States of America

16 15 14   5 4 3 2 1

First edition

CONTENTS

ACKNOWLEDGMENTS

I am very glad for the chance to express my gratitude to the many people who helped me in this work, without whom its completion would have remained an insurmountable problem (to use Maurice Blanchot's apt phrase). First and foremost, I would like to thank Ian Balfour, Howard Adelman, and Stephen Levine for their unwavering support, critical acuity, and seemingly endless patience. In addition to their support of this project in its earliest stages, they have offered me enduring models of intellectual generosity and rigor. A great many other colleagues and friends supported me in various ways, whether by reading portions of the work, suggesting resources, offering critiques, editing, catching mistakes, minding me, giving me a quiet room and uninterrupted time to work, nudging my thinking further, putting up with my intellectual obsessions, or offering much needed diversions. They include Mark Webber, Cathy Caruth, Michelle Cohen, Cory Stockwell, Rebecca Comay, Deborah Britzman, Scott Marratto, David Levine, Karen Valihora, Kir Kuiken, Ian Stewart, Dorota Glowacka, Alexandra Morrison, Doug Freake, Jonathan Bordo, Susan Dodd, Thomas Trezise, Rebecca Wittmann, Jean-Luc Nancy, John Zilkosky, Daniel Brandes, Aleida Assmann, Paul Antze, Gerald Butts, and Zsuzsa Baross. I would also like to extend my warmest thanks to the fantastic students in my upper-year seminar class on "The Concept of Memory in Late Modernity" at the University of King's College in Halifax. Their engagement with all things memorial over the past few years has been a huge inspiration for me and, above all, a powerful reminder of the point of it all.

Thanks are also due to the organizations and funding bodies that made possible my research and its dissemination: the Joseph Webber Memorial Scholarship, the Ontario–Baden-Württemberg exchange scholarship, the Freie Universität (Berlin) scholarship fund, the Ontario Graduate Scholarship fund, and the Social Sciences and Humanities Research Council of Canada. The University of King's College in Halifax provided a stimulating atmosphere within which I could bring this project to completion.

Finally, this book owes most of all to those who lived with it and saw the project through to the end with kindness, joy, and love—to Sherrill and Gerald Clift, Alison Clift, Uli vom Hagen, and above all to Tovah, who came along and changed everything.

Introduction

In the preface to the second edition of the *Science of Logic*, Hegel refers to "the peculiar restlessness and distraction of our modern consciousness."[1] Although the tone of this statement makes it sound like something to be avoided or at any rate minimized, a moment's reflection tells us that for Hegel, it is one of modernity's irreducible and most definitive components. Superficial though it may be, restlessness is nonetheless also the forerunner of negativity, what he calls elsewhere the "seriousness, the suffering, the patience and work of the negative."[2] Finally, for Hegel, this restlessness is the active dimension without which there would be no movement, no change, only stasis, and finally the sickness that leads to wholesale alienation and despair.

Despite the fact that the *Phenomenology of Spirit* famously and notoriously ends with a difficult scene of memory, Hegel could not have predicted the extent to which his notion of restlessness would become so concretely manifest in a world saturated with memory. But indeed, the political, ethical, and epistemological questions regarding how we remember have become some of the most important, and some of the most disquieted, questions of our time. The demonstrable rise of secular practices of historical memory attests to this disquiet, as do the proliferation of theoretical attempts to understand the significance of this phenomenon.[3]

As the diversity of the viewpoints presented in scholarship on memory attests, it is difficult to know exactly how to interpret this phenomenon—how to judge its social and cultural meanings, how to situate its explanation, or how to historicize its occurrence. But its presence is nonetheless palpable. As Jan Assmann—an Egyptologist by training whose work has led him to investigate the contemporary phenomenon of cultural memory—baldly states in the opening lines of *Das kulturelle Gedächtnis* (1992): "For some years now, we have been experiencing a virulence of memory."[4]

To describe memory in terms of virulence is, I think, a provocative gesture, suggesting as it does that memory operates under the sign of a condition whose power to reproduce itself lies in its ubiquity, its trajectory largely unknown, and reference to its origin circuitous and difficult. If memory has indeed long functioned as a synthesis or historical link between the past and the present, in our day it has also come to name a kind of reproductive dilemma and, by extension, a dilemma of representation. *Committing the Future to Memory* arises out of the conviction that there remains a great deal to be clarified regarding this virulence of historical memory, in its political and ethical dimensions, but also in relation to its media, to its social functions, and to the experiences of time that emerge out of it.

§

The general increase of the significance of historical memory in the public sphere suggests that there is widespread agreement, albeit perhaps a tacit one, on the limited social value of academic historical knowledge. While historical research and scholarship continue to provide important frameworks for the awareness of "what happens" in history and, to a lesser extent, while they also contribute to theoretical questions of historical methodology, they do not, for all that, provide the context for a greater understanding of the relation between the past and the present nor, for that matter, do they provide a clarification of what the implications of such an understanding might be.

The current engagement with memory suggests, then, not only that historical knowledge confronts its own limit in its inability to produce a subject who understands the past, but also that the rubric of historical memory is better suited to perform this role; it offers a more powerful and a more critical register in which to articulate the disasters that constitute the political "origins" of many contemporary collective and individual identities. This new importance of historical memory in the political sphere means that the ethos of "Never Forget" is neither tranquil recollection nor memorial celebration (as it is, for instance, in Hannah Arendt's assessment of ancient Greek memory) nor is it simply a recalling of the past, for the sake of poster-ity or national consolidation.[5] The knell that it sounds today is one of traumatic reminder, of warning, of threat: The injunction of "Never Forget" has become virtually indiscernible from the future-oriented promise of "Never Again." Memory has thus been given the task of creating a better future by virtue of past events that *must* remain passed—that is, located safely in the past.

Given that the deployment of memory is founded on the desire to ensure a better future and to ensure that atrocities will not be repeated, its efficacy as well as its conceptual coordinates only become legible in relation to that which weighs so heavily against its claim to bet-terment—that is, against the weight of the present to which it directs its attention and in association with which its social status has been secured. Nothing, in fact, seems more pressing than to invoke the succession of proper names—many of which have themselves already become history—in conjunction with this call for memory, of the "Never Again" of contemporary discourse. This list—"Sarajevo," "Bosnia," "Rwanda," . . . (Jean-Luc Nancy has spoken, elliptically, of the deadliness of the ellipsis in *Being Singular Plural*[6])—plagues the humanist discourse of memory, not as a call for an ever-renewed commitment to memory, but as pernicious testimony to its failure.

David Rieff has drawn attention to this failure in *Slaughterhouse: Bosnia and the Failure of the West*, situating it within a geographical and symbolic space (the "West") where memory has enjoyed a long cultural history and where it has recently attained renewed political and social importance. Rieff, in his grief and despair over the indif-ference of Western political figures and their publics toward the geno-cide of Bosnian Muslims, points to this prestige and indicts memory for its failure to have created the political will to act in Bosnia. His outrage is nowhere greater than when he comments on the abyssal disjunction between the imperative of public memory and the ethi-cal demand to intervene in the then-ongoing genocide. Bill Clinton's oratory at the inaugural opening of the US Holocaust Memorial in Washington receives the brunt of Rieff's outrage when, at the pre-cise moment when nothing was being done to prevent the genocide of Bosnian Muslims, Clinton forcefully aligned the "need to deploy memory" within the context of a future-oriented "Never Again." In Rieff's text, this public display of memorial piety is registered in a caustic mode—he calls it a "moral ballistic missile"—as the loss of an effective and responsible relation between the past and the present.[7]

The familiarity of this despair—and, we should note, its continuing force—notwithstanding, while Rieff calls into question the power of memory to ground the prevention of catastrophes, he does so by once again bringing memory into play in the form of "memoir," one of the most canonized of memory's forms. Caught between the object of its critique and the mode in which to elaborate this critique, the tension within the text bespeaks its own presupposition: The failure of memory is *not* due to our understanding of memory per se, but to its routinized and aestheticized instrumentalization; Rieff's suggestion, paradoxically enough, is that memory loses its political relevance as soon as it enters the realm of politics. For Rieff to call attention to this failure and to attempt, thereby, to close the gap between what we remember and what we do, he offers, precisely, more memory.

Pinpointing the problem of memory's political instrumentalization, however, has the regrettable consequence of leaving untouched the question of memory as such. At stake in the critique of memory that takes place on the pages of *Slaughterhouse*, then, is not only the loss of a vitalizing relation to the past; rather, it is also the index of a reentrenchment of the understanding as to how to overcome this loss. This understanding focuses on the suppositions that remembering recuperates the past, that the subject resists an indeterminate future through recourse to it and that the more memory we possess of the past, the better equipped we will be to confront the challenges that lie ahead.

The failure of memory to have secured this desired aim confronts us with an uncomfortable possibility—namely, that the widely held understanding of memory as that which binds the present to the past may, paradoxically enough, be complicit in making it irrelevant to the present. In other words, if the present suffers from an estrangement or alienation from the past, could it be *because* of the assumption that memory inaugurates a direct relation between them, and not in spite of it? Far from signaling a nightmarish scenario of a never-ending and empty "now" though, this crisis indicates the need for a more critical engagement with the notion that representations of the past serve to orient and stabilize the present. In particular, greater attention must be paid to the ways memory is conceptualized and a greater degree of complexity must be brought to bear on readings of the modern philosophical tradition out of which the current assumptions regarding memory could be said to have arisen.

My interrogation of historical memory began, then, with a series of questions: What if, contrary to the prevailing understanding of historical memory as what constitutes the ground of action in the present, the crisis in which our memories find themselves is not signaled by the loss of their ability to make sense of us and our own action in the present but rather, or also, in the investment that continues to be made in the presumption that such a project was ever possible in the first place? What if what is wrong with memory is that the more we continue to rely on the sense that historical memory generates a direct relation to the past—and as such, guarantees that political action will be grounded in that relation—the more we continue to shore up just the notion that may be implicated in the disasters to which memory is responding?

Committing the Future to Memory addresses these questions but it does so indirectly, by exploring a diversity of thinkers from various moments throughout the period of philosophical and literary modernity. Given how huge the differences are among the thinkers explored here—Hannah Arendt, Walter Benjamin, John Locke, Hegel, and Maurice Blanchot—what could possibly justify their shared company here? Though there is ultimately no justification that will succeed in concentrating them into a single shape, it is practically impossible to miss the call to remember in each of their works. As admittedly diverse as their expressions of that call are, they are all committed in one way or another to thinking about memory as the means by which the past comes to bear on the present, or emerges out of it. Furthermore, each of them suggests that this emergence involves articulation and representation, whether as history (Hegel), storytelling (Arendt and Benjamin), or testimony and retrospective self-accounting (Locke and Maurice Blanchot). In short, memory is a matter of language.

Obviously the emphatic role played by language is inseparable from the exigencies of communication and transmission lying at the heart of the memorial experience. In some sense, it will never be enough to remember; conventional ethics of memory take shape where remembrance is shared with others, where it is passed on so as to ensure it longevity, stability, and a capacity to orient future generations. The ethics of memory, lest we forget, is thus governed by a language that is capable of saying what it means more or less directly and that, as a consequence, can operate as a means of recuperating the past, of communicating knowledge or as a call to action.

In the course of my engagement with this group of writers, how-ever, another version of the linguistic register seemed to emerge that stopped short of saying what it has to say, that had no clear grasp on the past, that barely referred to anything beyond its own textual imagination, and that consequently undercut the clarity of its own position. So in these works, by now all fairly canonical, memory is at once laid out as a more or less direct imperative either for recupera-tion, enlightenment, orientation, or stability but at the same time, and at crucial junctures, that imperative is resisted, contested, and ulti-mately short-circuited.

Following where the texts meandered, tracing their indirections— all the while remaining mindful of where they more obviously lead— proved to be neither tangential nor beside the point. In fact, this mode of indirection seemed capable of posing challenges to a practice or ethics of memory at risk of becoming unquestioned or compulsive, akin to what Pierre Nora has dubbed "duty-memory."[8] To gauge those challenges, it will be a matter for us of exploring episodes pre-occupied with language in concrete ways, with reading and writing: as varied as Locke's report on a discoursing parrot and the illegible traces of writing on a tomb, a lugubrious account of a death-bed scene in Hegel's *Aesthetics* that demands of a scholar that he *read*, and the stammering undoing at the heart of Blanchot's attempt to account for his own literary past. Common to these dramatic events is the char-acter of a singular encounter or confrontation with the past as a kind of *instant de passage* or moment of discontinuity, moments at which those aspects of the past that resist incorporation into a self-under-standing come into stark relief. Resisting self-understanding, these aspects of the past are nonetheless still there; they remain as remnants that have yet *to be read*. I am wont to call these moments "textual events" insofar as they function as a kind of arrest or disjunction and, simultaneously, as an injunction to conceive of a dimension of futu-rity in excess of its straightforward temporal parameters. For at every turn, it is a question of considering how these discontinuous moments in the texts function in relation to the sense of progressive temporal-ity that otherwise governs memory, either explicitly in the text itself or indeed, in our own expectations or desires as readers.

The task of remembering in these works thus emerges as some-thing considerably other than that of simply "recuperating" the past. In particular, what my readings attempt to draw out is the sense that the future in these texts is not restricted to what "lies ahead" in the form of a calculated projection based on what knowledge is possessed of the past. As necessary and, in many cases, as deeply urgent as these calculations and predictions may be, I argue that the straightforward notion of the future—the one that lies ahead—is itself grounded in an immeasurable dimension of futurity *within* the representation of the past itself, one that both makes possible the future's prognostication but at the same time bears witness to other unforeseeable possibilities.

Representing the past thus becomes a complex double matter, both of reading the past and of writing it. The doubleness implicit to this reading-writing generates the sense in which any representation of the past necessarily presupposes a certain future, and in which therefore the very relation between the past and the present, precisely by being differentiated within this representation, conjures alternatives that would otherwise remain at best undetected and at worst foreclosed. The necessity of such a temporal relation points to the contingency of the representation it informs, and it also points to how this contingent representation gestures toward a necessary plurality of representations or interpretations.

What follows is no death knell for an outdated "ethics of memory," but it is a bid for vigilance in the difficult practices of reading and writing. If memory is something to be desired, if it is something toward which we feel a responsibility, we might find ourselves compelled perpetually to refuse the settling of accounts, to refuse the idolatry of the past, and to reconsider the interrelations among ethics, memory, and the specificities of individual acts of the past's interpretation, however allusive and non-normative the results may be. This is the risk of every act of reading history. As I hope the following chapters demonstrate, it might also be what is stake in opening up history to new possibilities.

CHAPTER ONE

Narrative Life Span, in the Wake

Benjamin and Arendt

The divine art is the story. In the beginning was the story. At the end we shall be privileged to view, and review, it—and that is what is named the day of judgment.

—Isak Dinesen

Jacques Derrida's lecture "Mnemosyne," written shortly after the death of Paul de Man and devoted both to his work and to the friendship they shared, opens with a statement that is as complex as it is succinct. Its tone is sorrowful, compounding the loss to which it testifies by indicating from the outset what the lecture will *lack*: "I," he writes, "have never known how to tell a story."[1]

His disquiet, Derrida goes on to explain in the lines that follow, is grounded in what is said to link storytelling to memory: "And since I love nothing better than remembering and Memory itself—Mnemosyne—I have always felt this inability as a sad infirmity. Why am I denied narration?" (*MdM* 3). Recalling Socrates's influential formulation of that relationship in the *Theaetetus*, that it is Mnemosyne or "Memory itself," *"tes tôn Mousôn metros*, the mother of all muses" who bestows the gift of narrative,[2] what Derrida has set in motion is, in fact, a renewed thinking of the complexity of both memory and narrative as well as of their relation to each other.

An apostrophe to an absent other, a lover scorned, withheld gifts, and memory sickness—it is not by ruse that Derrida's remarks are inflected with such erotic and melancholy accents. Indeed, far from obscuring the rigor of what is being claimed in those remarks, the precision of the formulation consists in rehearsing the union that would produce narration as its offspring. A self-professed "lover of Mnemosyne," Derrida begins by invoking echoes of a tryst, one restaged between Mnemosyne and the "I" of his own text. Though, unlike the ancient coupling that has—just barely—been invoked, its reflection, its echo and repetition in Derrida's text is an encounter that yields no gifts and bears no offspring.

Derrida's remarks attest to a blocked encounter: one that leaves no narration in its wake and so presumably permits no generation or transmission. Precisely the contrary, then, of how the West will so often have thought of memory and its origin, its offspring and its destiny. On the margins of this disjunction between memory and narration, however, one still senses an occasion for thought: "Why did I not receive this gift from Mnemosyne? From this complaint, and probably to protect myself from it, a suspicion continually steals into my thinking: Who can really tell a story? Is narrative possible? Who can claim to know what a narrative entails? Or, before that, the memory it lays claim to? What is memory?" (*MdM* 10).

In drawing attention to the long-established links between narration and memory and in underscoring the canonical figures according to which those linkages are normally understood—the figures of generation and procreation, of the lover-mother and her offspring—Derrida restages the inaugural moment of a tradition in which narrative, born of Mnemosyne, is given the task of preserving the past. But he restages that birth not in order to set a generative logic into motion but rather to expose the relation between memory and narration to thought, including even the most basic assurance that narrative memory guarantees continuity between generations. And this, too, is an act of restaging: It was Socrates who, on the verge of (his own) death, is reported to have said that he "was not good at inventing stories."[3]

At the risk of leveling down Derrida's complex gesture of invocation and citation, it might be possible to situate its questioning of narrative in relation to work done by Walter Benjamin and Hannah Arendt on narrative and memory. By asking the question of what is at stake when the relation between memory and narration is not simply given or assured, Derrida effectively inherits memory as a *dilemma*, a dilemma that had started to become especially pressing in Benjamin and Arendt's time. Both Benjamin's "The Storyteller" (1936) and Arendt's "The Concept of History" (published first in 1958 and again in *Between Past and Future: Eight Exercises in Political Thought* in 1961) recall the figure of Mnemosyne and, like Derrida, displace the operation of its traditional meaning as a force of unity between past and present. The motif functions as a kind of touchstone for their work, through which they are able to gauge the ruptures in memory itself—ruptures for which, according to Benjamin, Mnemosyne has become practically synonymous. The very name, he says, "takes the observer back to a parting of the ways in world history."[4]

Both Benjamin and Arendt undertake to examine aspects of the relation between memory and narrative and are both drawn into an encounter with the possibility of memory *without* narrative. In different ways, both thinkers are committed to the past and to thinking through this difficulty, not as a means by which to guarantee cultural generation through acts of commemorating the dead, but rather to mark out their absence, their invisibility, their lack of expression.

With Benjamin writing as Nazism was on the steady rise and Arendt writing in its long shadow, the violent shock of historical events intensified and accelerated what was already a precarious connection between past and present. On the one hand, neither Arendt nor Benjamin seemed to have had any doubts that historical discourse, determined in some measure by the legacy of nineteenth-century historicism, would prevail over all other forms of transmitting the past. Both were convinced, in this respect, of the need to submit historicism to a thoroughgoing critique, in particular by emphasizing the ways in which its own structures were complicit in the discontinuity between the past and the needs of the present. Critiques of its abstract notion of "humanity," of its own specific forms of selective memory and the violence of its ideas of progress and perfectibility, thus had to form the basis for a rethinking of historiography. And while Arendt's and Benjamin's essays both adopt the thematic of memory as the ground upon which to motivate certain aspects of this critique, it is not in order to set up a strict opposition between memory and history; rather it is to discern what remains legible of memory within modern historical discourse itself and, specifically, within its conception of time.

Arendt examines the potentially endless linear sequence of what Benjamin calls historicism's "homogeneous, empty time,"[5] seeking to establish the temporal conditions under which historicism as such could become possible. Historicism, she argues, is the apotheosis of a generalized temporal structure of modern historical discourse, one that became formalized in the chronological reforms of the eighteenth century. These reforms, wherein "the history of mankind reaches back into an infinite past . . . and stretches ahead into an infinite future," created the conditions within which mankind could achieve a "potential earthly immortality."[6] One of the most serious consequences of the formalization of this endless temporal sequence as "historical time"—and one of the potentially most violent—was how it inaugurated an alarming "lifelessness" at the heart of modernity's historical time, the endlessness of which bears no traces of human finitude.

Benjamin's well-known description of the Angel of History in the Ninth Thesis of the "Theses on the Philosophy of History" also addresses this continuous narrative of inexorable progress, transforming it into a nightmare of destruction and indecipherability: "Where we see a chain of events, he sees one catastrophe that keeps piling wreckage upon wreckage and hurls it in front of his feet. The angel would like to stay, awaken the dead, and make whole what has been smashed. But a storm is blowing from Paradise . . . this storm irresistibly propels him into the future to which his back is turned, while the pile of debris before him grows skyward. This storm is what we call progress" (TPH 257). The dangers of historicism are, for Benjamin, at their most legible in its notion of progress, the goal of which, while being assured as an ideal, is especially pernicious in that it is indefinitely, indeed infinitely, postponed. One of the strengths of this passage consists in the way it links "seeing [a continuous succession of events]" to language or more specifically to the only word explicitly registered as such, "progress." By drawing attention to the role played by language in determining what counts and becomes visible as history, his disastrous counterimage powerfully undermines the conception of language according to which words signify the "real"; this kind of language is turned into the very force of blindness itself. Moreover, it is also through this act of denaturalizing the word "progress" that Benjamin is able to register the need for another thinking of the language of history, one that can challenge historicism's notion of infinite progress and, perhaps, restore to history the potential of its own finitude.

Recent theoretical work in historiography has also responded to critiques of progress in ways that are relevant to Benjamin's and Arendt's critical interventions. Jacques Le Goff's *History and Memory* (1977), for instance, begins by soundly rejecting the notion of "a linear, continuous, irreversible progress" implicit to the dominant historiography of the nineteenth and early twentieth centuries: According to Le Goff, such a conception of history is "practically dead."[7] Along with many historians of his generation, Le Goff is concerned to undermine any residual power this notion of history may have, in part by problematizing the "category of the real" (*HM* 102) contained in the postulate that historical discourse represents the past "as it really happened." To that end, he attends to the complex textual operations involved in the historian's construction of a "real" historical event and in particular, to the irreducible groundedness of historical discourse in language.

If what is traditionally at issue for historiography is the epistemological status of "real" events and their transmission in historical discourse, the task of contemporary historiography is to develop criteria of truth that move beyond the naïve understanding that language is capable of representing a "real" past. As Le Goff asserts, "It is vain to believe in a past independent of the one constituted by the historian" (*HM* 102). Drawing out the implications of the contention that the historian does not have access to a "real" event but rather draws on the textual and social traces of memory in order to construct it, Le Goff cites with approval Barthes's notion of a "reality effect," that "in 'objective' history, the 'real' is never more than an unexpressed signified, sheltered behind the apparent omnipotence of the referent. This situation defines what could be called 'the reality effect.' . . . [H]istorical discourse does not follow the real, it only signifies it, ceaselessly repeating *it happened*, but that assertion can never be anything but the signified obverse of any historical narrative."[8]

The contention that the "real" event is an effect of discourse has, of course, a myriad of repercussions for the discipline of history, but one of them in particular has bearing on the critiques of Arendt and Benjamin: The notion that the "real" is a discursive effect allows Le Goff to bracket the claim of language's strict referentiality and to focus instead on how historical narratives—and indeed, all narratives—have internal structures and logics, ones for which close analysis provides a means of understanding how the time of historical narrative does not simply represent or mirror "real time" but is, in fact, a product of the text's narrative structure.[9] As such, the call Le Goff makes for a precise study of the temporal modalities operative both in the documents used by historians and in historical narrative itself can be understood as a means both to counteract the sense of an overarching and endless temporal process and to open up the notion of "historical time" to new understandings.[10]

In this regard, one cannot fail to mention Paul Ricoeur, who has also analyzed the temporal parameters of both literary and historical narratives and has drawn important links between narrative and human finitude on the basis of their shared temporality. In *Time and Narrative*, he writes that "time becomes human time to the extent that it is organized after the manner of a narrative; narrative, in turn, is meaningful to the extent that it portrays the features of temporal experience."[11]

The ways in which Arendt and Benjamin advance the notion of narrative memory as orientation for a theorization of history has relevance for the turn being made within contemporary historiography to the question of narrative time, especially for the possibility that narrative time be configured as a site or expression of finitude. Insofar as both thinkers articulate the structure of memory in terms of the affinities it shares with the structure of human life span, they also conceive of memory to be an expression, first and foremost, of the *time* of human finitude. As such, theorizing narrative memory in terms of "life span" will have implications both for an understanding of memory as well as for its temporal modality, beyond the strictly linear time of modern historical discourse.

MEMORIES OF LIFE SPAN

Were one to raise objections to the general framework within which memory is being conceived here—namely, as a relation to the past or as a form of anteriority at odds with the "historical time" of succession (past-present-future)—one might do so on the grounds that in fact, the historical record belongs among the most magisterial of memory's expressions. After all, does history not show itself to be a kind of memory when it rescues things from time and secures for them, as well as for the time of their unfolding, a more lasting resting place in its own discourse?

This objection is a good one and so deserves serious consideration. In "The Concept of History," Hannah Arendt argues to the effect that, at its inception in ancient Greece, historical narrative was unthinkable outside of the general rubric of memory, for which the task of immortalizing human action involved narrating historical events in accordance with the structure and the temporality specific to the life span of the individual human, or *bios*. By tracing the development of the concept of history from the Greeks up to that of the moderns, Arendt shows how, as historical narrative continued to be understood as the means for securing human immortality under the radically changed conditions of modernity, its chronicle of the events of human political life became gradually less and less tethered to the kind of temporality specific to human life.

The account Arendt provides of this gradual unmooring of historical discourse from the time of human lives serves as a basis upon which she can gauge the relevance of modern history for human memory and for the finitude to which memory was originally called upon to attest. As well, her formulation of the rift between human experience and modern history, both in the development of the essay's arguments as well as in its less clearly articulated aspects, will provide clues to an as-yet-unassimilated aspect of modernity's time.

§

For the Greeks, history consisted of preserving great political action, action deserving of remembrance. Invoking Herodotus, Arendt's claim is that history's aim was "to preserve that which owes its existence to men, lest it be obliterated by time, and to bestow upon the glorious, wondrous deeds of Greeks and barbarians sufficient praise to assure their remembrance by posterity and thus make their glory shine through the centuries" (BPF 41). By virtue of its capacity to safeguard that which is at risk of perishing, the writing of history for the Greeks was a form of memorial preservation: "the human capacity to achieve this was remembrance, Mnemosyne, who therefore was regarded as the mother of all the muses" (BPF 43).

Arendt argues that the key to understanding the importance of memory for the Greeks lies in their notion of human mortality: "Since the things of nature are ever-present," she writes, "they are not likely to be overlooked or forgotten; and since they are forever, they do not need human remembrance for their further existence" (BPF 42). Unlike this "ever-recurring life" of nature but also unlike "the deathless and ageless lives" of the gods, humans require memory because they are the "only mortal things there are" (BPF 42); that is to say, beyond being members of a species, they also exist as individuals. According to the Greek conception, it is only as individuals that humans can, strictly speaking, be said to be born, to live and to die.

Against the backdrop of this temporal passing, by virtue of which all human action was continuously subject to the threat of oblivion, memory was conceived as a means by which human mortality and the transient nature of human actions and deeds could be mitigated. As such, the Greek notion of memory was what enabled men to overcome their perishable nature and to foster truly divine aspirations: "By their capacity for the immortal deed, by their ability to leave nonperishable traces behind, men, their individual mortality notwithstanding, attain an immortality of their own and prove themselves to be of a 'divine' nature" (*Human Condition*, 19). The distinction between the mortality of men and the immortality of nature and the gods was the tacit assumption of these memorial practices. The passage of an action or deed from the transient, mortal world of men to the realm of immortality depended upon what Arendt describes as a kind of "translating" (*BPF* 45) into the written word: a recasting of human action and deed—that, on their own, "would never outlast the moment of their realization"—into a medium that could grant them longer life: This was the task uniting poet and historian (45).[12]

The line of inquiry that Arendt pursues in these discussions of mortality and immortality serves to emphasize what was generally at stake in ancient Greek memorial practices and what the underlying assumptions of those practices were. Memory, expressed as history or poetry, served as a bridge of sorts, between the transient, temporal realm of humans to the realm, both divine and natural, of "everlastingness."[13] The seeming irreconcilability of these two realms notwithstanding, to what do great actions of men owe their "translatability" or in other words, what characterizes mortality such that it can be "translated" into a kind of immortality? Probing this question, Arendt writes: "The mortality of man lies in the fact that individual life, a *bios* with a *recognizable life story from birth to death*, rises out of biological life, *zoe*. This individual life is distinguished from all other things by the *rectilinear course of its movement*, which, so to speak, cuts through the circular movements of biological life. This is mortality: to move along a *rectilinear line* in a universe where everything, if it moves at all, moves in a cyclical order" (*BPF* 42, emphasis added).

According to this description, the formal structure of *bios* corresponds to that of narrative; mortal life is not only life that is born, lives, and then passes away but is also one whose very life span provides the key to narrative immortalization. The strong affinities that the "form of life" or *bios* bears to a life story or plot show how difficult it is, at a certain level, to discern life story from life: At some level, the *bios* of individual life is always already *biography*.[14]

The most readily discernable temporal aspect of this movement is what Arendt, in the preface to *Between Past and Future*, refers to as "historical or biographical time" and describes as a "unidirectional flow of time. . . . [T]he traditional image according to which we think of time as moving in a straight line [is] a rectilinear temporal movement" (*BPF* 11–13). The linear chronology implied by an unfolding or sequence is, though, secondary in importance to what she calls in *The Human Condition*, "birth and death, natality and mortality."[15] This "general condition of human existence," she argues, provides the structure according to which a successive series of events or episodes is circumscribed and turned into something meaningful. In other words, the work of memory is said to immortalize the actions and deeds of humans as it gives expression to their emergence and their completion—actions, in other words, are inscribed within a structure bound to and by the facts of human birth and death.

Arendt's description of the structure of finitude bears strong resemblances to the theory of narrative structure advanced by Aristotle in the *Poetics*, in particular to the requirement that a narrative is complete only "if it has a beginning, a middle, and an end."[16] Notably, Ricoeur has taken up this requirement in *Time and Narrative* as "the pivot" of Aristotle's formulation, one that warrants consideration in terms of the temporality implicit to plot structure. While Aristotle himself did not articulate poetic structure in terms of its temporality—for Aristotle, poetry could only teach the universal on the condition that poetry itself maintain an "achronicity" (*TN* 170)—Ricoeur draws on the Aristotelian notion of "wholeness" to argue that "the act of emplotment combines in variable proportions two temporal dimensions, one chronological and the other not. The former constitutes the episodic dimension of narrative. It characterizes the story insofar as it is made up of events. The second is the configurational dimension properly speaking, thanks to which the plot transforms the events into a story. This configurational act consists of 'grasping together' the detailed actions. . . . It draws from this manifold of events the unity of one temporal whole" (*TN* 66).

Ricoeur conceives of the temporality of plot structure as a unified "double-time": on the one hand, the linear succession of events that is, for Aristotle, the domain of the plot's "middle" (*P* 50b31) and, on the other hand, the logical limits of the beginning and the end in accordance with which the contingent episodes become meaningful as part of a temporal whole. According to Ricoeur, the unexpected, the surprising, and the perplexing are what "the plot tends to make necessary and probable. And in so doing, it purifies them, or, better, purges them" (*TN* 44).

While no mention of Arendt is made in the context of Ricoeur's discussion,[17] her innovation is to have placed this narrative logic in relation to human finitude and to have discerned the paradoxical source of narrative's immortalizing power in the structure of *bios*. Moreover, the connection she makes between narrative structure and the finite structure of individual life becomes the basis upon which to draw out the importance of singularity in Greek history, for which historical events "are not seen as parts of either an encompassing whole or a process; on the contrary, the stress is always on single instances and single gestures" (*BPF* 43).

It might be useful, at this point, to clarify a possible difficulty: Although it can certainly be argued that Arendt's formulation—that the Greeks committed human action to the memorial structure of individual life span—reflects a broad humanist commitment and that hers is an attempt to "humanize" political action on the basis of the individual, her intention is certainly not to focus on how "great men" become immortal on the basis of an individualistic conception of personal biography. Rather, the task of her argument here is to show how Greek political action retains its singularity in historical discourse by virtue of being narrated *like* a human life. As she argues in *The Human Condition*, in contrast to an individualistic conception of politics, the basis of action—and all action was political, took place in the polis—was the human condition of plurality: "that men, not Man, live on the earth and inhabit the world" (*HC* 9). Moreover, for the Greeks, it simply would have been inconceivable that anyone outside of the polis—or, what amounts to the same thing, anyone not in possession of the potential to act that the "being-with" and the plurality of the polis enabled—could be conceived as a human (23ff.). So, rather than celebrating the individual as the agent of political action, her discussion of the relation between the structure of the individual human life and that of immortalizing narrative aims to demonstrate that the emphasis placed on singular instances in Greek historical discourse is due to its narrative structure, conceived in terms of natality and mortality.[18]

On that basis, Arendt insists on the following points: first, that history and poetry were given the task of inscribing politics into memory; second, that it is through the "acting in concert" of politics that humans were able to obviate their own individual mortality; and third, that insofar as political action and human life were thought to be inseparable, the memorial inscription of politics came to be emblematic of humanness as such.[19] This means that, for the Greeks, memory rids human life of its propensity simply to pass away by taking up its most memorable political actions and, within the structure of historical or poetic discourse, granting to those actions their singular and unique importance by narrating them in accordance with a specifically human form of temporality.

As Arendt is establishing remembrance as an expression of finitude, we are drawn to the sense of how profoundly, and how painfully, remembrance is linked to mourning and to expressions of grief. Her discussion pays homage to the mournful countenance of memory when she alludes to the strange and pitiful instance of Ulysses crying as he listens to the account of his own history. The passage bears quoting at some length:

> Not historically but poetically speaking, [history's] beginning lies in the moment when Ulysses . . . listened to the story of his own deeds and sufferings, to the story of his life, now a thing outside himself, an "object" for all to see and to hear. What had been sheer occurrence now became "history." The scene . . . is paradigmatic for both history and poetry; this "reconciliation with reality," the catharsis, which, according to Aristotle, was the essence of tragedy, and, according to Hegel, was the ultimate purpose of history, came about through the tears of remembrance. The deepest human motive for history and poetry appears here in unparalleled purity: since listener, actor, and sufferer are the same person, all motives of sheer curiosity and lust for new information, which, of course, have always played a large role in both historical inquiry and aesthetic pleasure, are naturally absent in Ulysses himself, who would have been bored rather than moved if history were only news and poetry only entertainment. (45)

By bringing the focus to bear on how "sheer occurrences" are turned into a unified and transmissible unity by virtue of their being narrated, Arendt reads Ulysses's emotion as the outward sign of an inward redemption. His tears are a sign of release from finitude's discord.

While the emotion is explained in terms of memory's unifying power, Arendt's description of the scene seems to insist upon a more alienating experience: "A thing outside himself," she calls it, "an 'object' for all to see and to hear." While it may indeed be true that the narration of Ulysses's life mitigates or tempers his finitude, at another level, Ulysses's tears also draw attention to the power of memory to arouse a deep and irremediable sense of finitude. We could perhaps say that Ulysses is at his most deeply divided precisely when he becomes the spectator—and the specter—to his own memorial account.

Something of a poetic reversal, in fact, is being put into play here, on a par with the scene's own extended reverse-simile in which his tears are compared to those of a widow weeping over the body of her dead husband: More woman than man, it is by virtue of the peculiar power of language that Ulysses is also more dead than alive. The poetic genius of having Ulysses weep as he hears his life narrated as history lies in how those tears almost inaudibly attest to a tear or rupture in the very economy of life and death upon which the logic of narrative biography depends: Because the life story has achieved an independence that will ensure its survival after his death, it also seems to possess a vitality and a life that exceed Ulysses's own. In bearing witness to his own life story taking leave of him, how could Ulysses experience himself if not, in some way, as always already dead?

That Ulysses, poetically speaking, need not wait for his *actual* death in order to "experience" it through his own biographical narrative points to a rupture within which language stakes a claim to immortality. Somewhere between finite existence and immortalizing narrative (or *within* the moment of their commingling), the impossibility of their reconciliation is given expression, quite simply, as tears. As unassimilated remainder, those tears mark the scene not only with a sense of how mortals become immortal through the language of memory, but also of how deeply tied that memorial expression is to a singularly difficult mourning.

The force of Arendt's interpretation notwithstanding (and in particular, her attention to the specific power of language to generate history, one that we will encounter again in our discussion of Benjamin), these tears seem to mark the precise instant at which Ulysses is confronted with the irreducibility of his own finitude.[20] As such, one of the things that make this scene so moving is the way it gives expression to the possibility that, aside from the task of enabling men to go beyond the border of their despairingly finite condition, remembrance also forces them to recognize the enigma of that border as well as to confront life as an ongoing negotiation with it.

§

Arendt gives a preliminary idea of just how unfamiliar and foreign these notions of history and poetry would become by noting the radical changes introduced by the so-called Socratic school of philosophy into the conception of human immortality. In this respect, Arendt describes Plato's philosophy as a "culmination" (*BPF* 46). In addition to various other attacks launched against the attempts made by humans to immortalize themselves, the philosopher famously has Diotima suggest in the *Symposium* that the impulse be satisfied by encouraging the masses to procreate.[21] Otherwise, it is a vain and imprudent undertaking.

The emergent authority of metaphysics is grounded in a more or less explicit rejection of the framework of mortal life in accordance with which the memorial forms of poetry and history had been structured. Nowhere is this metaphysical transformation exemplified with greater clarity than in Plato's dialogue *Phaedo*, wherein testimony is given of Socrates's final conversation with his disciples and a perspective on immortality and human finitude developed that differs in almost every respect from the notion that memory is moored to human life span.

In order to give his listeners a sense of the serenity he is experiencing in the face of death, Socrates puts forward the famous argument that what is worthy of remembrance and recollection exceeds the boundaries of human life. Death, the separation of body and soul, is welcomed by the philosopher, given that all things proper to the mortal body—what in the *Symposium* is described in graphic and disparaging fashion as "a process of loss and reparation: hair, flesh, bones, blood, and the whole body are always changing" (S 209b-c)—must be abandoned as worthless or dangerously seductive if the soul is to perceive the eternal and unchanging world of the ideas.

Philosophical recollection is, thus, death rehearsal. In the *Phaedo*, Socrates approves the popular understanding that philosophers are half-dead: "Anyone who thinks nothing of physical pleasures has one foot in the grave" (P 65a). The philosopher gains access to an eternal realm only by denying the fugacity of mortal life; he has always allied himself to what does not pass away, change or grow old. Thus the philosopher need not fear death since he has been preparing himself for it all along.

What is especially significant for our purposes is the enormity of the changes in perspective on human life being proposed here: Whereas poetry and history found the form of immortalizing memory within the very structure of mortal life, philosophy will overturn this valorization and conceive of human life as deeply corruptive for all that is truly immortal.[22] Memory, no longer cast as a narrative repetition of the temporal structure of human life, is a struggle away from the temporality of all things mortal. Socrates evokes this struggle as he discusses what happens to the soul when it is forced to take shelter in the body: "It is dragged away by the body into the realm of the variable, and loses its way and becomes confused and dizzy, as though it were fuddled. . . . But when it investigates by itself, it passes into the realm of the pure and everlasting and immortal and changeless, and being of a kindred spirit . . . strays no longer, but remains in that realm of the absolute, constant and invariable, through contact with beings of a similar nature" (P 79d–e).

According to this perspective, for as long as the immortal soul is embodied, it is condemned to an existence that is "human, mortal, multiform, unintelligible, dissoluble, and never self-consistent" (P 80b). The embodied soul is errant, its state one of temporary confusion. Leaving aside the question of whether or not the temporariness of this confused state—and so, the fact of its temporality—compromises the radically unchangeable nature of the soul, the official meaning of these statements is clear: Since truth does not change, it is neither subject to processes of aging or decay, nor could it ever be made manifest in the processes of human finitude. It is not, like mortals are, enslaved by time. Wholly immersed in their bodily finitude, humans are incapable of truth.

It would be difficult to overstate the influence that these formulations have had on Western thinking, particularly in terms of the opposition they set up between thinking and other, more worldly activities, and in terms of the disdain they authorize for the body, one that has scarcely abated since.[23] Less obvious, perhaps, but no less decisive are the consequences that this estimation of human life has for memory. When, for instance, Plato has Socrates denounce "wars and revolutions and battles" by virtue of their belonging to the realm of "the body and its desires" (66c), it is to disqualify politics *tout court* as the site of memory. Since political events happen in time as a dimension of human finitude, they only serve to distract the philosopher, whose recollection is directed toward what is timeless.[24] Philosophical memory, out of step with the time of politics, is also patently nonpolitical: Attempting to rid itself of the traces of human temporality, it is a form of resistance to politics and to finitude as such.

These conceptions of life, death, and memory are a reversal of all the themes and formal structures that had been established within Greek history and poetry: Death for philosophy, as the radical separation or separability of the soul from the constraints of finitude, is the condition upon which philosophy stakes its claim to memory's ultimate timelessness. According to this schema, human death is not what it was for the pre-Socratic narrative arts: not an end or a loss to which narrative responds by ensuring an ongoing relation to that loss (in the memorial form of its own temporality). Philosophy conceives of human death in a more radically upbeat sense, according to which whatever loss it entails is registered as pure gain.[25] And in direct proportion to how philosophy tends to value death as a force of unqualified redemptive potential, it also subjects human birth to a radical depreciation, decrying it as the soul's catastrophic fall into the mortal world of humans. Amnesia-inducing, it is a kind of trauma *avant la lettre* (P 75c–76b).[26]

§

This lengthy exposition has, I hope, served to lend a measure of clarity to two dominant understandings of memory and to the lines along which their opposition can be understood. On the one hand, the immortalizing potential of narrative resides in the chronicle it produces of human political events, a chronicle structured like a human life. On the other hand, disdain for the mortal life of humans is central to a radically different notion of memory: one that, having as little as possible to do with human life, could be defined as a form of pure and a-temporal contemplation or recollection. The aim of this contemplation—knowledge of the ideas—lay at the end of a long metaphysical journey that resembled death and that had to be taken largely alone.

In other words, philosophy did not just take memory in a direction that turned out to be incompatible with the political realm or with the social world of humans; rather, it actively turned memory *against* human life. Arendt emphasizes how philosophy had turned memory away from the world of humans when she draws attention to the silence of its ultimate undertaking: "Thus the proper attitude of mortals, once they had reached the neighborhood of the immortal, was actionless and even speechless contemplation: The Aristotelian νοῦς, the highest and most human capacity of pure vision, cannot translate into words what it beholds, and the ultimate truth that the vision of ideas disclosed to Plato is likewise an ἄρρητον, something that cannot be caught in words" (*BPF* 47). When memory enters the domain of solitary or philosophical-sectarian contemplation, it is severed from the world of human affairs. By highlighting the ineffability of philosophical memory, Arendt is again laying particular stress on the centrality of language for action and its immortalizing memory.[27]

In many ways, the gap dividing Greek memory into the immortal-izing narrative account of political events on the one side and the tran-scendent and eternal realm of the ineffable on the other, is a legacy that Christianity would inherit and attempt to resolve. For, how else are we to specify the uniqueness of Christianity if not in its having given its god a life span? Hegel's description of Christianity proceeds along these lines: "The fact that Christ is a child," he writes in the *Aesthetics*, "does in one way definitely express the meaning he has in our religion: he is God who becomes man and therefore goes through the stages of human life."[28] If the specificity of Christianity does indeed lie in its granting to God a human life span—submitting him to a birth and, even more scandalously, to suffering and death—then the process by which he is immortalized, if he is not to be subject to an internal division (and so consequently not absolute at all), must also be articulated in terms of this life span. The Christian God is thus made immortal by virtue of the immortalization of his human life span, a process that Catherine Malabou has described in terms of the "absolutizing of finitude."[29]

Christianity attempted to resolve the dual nature of the claim to immortality through its deification of life span. In so many ways a parallel to Plato's parable of the cave, just as the philosopher must first leave the cave that is humanity's earthly prison, so too is Christ's departure from his earthly tomb the condition upon which his place in eternity is assured. Though, as Christianity immortalizes human life span and so resolves the contradiction between two competing notions of memory, it produced another tension, one between politics and memory.

Arendt argues that by immortalizing the life span of the single human individual, Christianity affectively reversed the Greek order according to which men could aspire to everlastingness. She makes the point as follows: "In Christianity neither the world nor the ever-recurring cycle of life is immortal, only the single living individual. It is the world that will pass away; men will live forever" (*BPF* 52). In order for Christianity to immortalize human life span (noting that its immortalization is predicated upon departure from *this* world), life span will have had to forfeit any attachment to a changing and changeable world.[30] Beyond the assurance Christianity gives of mem-bership in a community of the faithful, Christianity's resolution of Greece's two competing claims to immortality means that life span and finitude have had to take leave of their specifically political and "worldly" character.[31]

The effects of the Christianization of life span are not limited to a transformed notion of immortality vis-à-vis human life; it
also brought about transformations in how the unpredictable and
changeable world of politics was to be narrated. To the extent that
Christianity draws a distinction between the human life span and the
world of politics and raises the former above the latter, it also provides Arendt with a backdrop against which to examine what little
has remained of human finitude within the discourse of modern history. Very much in contrast to the more life-affirming aspects of the
Greek narrative arts, the story she tells of modern history is that of its
radical depopulation.

§

The characterization Arendt gives of modern history underscores
how decisively it differs from the Greek conception of history. Modern history, she argues, is incompatible with the notion of history as
narrative life span insofar as "since the seventeenth century the chief
preoccupation of all scientific inquiry, natural as well as historical,
has been with processes. . . . In the modern age history emerged as
something it never had been before. It was no longer composed of the
deeds and sufferings of men; it became a man-made process, the only
all-comprehending process that owed its existence exclusively to the
human race" (BPF 57–58).

Just as she had linked the Greek conception of history to its conception of nature on the grounds that history allowed humans to
escape their transience and to partake of immortality, so too does she
link modern history to nature, but for different reasons. The common
basis of their claims to immortality, Arendt argues, lies in the quintessentially modern concept of process: "both [history and nature] imply
that we think and consider everything in terms of processes and are
not concerned with single entities or individual occurrences and their
special separate causes" (61).

As Arendt directs her attention to the consequences of this process-
oriented thinking for human life, her discussion becomes increasingly critical of its dehumanizing aspects. Regarding the decline
of the humanities and the rise of the social sciences as the logical
heir of modern history, she writes, "If their vocabulary is repulsive
and . . . our deplored impotence to 'manage' human affairs through
an engineering science of human relations sounds frightening, it is

only because they have decided to treat man as an entirely natural being whose life process can be handled the same way as all other processes" (*BPF* 59).

When meaning is generated solely on the basis of an overarching process, the repercussions are potentially catastrophic, beginning with how the plurality of individual beings is reduced to a function within a process that itself cannot be made the subject of human experience. "Invisible processes," she writes, "have engulfed every tangible thing, every individual entity that is visible to us, degrading them into functions of an over-all process" (63).

When Arendt raises the issue of the chronological reforms introduced in the eighteenth century, it is to show what impact the modern conception of historical process had on notions of temporality once the former had been freed from the constraints of life span. Arguing that modernity bestows "upon mere time-sequence an importance and dignity it never had before" (65), she goes on to suggest that what is truly decisive about those reforms is that "the birth of Christ becomes a turning point from which to count time both backward and forward," and that for the very first time, "the history of mankind reaches back into an infinite past to which we can add at will and into which we can inquire further as it stretches ahead into an infinite future. This two-fold infinity of past and future eliminates all notions of beginning and end, establishing mankind in a potential earthly immortality . . . as far as secular history is concerned, we live in a process which knows no beginning and no end" (67–68). According to this understanding, what is distinctive about the temporality of modern history is how it continues to be dependent upon the rectilinear time of *bios* but only after the latter has been stripped of birth and death. Thus, the temporal standard adopted from the life span of the human individual has given way to a rather more alarming constellation: one in which the history of modernity's mankind, because it is neither born nor dies, is told in a kind of infinite and undead narrative time.

In contrast to the description of Greek historiography, the discourse of modern history emerges in Arendt's thinking as the site of a two-fold dehumanization: first, since historical events only become meaningful when seen as part of an ever-expanding historical process that neither begins nor ends, history in the modern period ceases to derive its narrative form from the temporal structure of human life span, the result of which being that birth and death no longer figure in the formal structure of the modern historical account. In modern history, nothing ever begins or ends. Secondly, in its unmooring from the conditions of finite existence, historical discourse is deeply complicit with the broader modern phenomenon of the gradual disappearance of representations of finitude from the public sphere, a disappearance that, according to one prominent historian of death, is practically complete.[32]

Arendt's account shows how decisively the structure of modern historiography differs from that of Greek historiography. Grounding her distinction in the uncanny sense that the structure and temporality of human life span have "gone missing" from modern historiography, her account invites us to consider modernity as an epoch whose historical discourse generates no narrative memory proper to human finitude. And, although not explicitly stated in these terms, in a sense she is also asking us to consider modernity as an epoch to which no one can truly bear witness.

Less despairingly, perhaps, another question raised by Arendt's theory of narrative memory involves what might remain of finitude *within* modern history's open-ended and linear succession, especially since this claim of open-endedness is made as a function of historical time. For if the time of modern history is understood as an endless succession of distinct moments, could it not also be argued that *bios* is *everywhere* at work within this temporality, governing its operation of almost constant rupture whereby every moment is constituted by virtue of the break it makes from the one preceding it?

Philosopher Michel de Certeau has claimed as much, grounding his description of historiographical time in the relation it bears to death. Like Arendt, he too suggests that modern history presumes to have evacuated death from its own temporality. But de Certeau's account also differs from Arendt's; he discerns in this temporality of endless succession not the radical purging of death but its curious ubiquity. The source of this ubiquity, he argues, lies precisely in the modern notion of time as a constant *rupture*—that is, as a process of constant differentiation by means of which the production of the new "provides the place for a discourse considering whatever preceded it to be 'dead.' . . . Breakage is therefore the postulate of interpretation (which is constructed as of the present time)."[33] De Certeau's account draws out the implications of history's relation to the past when its "heterology" consists of a weighty deadness:

> On its own account, historiography takes for granted the fact that it has become impossible to believe in this presence of the dead that has

organized (or organizes) the experience of entire civilizations; and the fact too that it is nonetheless impossible "to get over it," to accept the loss of a living solidarity with what is gone, or to confirm an irreducible limit. What is *perishable* is its data; *progress* is its motto. . . . It is an odd procedure that posits death . . . and that yet denies loss by appropriating to the present the privilege of recapitulating the past as a form of knowledge. A labor of death and a labor against death (5).

What de Certeau's formulation suggests is not so much that modern history has evacuated finitude from its discourse as that its own temporal structure has inadvertently multiplied and intensified it. From this perspective, the chronological time of modern historical discourse appears to have formalized *bios* as its own temporal principle; the claim of every moment, epoch, or period is asserted by virtue of the "death" of the one preceding it. Consequently, we might say that every moment of a historical succession has itself become finite: Indeed, it possesses a "life of its own," as well as a death, one that historiography can no more readily mourn than abandon.

Insofar as Arendt limits her discussion of memory in modernity to the perils of modern historical discourse, she leaves open the question of the relation between memory and human finitude in art. Indeed, while both Greek history and poetry are clearly tethered to the exigencies of immortalizing memory in Arendt's thought, her silence on the question of the language arts of modernity raises the possibility that perhaps their own sustained relation to finitude may help to draw out the implications of a *bios* that has not simply disappeared but that occurs at every single moment.

MOURNING STORIES

The past carries with it a temporal index by which it is referred to redemption. There is a secret agreement between past generations and the present one.
—Walter Benjamin

Some twenty years before Arendt, Walter Benjamin had directed his attention to the question of narrative and cultural transmission, inflecting what he saw as the widening disjunction between them with a kind of historical specificity. In his essay "The Storyteller,"[34] Benjamin offers clues to suggest not only that consideration of the relation between modern culture and story-telling must take into account the demise of story-telling as a means of cultural transmission but also—and more oddly—that it is *only* with the demise of story-telling that such a relation can be accurately characterized at all. Beyond the at-times awkwardly nostalgic feel to the essay (which perhaps accounts for why it is not read as rigorously or as systematically as many of his other writings), Benjamin wishes to situate the end of narrative in light of a broader, markedly nonnostalgic question: what it might mean—namely, for a culture to be no longer transmissible by narrative. So, as well as attempting to clarify what might be implied by storytelling's loss of authority as a "medium" for cultural transmission, the essay thus also asks what it might mean for a culture to take stock of that loss, in a mode that resists simply capitalizing on it, as part of its own continued survival.

Given these aims, it seems fitting that the essay begins by developing an image of the storyteller using a dense interplay of remoteness and proximity, of the immediacy of "living presence" and more complex modes of encounter. For, it is only from a perspective of this sort—near and far, visible and yet barely discernable, accessible only in its inaccessibility and so on—that, Benjamin suggests, we will be able to "see" what is at stake in the end of storytelling. Then he goes on to suggest that "the art of storytelling is coming to an end. Less and less frequently do we encounter people with the ability to tell a tale properly. More and more often there is embarrassment all around when the wish to hear a story is expressed. It is as if something that seemed inalienable to us, the securest among our possessions [*Vermögen*], were taken from us: the ability to exchange experiences [*nämlich, das Vermögen, Erfahrungen auszutauschen*]" (ST 83/380).

What Benjamin here claims is assured property, and what is at stake when stories are no longer told is not really a possession at all, at least not in the strict sense of the word. To the contrary, what is called "possession" here actually seems more like the relinquishment of one: the act of transmission itself is what Benjamin suggests may be at stake in the loss of storytelling. And, if storytelling is no longer able to act as a means by which people are able to share their experiences with one another—if, as Benjamin contends, people experience embarrassment at the mere mention of the word—then presumably, changes undergone at the level of experience have played a decisive role in this demise, changes that have made experience incompatible with the narrative mode of language.

In fact, while the essay's title "The Storyteller" ("*Der* Erzähler" and not, say, "*Ein* Erzähler") draws attention to the work of Russian storyteller Nikolai Leskov (whose writings had already been largely consigned to literary oblivion in Benjamin's own time) as a figure of utter singularity, the essay's most powerful and provocative moments are provided by a double sense of Leskov's exemplarity—that is, both his singularity *and* his example—of which the "pastness" of his literary achievement is a not insignificant trait. In fact, Leskov's exemplarity seems most productive for Benjamin at the level of the more general insights it affords regarding this loss of narrative as an articulation of experience. For Benjamin openly contends that the loss of a literary means to express experience cannot be isolated from other, graver ruptures in experience, the historical weight of which is brought to bear on the text as a whole. As he describes it in the first paragraphs of the essay, every aspect of experience has been brought face-to-face with what has the power to overwhelm it. Beginning with the limit experience of men returning from the battlefields of WW I, "grown silent—not richer, but poorer in communicable experience," Benjamin writes: "And there was nothing remarkable about that. For never has experience been contradicted more thoroughly than strategic experience by tactical warfare, economic experience by inflation, bodily experience by mechanical warfare, moral experience by those in power. A generation that had gone to school on a horse-drawn streetcar now stood under the open sky in a countryside in which nothing remained unchanged but the clouds, and beneath these clouds, in a field of force of destructive torrents and explosions, was the tiny, fragile human body" (ST 84).

Describing a world in which the only constant are clouds—which, in most people's estimation, do nothing if not change—the essay's very first impulses are to insist on the disjointedness of experience and of time as a way of explaining why narrative practices have become impossible to sustain, either as a literary genre or as a discursive mode of everyday life. The return home of soldiers burdened with extreme and unnarratable experience is itself marked as a historical threshold by virtue of which modernity's generalized crisis of experience has become legible.[35] Benjamin articulates this crisis as a confrontation with an unrecognizable world, one that has made an anathema of human life: It offers no orientation or scale with which the measure of human lives could be taken. Assurances of this kind belong to the past, of which even the most recent moments seem so remote that they can only be conjured through the nostalgic, almost quaint image of going to school "on a horse-drawn streetcar."

This invocation of a bygone era has a melancholy ring to it—longing, perhaps, for a *temps perdu*—but on a more formal level, the contrast that it effects captures a sense of the gap separating past from present. Reducing even the very recent past to the status of a faded cliché accentuates the toll that the destructive violence of the world has taken on time and memory. For a world whose only continuity is provided by the strange permanence of clouds in the sky, the past can no longer be appropriated or understood by the present, much less can it offer meaningful and narratable orientation for the future: it can only be invoked mechanically, as drearily unassimilated and unassimilable as a stale metaphor.

It is in the context of this rift between the past and the present that the critical force of Benjamin's reflections on the possible end of narrative as well as its implications for experience are to be situated. For, both here and elsewhere, Benjamin is resistant to the notion that experience constitutes the "raw material" for memory, narrative or otherwise; rather, experience for Benjamin is already implicated in memory and is, as we shall see momentarily, already irreducibly literary. For instance, in the Baudelaire essay published just a few years later, Benjamin writes approvingly of Bergson's contention in *Matière et mémoire* that "the structure of memory [i]s decisive for the philosophical pattern of experience [*Erfahrung*]."[36] It is partially on the basis of memory's primacy that Benjamin effects the contrast between *Erfahrung* and *Erlebnis*: whereas *Erfahrung* is the name given to impressions that have already been lifted out of the time of their occurrence by memory, *Erlebnis* elicits the impression of events that have remained "at a certain hour in one's life" and that as a result have proven resistant to narration.[37]

While certainly this stance had become more explicit in the later essay, one can sense the urgency with which it is beginning to emerge in the descriptions of "The Storyteller." The excessive and violent stimuli of the modern world threaten narrative memory, making the structures of memory unstable and, even more radically, calling into question the very possibility of experience itself. Over and against a past that yields only silence or neutralized clichés when confronted with an overwhelming present though, Benjamin seems to postulate hidden conjunctions between what is passing—storytelling—and the needs of the present. This he does by locating affinities between the temporal register of the life and death of narrative and that of the "tiny, fragile human body." Thus, he lingers at the end of storytelling, draws it out, and lets it take its time in order to make a point, precisely, about time.

Among the various factors that contribute to the demise of storytelling—the novel and its solitary individual, the rise of the middle class, the invention of the printing press, capitalism, and so on—Benjamin singles out one factor in light of the seriousness of the threat it poses. After having discussed the emergence and transformation of epic narrative forms in terms that hyperbolize the tectonic slowness of their tempo (in rhythms, he emphasizes, which are "comparable to those of the change that has come over the earth's surface in the course of thousands of centuries"), he writes:

> We recognize that with the full control of the middle class, which has the press as one of its most important instruments in fully developed capitalism, there emerges a form of communication which, no matter how far back its origin may lie, never before influenced the epic form in a decisive way. But now it does exert such an influence. And it turns out that it confronts storytelling as no less of a stranger than did the novel, but in a more menacing way, and that it also brings about a crisis in the novel. This new form of communication is information. (88)

As information is brought into sharper focus, greater and greater emphasis is placed on the character of its temporality. And pointedly, Benjamin accentuates how it is that as information becomes more and more pervasive, its rationalization and acceleration of time stand to annul questions of time altogether.

One aspect of information targeted by Benjamin involves its sense of immediacy, beginning with the prerequisite that it "appear 'understandable in itself'" and that it be subject to "prompt verifiability" by means of other sources (89). These requirements suggest that information has direct and immediate access to the real and that it is somehow able to circumvent language's potential complications, including questions of authority, translation, uses of rhetoric and trope, and those involving referentiality itself.[38]

Benjamin draws attention to the temporal implications of this kind of language by noting how value is accorded to information on the basis of how *little* time it takes. By definition, he notes disparagingly, information is transitory and short-lived: it is almost always rushed. So tightly wedded to the present, information is produced and exhausted within the space of a single moment, a moment disconnected and separated off from all other moments. Evoking a kind of confrontation with the law, he writes that information "does not survive the moment [*dem Augenblick*][39] in which it was new. It lives only at that moment; it has to surrender to it completely and explain itself to it without losing any time" (90) and he quotes Valéry that "the time is past in which time did not matter [*Die Zeit ist vorbei, in der es auf Zeit nicht ankam*]. Modern man no longer works at what cannot be abbreviated" (93).

Storytelling, on the other hand, takes time. In what, at a certain level, seems like an implausible comparison, Benjamin contrasts information's *Augenblick* with what is so exemplary about a story by Herodotus, its potential for practically infinite generation—a trope for earthly immortality if ever there was one. Benjamin renders the story with a clear focus on its enigmatic expression of mourning:

> When the Egyptian king Psammenitus had been beaten and captured by the Persian king Cambyses, Cambyses was bent on humbling his prisoner. He gave orders to place Psammenitus on the road along which the Persian triumphal procession was to pass. And he further arranged that the prisoner should see his daughter pass by as a maid going to the well with her pitcher. While all the Egyptians were lamenting and bewailing this spectacle, Psammenitus stood alone, mute and motionless, his eyes fixed on the ground; and when presently he saw his son, who was being taken along in the procession to be executed, he likewise remained unmoved. But when afterwards he recognized one of his servants, an old, impoverished man, in the ranks of the prisoners, he beat his fists against his head and gave all the signs of deepest mourning. (89–90)

Benjamin likens the story to "seeds of grain which have lain for millennia [*jahrtausendelange*] in the chambers of the pyramids . . . and have retained their germinative power up to the present day [*bis auf den heutigen Tag*]" (90, translation modified).

Despite the almost Biblical hyperbole of the passage, the simile is no mere flight of fancy. In fact it does not seem to be an ordinary simile at all, but rather the citation of one: It is difficult not to read in Benjamin's reference an invocation of the pyramid that had figured so prominently in Hegel's theory of the sign in the *Encyclopedia of the Philosophical Sciences*, among other places. Set in contrast to Benjamin's highly critical appraisal of information's language of immediacy preceding it, one is reminded of how Hegel uses the pyramid's formal structure to explain the disjunction of the sign: How its inside and its outside are irresolvably disjoined.[40] The visibility of its exterior can, for Hegel, never be subjected to processes of reconciliation with the invisibility and indeterminacy of what, if anything at all, resides on its interior.[41]

There is, thus, a sense in which Benjamin's pyramid demands a two-fold reading: On the one hand, as a citation or echo of Hegelian motifs, it acts as a critique of the assumption that language refers directly to what is outside it. On the other hand, it is also drawing our attention to the story's incredible longevity, by accentuating the role that a *different* kind of language plays in that longevity.[42]

Indeed, the language of the story being privileged here appears to have little in common with the kind used in the transmission of information. The story endures, Benjamin seems to suggest, precisely because of how its language fails to guarantee any kind of direct relation to the real: It is likened to a pyramid after all and so, to the irresolvable indeterminacy of its content. In other words, language does not simply register what, beyond language, is of enduring value, by granting form to the formlessness of "timeless truths" or the like. Rather, the language of the story seems to point to another kind of endurance, one focused more on the inexhaustible richness of language than on a mimetic understanding of representation. In short, for Benjamin, it seems to be *because* language does not signify in any direct or natural way that it is able to generate any history at all.

Beyond the manner in which the story's own history gets generated, there is also the decidedly enigmatic instance of mourning that takes place within the story and in which Benjamin clearly locates the source of the story's lasting power. Mourning, like memory, is most often understood in terms of the clear temporal parameters according to which the present turns toward the past or toward what has assuredly passed. There is a majestic stability to this backward gaze; so rarely shaken, it seems to come from the work of mourning itself. Nothing, in fact, would seem more detrimental to mourning than doubt or confusion. Here though, the story's scene of mourning is just such an arresting instance of unpredictability, one that takes its readers—of the past, present, and future, says Benjamin—by surprise. But what kind of mourning is it that comes on so quickly and in so unexpected a way that it seems practically to come from the future?

Let us defer the question of the futurity of mourning for a few moments and pursue another one related to it: the suggestion Benjamin makes at the beginning of the essay regarding the relation between storytelling and experience. To what aspect of narrative language could experience ever have possibly owed its transmissibility, especially when the story is praised for a kind of language that does not in the first instance transmit content? Although Benjamin is clear on the point that an ostensibly transparent language is incompatible with the narrative transmission of experience, he is less clear on what it is about narrative that allows it to generate insights about experience. In that light, it makes sense to turn to a more complicated sense of the affinities between narrative and experience beyond those generated by an understanding of representation as imitation or copy. The essay's almost constant preoccupation with time suggests that affinities between the literary structure of narrative and the structure of experience are to be found in the kinds of temporality that they share.

Benjamin will specify these affinities by inquiring into how the two prose genres of the story and the novel manage to negotiate the question of their own endings. In some respects similar to how Arendt praised Greek narrative for the relation it sustains to human finitude and life span, Benjamin had nonetheless already gone further than Arendt by taking the notion of life span beyond its objective representation in language—that is, beyond the notion of life span as seen from the perspective of its completion. By exposing the limits of such an objective representation, he had also already exposed the conventional understanding of the relation between experience and narrative memory to what, in the Baudelaire essay, he would call the "shock experience" of modern life.

§

In the final analysis, the range of life must be determined by history.

—Walter Benjamin

In part to explain how the notion of eternity and, along with it, memory's immortalizing claim both get eclipsed by an increasingly rationalized temporal structure, Benjamin begins by pointing out a paradox: that eternity is related to death. "The idea of eternity," he writes, "has ever had its strongest source in death" (93). Relating death's disappearance to the decline of this idea, he suggests that the moment in which information—along with its reduction of time to *mere* moments—has flourished is also the epoch in which "people [can] avoid the sight of the dying": "In the course of modern times dying has been pushed further and further out of the perceptual world of the living. . . . Today people live in rooms that have never been touched by death, dry dwellers of eternity, and when their end approaches they are stowed away in sanatoria or hospitals by their heirs" (93–94). Thus, modernity is an epoch that, "by means of hygienic and social, private and public institutions," has almost entirely succeeded in evacuating death and dying from its midst.

Unsurprisingly, Benjamin's rendering of the phenomenon emphasizes its literary dimension by tying Ariès's "denial of death" to the demise of narrative. What Benjamin asserts will later resonate in Arendt's claim that the authority of narrative is furnished by the relationship it sustains to human finitude, a relation that modernity threatens to make superfluous or to negate altogether. Thus Benjamin can state that "death is the sanction of everything that the storyteller can tell" and that "it is . . . characteristic that not only a man's knowledge or wisdom, but above all his real life—and this is the stuff that stories are made of—first assumes transmissible form [*tradierbare Form am ersten*] at the moment of his death" (94).

No sooner does Benjamin make the claim that death plays a singular and authoritative role in literature than he complicates it by multiplying the essay's perspectives on death. In the passage just cited, for instance, Benjamin situates death's authority in terms of the kind of "closure" it affords. Structurally similar to the force exerted by death in Arendt's account of narrative life span, in order to radicalize the sense of what is at stake in the loss of narrative Benjamin's account places decidedly greater emphasis on how narrative gives meaning and form to life *for the very first time*.

Although this stance might seem to indicate a rather uncomfortable slide toward an aestheticization of human existence, Benjamin's deep conviction of the all-encompassing scope of language demands that it be read otherwise than as an aestheticizing trivialization or denigration. The possibility that literature might offer insights into experience that experience itself cannot offer—especially in light of the breakdown of experience sealed by modernity—is brought to bear on his discussion of the novel, for example, the appeal of which is explained by what can be gleaned from the lives of the characters through their deaths. As well, Benjamin suggests that the death of a character can reveal something about a future death to which the reader will never have access—his or her own: "This stranger's fate by virtue of the flame that consumes it yields us the warmth that we never draw from our own fate. What draws the reader to the novel is the hope of warming his shivering life with a death he reads about" (ST 101).

What might it mean, in accordance with this formulation, that death—a death that, paradoxically, has the power to warm—has gone missing? On the one hand, if death is the condition upon which a life in its totality first becomes meaningful, then death's absence is clearly going to have massive repercussions, both within literary discourse and outside of it, for issues of cultural transmission, continuity, and for what Benjamin calls "the chain of tradition which passes a happening on from generation to generation" (ST 93). Arendt too alludes to this crisis of transmission, seeing it exemplified by the postwar experience of the French Resistance after a return to normalcy had made the "essential years" of the Resistance fundamentally incommunicable. For Arendt, this experience is best encapsulated by René Char's aphorism, "Notre héritage n'est précédé d'aucun testament," a claim that she explains in the preface to *Between Past and Future* in the following terms: "The point of the matter is that the 'completion,' which indeed every enacted event must have in the minds of those who then are to tell the story and to convey its meaning, eluded them, and without this thinking completion after the act, without the articulation accomplished by remembrance, there simply was no story left that could be told."[43] As was suggested at the beginning of the chapter, both Arendt and Benjamin were only too aware—and not just in theory—that a world in which death only ever takes place off-stage distorts the task of remembrance, threatening to turn it into an endless "triumphant procession" in which human death has only instrumental value. A central aspect to Benjamin's critique of history was thus to situate the violence of this "deathless" and progressive history in relation to its temporality. "The concept of the historical progress of mankind," he writes toward the end of the Thirteenth Thesis, "cannot be sundered from the concept of its progression through a homogeneous, empty time. A critique of such a progression must be the basis of any criticism of the concept of progress itself" (TPH 261). Given the contention that a critique of progress must begin with a critique of the temporal parameters of progression, what insights does Benjamin's analysis of temporality in literature bring to bear on this critique of progress?

Let us pick up the thread of the argument regarding literature and time. We saw how Benjamin had begun outlining the temporality of the novel by situating it in relation to the finality that comes with death, be it a figurative death (the end of the novel) or an "actual" one (the death of a character). We saw too how important this sense of closure was for the kind of memory inhabiting the novel. But what of its time? Subscribing to Georg Lukács's dictum that "the novel is the only art form which includes time among its constitutive principles," Benjamin's formulation bears quoting at some length, beginning with the claim it makes of the novel's inherent suspense:

> The suspense which permeates the novel is very much like the draft which stimulates the flame in the fireplace and enlivens its play.
>   It is a dry material on which the burning interest of the reader feeds. "A man who dies at the age of thirty-five," said Moritz Heimann once, "is at every point of his life a man who dies at the age of thirty-five." Nothing is more dubious than this sentence—but for the sole reason that the tense [*Tempus*] is wrong. A man—so says the truth that was meant here—who died at thirty-five will appear to *remembrance* at every point in his life as a man who dies at the age of thirty-five. In other words, the statement that makes no sense for real life becomes indisputable for remembered life. The nature of the character in a novel cannot be presented any better than is done in this statement, which says that the "meaning" [*der "Sinn"*] of his life is revealed only in his death. (ST 100–101)

According to this description, the form of remembrance best exemplified by the novel is one in which each of its moments is infused with its end. According to Benjamin this means that the moments of a remembered life cannot be "read" in isolation from other moments (which is another way of saying that they are never, or never quite, *momentary*), nor are they to be read as simply part of a continuous sequence. Rather, these remembered moments are shot through with a deep and irrevocable sense of the end to which they are directed.[44] Not to be confused with how conventional wisdom usually associates "knowing how a story ends" with the deadening boredom of predictability, Benjamin attributes what is so suspenseful about a novel—a quality that gives it its life, its breath—to a structure within which remembrance is literally inseparable from anticipation.

The novel inaugurates a particularly *suspenseful* experience of reading in part because of how it is able to *suspend* or complicate its own narrative and temporal sequence of a past-present-future unfolding. While linearity doubtless plays a role in the novel, it is supplemented—and its temporal hegemony ultimately compromised—by the force of the novel's end that is given by remembrance and that should, theoretically at least, make itself felt at every moment. The end of the novel is able to exert this kind of force, not because the novel makes no claim to truth but because of the irreducible textuality of its structure, its inscriptive aspect or quality not being subordinated by language's representational function. Each moment of a novel is, then, divided within and against itself, to be read both in terms of the unfolding temporal sequence and in terms of how it is filled with a sense of its own fulfillment and completion, its own memory. Thus, no moment of the novel—nor any minimally discursive moment at all, for that matter, save those saturated with information—can be read in a pure way, isolated from other moments or from its own internal doubling; rather, each moment is inextricably linked to the end.

Whereas Benjamin locates the force of the novel's temporality in the finality of its end, by virtue of which each of its moments is filled with the virtual presence of that end, a remark made in an unaccountably offhand way suggests that something else is at stake at the end of a story. The contrast between the novel and the story is affected, in Benjamin's account, by how their temporal and narrative parameters are differently oriented toward their respective endings: "Actually there is no story for which the question as to how it continued [*Wie ging es weiter?*] would not be legitimate. The novelist, on the other hand, cannot hope to take the smallest step beyond that limit at which he invites the reader to a divinatory realization of the meaning of life [*den Lebenssinn ahnend sich zu vergegenwärtigen*] by writing 'Finis'" (ST 100).

What we read here as the novel's requirement of completion contrasts with the story's withheld ending, with its literal "open-endedness." That the end of the story is conceived as "to be continued" does not mean that the story is itself meaningless, just that it offers no promises or guarantees of meaning. Nor does it mean that the story's time is one of an endless linearity. All along Benjamin has been clear on this last point: that, like the novel, the story's authority is also given by the relation it sustains with death. The challenge of the remark lies, I think, in understanding what the authority of death might mean in the context of its being *withheld*.

The challenge might be taken up in the context of the insights that Benjamin has just generated around the question of the novel's temporality. The temporality of the story is marked by a future that is more uncertain and open than that of the novel; nonetheless, its temporality is still structured around futurity—around the *Wie ging es weiter?*—and needs to be considered as such. Whereas the novel's future is given in each and every one of its moments as a kind of Marquezian "death foretold," the story's futurity permeates every one of its moments with a kind of restlessness, a power that could arrest time or explode its continuity. Filled with an unforeseeable future, every moment of the story harbors the possibility of a surprise yet to come.[45]

§

In order to see how Benjamin's analysis of literature's temporality might bear on his critique of historicist time, let us return briefly to one of the *Theses*' most celebrated statements. "To historians who wish to relive an era," Benjamin writes in the Seventh Thesis, "Fustel de Coulanges recommends that they blot out everything they know about the later course of history. There is no better way of characterizing the method with which historical materialism has broken" (TPH 256). Here, Benjamin describes the violence of a historicist approach to the past in terms of how "its process of empathy" sacrifices the present to a past supposedly untouched by futurity. In its drive to identify with the past, historicism effaces any sense of the foreignness that accrues by virtue of lapsed time. It is to a power inherent to this lapse of time—precisely, to what we have seen emerge in the analysis of literary time as the past's imminent and surprising futurity—that Benjamin is drawing attention in the first supplement to the *Theses* when he describes the necessary, structural belatedness of history as "posthumous":

> Historicism contents itself with establishing a causal connection between various moments in history. But no fact that is a cause is for that very reason historical. It became historical posthumously, as it were, through events that may be separated from it by thousands of years. A historian who takes this as his point of departure stops telling the sequence of events like the beads of a rosary. Instead, he grasps the constellation which his own era has formed with a definite earlier one. Thus he establishes a conception of the present as the "time of the now" which is shot through with chips of Messianic time. (TPH 263)

Despite the haste with which these thoughts likely had to have been formulated—they were among his very last—it is nonetheless not simply a shortage of time that leads Benjamin to move from a discussion of the history of historicism to a kind of history that is not even identified or named as such. Rather, "a conception of the present as the 'time of the now'" in which the past makes its futurity felt registers what no historicism ever could, that a historical moment is never entirely at one with itself, and that the time for its futurity is, literally, "now."

How seriously should this proposal be taken, that literature serve as a model for historical discourse? It would have the definite advantage of denaturalizing history and of making its discourse and its temporality matters for reading and writing—a far cry from the modes of transparency and idealist reflection of much nineteenth-century historiography. As well, it could help to open up the texts of the past onto other temporal modalities and onto other modes of expressing the past in relation to the needs of the present. Far from simply turning history into an eclectic literary genre wherein anything goes, if an approach to history is conceivable along lines similar to those that Benjamin ascribes to the reading of a story—and in particular, to the indeterminacy of its *to be continued . . .* —the implications of modernity's own withheld ending can be drawn to a conclusion quite different from the one leading to a despairing sense of the future's emptiness—namely, that none of the moments of modernity's past are ever really or simply passed and that each one of them is powerfully infused with the possibility and the potential for a deeply surprising future.

On another level, it seems highly significant that the reemergence of literary time in Benjamin's notion of historical discourse is so utterly in keeping with the itinerary he follows as he traces the passing of literary modes of experience. The passing of the literary narration of experience turns out to be the very condition for it to yield a temporal modality that is directed toward an as-yet unarticulated future. As such, the unforeseeable emergence of that temporality in the mode of a history "to come" is as much a performance of the theory, as it is its suspenseful affirmation.

What happens to experience in modernity, though, when it can no longer be articulated, shared or sustained by means of literary narrative? In the next chapter, the task will be to discover what it might mean to bear witness to one's own history in modernity—especially since, as we have seen, the conditions of modernity produce a form of historical memory that can hardly be called human, let alone "one's own."

CHAPTER TWO

Memory in Theory

The Childhood Memories of John Locke
(Persons, Parrots)

LOCKE'S MOMENTUM

As we saw in Chapter 1, one of the achievements of Arendt's and Benjamin's critiques of history is to have drawn attention to the ways in which modern history effectively eliminates the dimension of human experience from its discursive structure. The question remains, though, as to how to situate the concept of experience with respect to this devaluation, especially given that one of the single most important innovations of modern philosophy was to have grounded knowledge in experience itself. In short: If modern history all but eliminates experience from its discourse, it is no less the case that the modern concept of experience is grounded in an elimination of history.

In this respect, the philosophy of John Locke is a case in point. In *The Second Treatise of Government*, Locke tries to preempt objections to his claim that existing political societies began as gatherings of men in the "state of nature." The first of these objections involves the scant historical evidence that can be amassed in support of such a claim. Locke addresses the objection twice, first summarizing it as follows: "It is often asked as a mighty objection, *where are*, or ever were there any *men in such a state of nature?*"[1] and then, later in the treatise, "*That there are no instances to be found in story* [sic], *of a company of men independent, and equal one amongst another, that met together, and in this way began and set up a* government" (*STG* §100).

His preliminary impulse is simply to deny the objection outright: "It is plain," he writes, "the world never was, nor ever will be, without

numbers of men in that state" (*STG* §14). After making a few obscure
references to "two men in the desert" of Peru, to the promises made
between a European and an Indian in the woods of America and so
on, Locke concludes on shaky ground: "I moreover affirm, that all
men are naturally in that state" (*STG* §15).

His second response, while no different from the first in its conclusion, is substantially more interesting for its argumentation. In granting to his critics the difficulty of finding historical evidence to support
the claim that associations of men in a state of nature ever existed,
Locke takes the opportunity to muse over why this might be the case:

> It is not at all to be wondered, that *history* gives us but a very little
> account of *men, that lived together in the state of nature.* . . . And
> if we may not suppose *men* ever to have been *in the state of nature*,
> because we hear not much of them in such a state, we may as well
> suppose the armies of *Salmanasser* or *Xerxes* were never children,
> because we hear little of them, till they were men, and imbodied in
> armies. . . . [F]or it is with common-wealths as with particular per-
> sons, they are commonly ignorant of their own births and infancies:
> and if they know any thing of their original, they are beholden for it,
> to the accidental records that others have kept of it. (*STG* §101)

As C. B. Macpherson argues in the introduction to Locke's text,
the "natural condition" of mankind that Locke develops cannot
be grounded in history; as such, it is to be understood as a "logical
abstraction" or deduction (xiii).

By dispensing with a consideration of history, Locke's "state of
nature" is certainly in good company. Both Hobbes's "state of nature"
and, even more so, that of Rousseau some sixty years after Locke's
were preoccupied with an origin that could be neither captured by
history nor even discerned in it retrospectively. Concerning the latter, in what is perhaps one of the most famous statements of "On the
Origins of Inequality," Rousseau does not so much invoke the dustbin of history as he contends that all history, written hitherto, *is* a
dustbin: "Let us therefore begin by putting aside all the facts, for they
have no bearing on the question. . . . O man, whatever country you
may be from, whatever your opinions may be, listen: here is your history, as I have thought to read it, not in the books of your fellowman,
who are liars, but in nature, who never lies."[2]

Locke's bracketing of history is certainly less robust and rhetori-
cally forceful than Rousseau's, but what is nevertheless striking about
it is that the "logical abstraction" on which it is said to rest is *not* very

logical or abstract at all, or at least it is made demonstrably less so by the resource it makes of the natural phenomenon of aging and its accompanying memory loss. Of interest here is not so much the fact that Locke evades the question of history as *how* he offers an explanation of it: the benighted state of a commonwealth regarding the question of its own origin in the state of nature is analogous to, and thus ostensibly explained by, the physiological and mental experience of a single individual, in particular, through recourse to that individual's loss of childhood and to the seemingly natural "fact" of his or her amnesia regarding that childhood.

In other words, to explain the lack of historical origin of men in a state of nature, Locke must resort to yet another ahistorical "natural man": the latter's forgetting its childhood appears to explain the lack of origin of the former. At one level, of course, the explanation is successful precisely to the extent that it explains nothing—it merely points to a lack of explanation or a "blank" and attempts to give it solid empirical grounding. At another level, the resource Locke makes here of "particular persons" and the experiences they undergo, those involving the physiological effects of aging—the transition from childhood to adulthood—and the memory loss that supposedly accompanies this transition, seem difficult to take at face value as phenomena with any real explanatory value. In fact, what is given here as the "explanation" of a lack of historicity simply begs the question of memory loss as such.

Like the "state of nature" whose lack of history it is called upon to explain, Locke's "person" emerges with no discernible historical ground beneath its feet. Its emergence would, however, turn out to be "history-in-the-making": The influence of *An Essay Concerning Human Understanding*—also published in 1690 and in which extensive treatment is given to those issues of personhood, identity, and memory that the *Second Treatise* only mentions in passing—was and continues to be far-reaching. Neil Wood attests to its momentum in his study of the politics of Locke's empiricism with the following contention: "John Locke's *Essay Concerning Human Understanding* (1690) is one of our most widely read and influential philosophic masterpieces. Seldom has a book so shaped the mind of a culture . . . perhaps no single volume can so justifiably be called the intellectual foundation of the eighteenth-century Enlightenment that ushered in the modern world of ideas."[3] Likewise Nicholas Jolley, in arguing for Locke's particular relevance in the context of contemporary discussions of memory and identity, has also pointed to the text's canonical status. "It is hardly an exaggeration," he suggests, "to say that Locke invented the problem [of personal identity] in the form in which it is known today. The recent upsurge of interest in the topic is often clearly Lockean in inspiration; either explicitly or implicitly, many contemporary writers seek to remodel Locke's basic program." Furthermore, writes Jolley, "the project of analysing personal identity over time in terms of memory has attracted many philosophers, and even today Locke's theory continues to be a source of inspiration."[4] Perhaps, though, it is Hans Aarsleff who has articulated this influence in the most compelling, if enigmatic, temporal terms: "the *Essay*" he writes, "has no other history than that which was its own future."[5]

§

Despite the fact that Locke himself saw fit to invoke a failure of memory as constitutive of personhood in the *Second Treatise on Government*, the scholarly attention paid to the issue of memory in *An Essay Concerning Human Understanding* has generally been limited to the edifying role that memory plays in the constitution of persons. Paradigmatic in this respect is the reference we find to it in the section on "Of Identity and Diversity." "To find wherein *personal identity* consists," Locke writes, "we must consider what *person* stands for; which, I think, is a thinking intelligent being, that has reason and reflection, and can consider itself as itself, the same thinking thing, in different times and places."[6]

If Locke's *Essay* does continue in large measure to ground current understandings of identity and memory, what seems most significant about the historicity of Locke's *Essay* is precisely that it is not limited to the historical moment in which the text was written: In light of its continued relevance, it seems especially urgent to trace the ways in which Locke produces the unifying version of memory that has become the standard interpretation of his text.[7] Reading "against the grain" of the text's doctrine, one could, albeit in a preliminary way, emphasize that within the development of Locke's argument concerning memory and identity, the staging of a triumphant self reflecting on its own fully accessible and remembered past is itself framed in the text as a recovery from a life-threatening form of self-alienation, embodied in and around the fundamental *foreignness* of memory.

That Locke's doctrinal project can be called into question, however, certainly does not imply that it is emptied of all instruction. To
the contrary, the ways in which memory, its failures, and its impos-
sibilities are staged in *The Essay*, and the ways in which "voice" is
recuperated in these failures, give a sense of what is at stake—perhaps
even today—in testimonial or autobiographical claims to memory. In
his goal to put a human face on memory, he highlights what is at stake
every time we speak, as "persons," in the guise of memory.

§

Early in Book 2 of *The Essay Concerning Human Understanding*, in
the section "Of Retention," Locke spells out the position of memory
within his empirical system. Memory is subordinate to the perceptual
activities of the mind (that is, one can perceive without the aid of the
faculty of memory); yet for the more developed faculties of the understanding, it acts as a crucial foundation without which the mind would
remained stalled at a stage of infancy. For the human understanding,
he writes, memory "is necessary in the next degree to perception. It
is of so great moment that, where it is wanting, all the rest of the faculties are in a great measure useless; and we in our thoughts, reason-
ings, and knowledge, could not proceed beyond present objects, were
it not for the assistance of our memories" (*Essay* 2.10.7). Consistent
with his critique of the doctrine of innate principles—a critique central to the development of his own doctrine of experience, one whose
implications are as much social as they are philosophical, according
to several of his later commentators[8]—Locke contends that memory
follows on the heels of sense-experience, that in other words memory
does not recall anything that does not have its origin in sense-perception. Locke writes that "to say a notion is imprinted on the mind,
and yet at the same time to say that the mind is ignorant of it, and
never yet took notice of it, is to make this impression nothing" (*Essay*
1.2.5), and some sections later, that "whatever idea comes into the
mind is new, and not remembered; this consciousness of its having
been in the mind before being that which distinguishes remembering
from all other ways of thinking" (*Essay* 1.2.21).

   As Leibniz would contend in his critique of Locke's text, Locke's
work differs from his own to the extent that Locke's "is closer to
Aristotle's and mine to Plato's."[9] In relating Lockean empiricism to
Aristotelian philosophy in this way, Leibniz is recalling the radical

shift that Aristotle had inaugurated in relation to the metaphysics of Plato. Indeed, the presuppositions that Aristotle was able to articulate by virtue of this shift would be the very ones upon which Locke would later draw. However, as Leibniz also contends, both moderns differ "at many points from the teachings of both of these ancient writers" (48). Nowhere is this claim more compellingly demonstrated than in the difference between Locke and Aristotle on memory and, in particular, on the relation between memory and subject-constitution, or identity.

Aristotle's short treatise *On Memory* yields his most comprehensive statements on the phenomenon of memory. In it, his dispute with his predecessor clearly comes into focus. "We must first consider the objects of memory," Aristotle writes in the opening lines of the text, "a point on which mistakes are often made. Now to remember the future is not possible—that is an object of opinion or expectation. . . ; nor is there memory of the present, but only sense-perception. For by the latter we know not the future, nor the past, but the present only. But memory relates to what is past."[10]

This position is in stark contrast to Plato's, which characterizes sense perception as the ephemeral and all-too-seductive shadow of eternal and unchanging truths. As we saw in Chapter 1, the tensions between the pre-Socratic memory arts and philosophy arise out of two differing conceptions of memory, philosophical reminiscence for Plato being of what *is* eternally. By virtue of the ontological priority given to memory over sense-perception, Socrates advances the famous thesis that learning is, in truth, reminiscence.

Whereas for Aristotle memory is a capacity that both human beings and the more developed animal species possess, the faculty of reminiscence or recollection is restricted to humans. Memory, according to this schema, involves the mere retention of sense images, imprinted on the mind to varying degrees depending on the strength of the initial impression and on the receptivity of the imprinting surface.[11] Reminiscence, on the other hand, is the human ability to call up past images in a deliberate and conscious manner. The decisive point for our purposes is that reminiscence employs mental images that originate in sense-perception. On this point, Aristotle is insistent: "Recollection is not the recovery or acquisition of memory; since at the instant when one at first learns or experiences, he does not thereby recover a memory, inasmuch as none has preceded, nor does he acquire one ab initio. It is only at the instant when the aforesaid state or affection is implanted in the soul that memory exists, and therefore memory is not itself implanted concurrently with the continuous implantation of the sensory experience."[12] Unlike for Plato, Aristotelian reminiscence does not recall a priori ideas, of which objects perceptible by the senses would be considered mere copies, but recalls images derived from sense experience. The scope of reminiscence, for Aristotle, is confined to the horizon of sense experience. The affinity between memory images and those produced by the imagination—and the potential slippage between the two—is rooted in the contention that they are both paler images derived from the perception of sensory objects.[13]

Although Aristotle's and Locke's theories of memory hold much common ground and although the former unquestionably instructs the latter, Locke nonetheless (as Leibniz suggests) departed in important ways from his ancient predecessor. One of the most significant of these departures, as Jeffrey Andrew Barash has pointed out, is Locke's contention that not only are imagination and reminiscence dependent upon what is furnished by the senses as they are also in the Aristotelian system, but that so too is the intellect itself dependent upon sense-experience.[14] In this, Locke's conception of the intellect contrasts starkly with that of Aristotle, which experiences no change over time and which "is separable, impassable, unmixed, since it is in its essential nature activity . . . in the individual, potential knowledge is in time prior to actual knowledge, but absolutely it is not prior even in time. . . . When separated it is alone just what it is and this alone is immortal and eternal . . . and without this nothing thinks."[15] For Aristotle, limiting the scope of recollection to the sphere of sense experience did not impair the intellect in its quest to make "intelligible the eternal structure of Being,"[16] provided the (implausible) condition was met that it be detached from its present conditions or, as Aristotle puts it, "separated" from its particularity. For Locke, on the other hand, the human intellect is just as dependent on the experience of sense perception as are the imagination and reminiscence.[17]

In what is perhaps his most famous statement, Locke contends that all aspects of the human understanding are generated by experience. In "Of Ideas in General, and their Original," Locke writes, "Let us suppose the mind to be, as we say, white paper, void of all characters, without any *ideas*. How comes it to be furnished? Whence comes it by that vast store which the busy and boundless fancy of man has painted on it with an almost endless variety? To this I answer, in one word, from *experience*. In that all our knowledge is founded, and from that it ultimately derives itself" (*Essay* 2.1.2). As such, Lockean self-understanding is attained through experience rather than through intellectual or metaphysical insight into the substantive principle of the soul. All aspects of human understanding are located in empirical time and space and are, as such, accessible to the under-standing by means of its own powers of self-observation. Such is the aim of the *Essay*, to comprehend the structure of the understanding as the product of nothing outside of its own purview; it is accessible to its own reasoning because it is itself reason. Locke's stated goal is to "take a survey of our own understandings, examine our own powers, and see to what things they were adapted" (*Essay* 1.1.7). This method of self-examination has, for Locke, a regulatory function: It is about examining the boundaries between the known and the unknown, or between the "enlightened and dark parts of things," so that "men would perhaps with less scruple acquiesce in the avowed Ignorance of the one, and employ their thoughts and discourse with more advan-tage and satisfaction in the other" (*Essay* 1.1.7).

The prudence that this passage advocates for the exploration of the powers of the human understanding—to know the regions in which it is capable of exerting its own reasoning power and those in which it is not—belies a deeper and more enigmatic principle of the Enlightenment, that of the unboundedness of its own powers. The modesty of Locke's stated aim notwithstanding, his flurry of philosophical humility about limits, boundaries, and acquiescence turns into an account of the vastness of the mind's capabilities.[18] In a moment of poetic inspiration worthy of Coleridge, Wordsworth or of the later Kant, Locke writes, "All those sublime thoughts, which tower above the clouds and reach as high as heaven itself, take their rise and footing here: in all that great extent wherein the mind wan-ders, in those remote speculations it may seem to be elevated with, it stirs not one jot beyond those *ideas* which *sense* or *reflection* have offered for its contemplation" (*Essay* 2.1.24). The implications of this shift—from the grounding of the self in the metaphysical realm to the ground provided by its own power of reason—are far-reaching. The claims made for the experience of the self are wholly provided "by the powers intrinsical and proper to itself." The understanding is, for Locke, utterly self-grounding.

When the individual is conceived in terms of the events of his or her own experience, the scope of memory itself changes. In fact, in

Chapter 27 of the *Essay*, memory is one of the key characteristics used to distinguish personal identity:

> To find wherein *personal identity* consists, we must consider what *person* stands for; which, I think, is a thinking and intelligent being, that has reason and reflection and can consider itself as itself, the same thinking thing in different times and places . . . For since consciousness always accompanies thinking, and it is that that makes every one to be what he calls *self*, and thereby distinguishes himself from all other thinking things: in this alone consists personal identity, *i.e.*, the sameness of a rational being. And as far as this consciousness can be extended backwards to any past action or thought, so far reaches the identity of that person. (*Essay* 2.27.9)

In jettisoning the principle of unity that the Greeks sought in Being beyond finite being, Locke seeks to recover a principle of unity in the experience of the finite self, experience that includes and is indeed defined by memory of experience over time. By bracketing physical constitution or biological structure, Locke affirms that self-consciousness is the defining feature of humanness. Continuity is the key to personhood; its vehicle, according to Locke, is consciousness itself: "Nothing but consciousness can unite remote existences into the same person" (*Essay* 2.27.23).

So far as present consciousness includes the past experiences of an individual, so far extends the identity of that person: "For as far as any intelligent being can repeat the *idea* of any past action with the same consciousness it had of it at first, and with the same consciousness it has of any present action, so far as it is the same *personal self*. For it is by the consciousness it has of its present thoughts and actions, that it is *self to itself* now, and so will be the same self, as far as the same consciousness can extend to actions past or to come" (*Essay* 2.27.10). Personal selfhood is constituted not only by the immediate transparency of the self to itself—that is, in the present—but also by a reflection of consciousness on past thoughts, actions, and experiences. Insofar as a person can claim a set of past experiences as their own by testifying to the sameness of the consciousness that had such experiences and that "remembers" them, such consistency over time itself attests to personal identity; it is "the same self now as it was then, and it is by the same self with this present one that now reflects on it, that that action was done" (*Essay* 2.27.9).

The influence these formulations have exerted over the centuries is matched only by the criticism they have met, beginning with

Joseph Butler's famous objection. He charges that the theory involves Locke in an inescapable circularity: "One should really think it self-evident," he writes, "that Consciousness of personal Identity presupposes, and therefore cannot constitute, personal Identity."[19] In other words, conscious memory cannot possibly serve as the basis for one's identity, because if I remember visiting the Eiffel Tower, then what I remember is that *I* visited the Eiffel Tower. Of course, Butler's objection raises the issue of the argument's circularity in order to highlight the primacy and the anteriority of identity over and above its experience. According to Butler's criticism, if the self can be said to bear witness to its own experience in the form of memory, then it follows that the self must precede—both logically and temporally—all experience. What Butler is, in effect, calling into question is the *finite* status that Locke grants to the self, grounded entirely in its own experience. This is, of course, meant to deal a blow to Locke's entire project but only, it should be stressed, as Butler and many critics after him have construed it.[20]

The theory also met with another charge, first developed by Thomas Reid and similar in many respects to Butler's, that memory cannot serve as a necessary condition for personal identity because memory is always flawed, partial, or even selective. For Reid, we would be hard-pressed to grant—as he suggests Locke demands that we do—that experiences and events that the self is unable to remember form no part whatsoever of their identity.[21]

One could come to Locke's defense by arguing that his notion of memory amounts to an ability in principle and not necessarily in fact—that his theory of memory is, precisely, memory *in theory*—but one would still have to admit that many of the paradoxes and aporias of memory that Locke's critics raise are ones that can be gleaned from the pages of Locke's own text; indeed, Locke himself had already addressed some of those difficulties, albeit in oblique or even at times hyperbolic fashion, in the *Essay*. This indicates two things: firstly, that Locke was far more aware of the difficulties raised by his formulations than many of his critics are willing to admit and secondly, that these dilemmas already form an important, even integral, aspect of Locke's own exposition of the problem of the finitude of human identity. To do justice to Locke, then, one must do more than simply reveal the holes in the theory, for those holes are themselves part of the theory. Rather, one must seek to understand his version of personal identity *both* in terms of the fiction of self-enclosure that it inaugurates—and one in which we all, as Locke's unwitting heirs, participate to some extent—*and* in terms of how that self-enclosure generates its own openings, ruptures, nicks, and tears, precisely when the Lockean self is called upon to testify to itself in the form of memory and when Locke is forced to concede memory's irreducibly social and linguistic dimensions. For in the end, what is at stake for Locke's project of self-attestation and for the aporias, paradoxes, and circularities that it may generate is the possibility of testifying to the finitude of the self, in the absence of a notion of immortality or of a persisting substance.

With this in mind, let us return to Locke's argument. The admittedly problematic formulations with which we left off perhaps help to clarify a contention made earlier in "Of Identity and Diversity," which is that, as concerns the identity of finite intelligences, the specific time and place of their coming into existence—that is, their birth—determines their identity. In fact, placed in the context of Locke's relentless critique of innatist principles, it could be suggested that knowledge of one's own origin takes on an inordinately important role in the theorization of personal identity as that which is determined by nothing outside of its own purview. Locke writes, "for we never finding, nor conceiving it possible, that two things of the same kind should exist in the same place at the same time, we rightly conclude that whatever exists anywhere at any time excludes all of the same kind" (*Essay* 2.27.1), that "one thing cannot have two beginnings of existence, nor two things one beginning" (*Essay* 2.27.1), and that "finite spirits having had each its determinate time and place of beginning to exist, the relation to that time and place will always determine to each of them its identity, as long as it exists" (*Essay* 2.27.2).

The contention that identity is determined by its temporal and spatial origin suggests that a finite notion of personal identity depends upon its having a memory of its origin and that this origin is one to which the self can attest in the form of testimonial knowledge about itself. What is registered here is nothing less than the control of the understanding over all of its previous moments, as well as the means to its expression: a kind of totalized self-attestation that, as the understanding's means of expression, constitutes the most decisive proof of its finitude.

At the end of the section, however, the subjective dominion so confidently articulated in the earlier sections is expressed in somewhat more uncertain terms. The hesitation of the argument that insists on

the appropriation of the past for the self is expressed in the form of
the self on trial:

> *Person*, as I take it, is the name for this *self*. Wherever a *man finds*
> *what he calls himself*, there, I think *another may say* is the same per-
> son. It is a forensic term, appropriating actions and their merit, and
> so belongs only to intelligent agents, capable of a law, and happiness
> and misery. This personality extends *itself* beyond present existence
> to what is past, only by consciousness, whereby it becomes concerned
> and accountable, owns and imputes to *itself* past actions, just upon
> the same ground and for the same reason as it does in the present.
> (*Essay* 2.27.26, emphasis added)

In keeping with the appeals Locke regularly makes to common sense
and realism, immediately after having contended that selfhood is
grounded in the accessibility of its past (including the event of the
self's own origin), he tempers that claim by submitting it to procedures of external verification. That testimony is insufficient on
its own and must, by virtue of the potential of its own errancy, be
attested to by another suggests that the self may not be as uniquely
determined by consciousness of its past as Locke himself may have
preferred. In other words, what had been elaborated in the earlier
sections as an exercise in hermetic self-observation here becomes subject to the demand that another attest to the self through the figure of
person. As Locke suggests in no uncertain terms, "person" is a figure
of and for sociality. Insofar as he *"must find what he calls himself,"*
"person" is less a legalized nomenclature for self-assured sovereignty
than it instantiates the insecure figure of *relation*.

We should, of course, take care not to gloss over the multiple tensions that this form of testimony poses for Locke's explication of selfhood. For although Locke insists on the ability of the understanding to know itself through consciousness of all its previous moments
and ultimately to reign supreme over them, both the terminology of
"finding oneself" and the introduction of the third-person witness
suggest that this knowing is flawed; namely, it is vulnerable to fal-
sification. Furthermore, because testimony occupies the shady area
between subjective constitution and objective verification, it instantiates a rift to be overcome, that between knowing or telling and being.
For, if personal memory is what is most proper to and constitutive of
the individual's identity, as Locke has suggested, then recourse to the
witnessing function of a third party seems to violate the very conditions upon which identity is constituted. Put otherwise, what is said

to be most proper to and constitutive of the individual also seems to be what most needs substantiation by another.

This structure of self-testimony gives some sense of what is at stake for Locke in his discussion of identity and memory. In the first instance, it tells us that the reconciliation of the past with the present of the individual does not take place within a sealed chamber of self-knowledge—that is, that the autobiography of personhood has a more or less explicit social function and that its substantial existence is to be found outside of the self. Secondly, it tells us that the relation of the self to the events of its own past is enabled by its capacity for expression—the ability to speak, to call oneself *self*—as the means by which one can attest to actions and events as one's own.

These two imperatives—the social context of personal memory and the verbal ability to appropriate the past as one's own property—converge in the event of *calling* oneself "self": "Everyone is to himself that which he calls *self*. . . . For since consciousness always accompanies thinking, and it is that that makes everyone to be what he calls self, and thereby distinguishes himself from all other thinking things, in this alone consists *personal identity*" (*Essay* 2.27.9).

Although Locke repeatedly insists on the role of consciousness in the singularly human ability to experience sameness over time, what is highlighted in this passage (and others like it) is that the self's finite singularity—that is, its experience and its consciousness of temporal duration over time—is itself experienced *not* through consciousness or even thought but through narration and voice. However foundational a position Locke would like to maintain for consciousness and the experience that it reflects upon, the ability to pay *verbal* testimony seems to be the basic condition through which memory comes to be a cornerstone of personal identity. Identity is the stabilized experience of oneself, not as it is experienced in a moment of pure and unfettered self-observation; rather, identity is stabilized through language—namely, through the act of *calling* oneself "self" before the scrutiny of others. The voice, then, quite independent of consciousness's claim to preside over it, becomes not only the means by which actions and experiences in the past are unified, but also the means by which the subject guarantees the singularity—however qualified, mitigated or mediated by language—of its identity.

One thing Locke fails to explore in his discussion of the voice of the "person" is the resonance that the term has with its own origin in the Latin term *persona* or "mask."[22] This omission is not especially surprising given that Locke appeared never to show any interest in ety-mology;[23] however, the *Oxford English Dictionary* explicitly suggests that the term "person" in the seventeenth century not only carried all the Lockean connotations of a "self-conscious or rational being" but that it also hearkened to its roots in similitude, dissimulation, and indeed, dra-matic representation.[24] In this regard, "person" denotes "a part played in a drama or in real life," "an individual . . . regarded as having rights or duties before the Law," and "in the character of, representing." If the definition of personhood implies its own integrity and accountability in a judicial realm—if it is, as Locke contends, a "forensic" term—it also implies that in order to pay testimony, one must assume a mask in order to play a part in a certain kind of social drama. In certain respects, that "personhood" implies this potential duplicity, that it can also be a mask, a ruse, a means of disguise, and importantly, a fiction through which one could assume the guise of another, makes sense of Locke's concluding recourse to the certainty of divine justice. When at the end of the section, Locke highlights divine justice as the dissolution of the rift between subjective knowledge and objective truth, he is only further emphasizing the aporias inherent to human testimony.[25]

The threat of counterfeit testimony, as well as the unpropitious rift between consciousness and voice that makes possible such a threat, provides one way of thinking about the mask of "personhood" and the subtle anxieties that inhabit Locke's discussion of it. That "person-hood" can be a mask and that it can act as a disguise suggests, on the one hand, that what lies beneath this *persona* is a true self, one that can "find itself" adequate to all its moments, and one that is able to repre-sent the true empirical origins of its memories. Locke's text testifies to this possibility in the form of "false memories," and of various forms and degrees of amnesia that might otherwise impair the adequation of all moments in the past with present consciousness (*Essay* 2.27.13–14).

On the other hand, the mask of personhood itself conceals another possibility, one even more devastating than the possibility of an improper or false *persona*. It is one that suggests the mask's abso-lute necessity; the mask does not hide a more authentic or "proper" (one of Locke's favorite words) variant of "personhood" but more precisely, it hides the fact that it hides *nothing* proper to the person—that is, that *person*, as a mask, does not hide an otherwise sound rela-tion of consciousness to its past which might be subject to various kinds of distortions but that an impropriety is involved even in the most intimate and faithful of testimonials.

Lest this argument itself be taken as unduly importing what is foreign to Locke's assured system of self-representation and of imposing a certain problem where there is none, let us examine two moments in Locke's argument where this anxiety comes more clearly into focus. The first is found in "Of Identity and Diversity" when Locke attempts to delineate the boundaries between species, but ends up entwining his argument together with the telling of an incredible fable; the second occurs in his theory of language. In both cases, we are confronted with what could be construed as the human's double: the anticlimactic, perhaps even banal, exemplarity of the parrot.

In attempting to construe the definitive boundaries that separate species, Locke seeks recourse to the definition of "man" and takes note of the ways in which the idea "man" is related to the sound of the word "man." According to Locke, such a relation—between the idea and the word—is sufficient to suggest that whatever "man" means, its definition is closely related to its bodily form and as such, excludes all other animal forms:

> And, whatever is talked of other definitions, ingenuous observation puts it past doubt that the *idea* in our minds of which the sound *man* in our mouths is the sign, is nothing else but of an animal of such a certain form: since I think I may be confident, that whoever should see a creature of his own shape or make, though it had no more reason all its life than a *cat* or a *parrot*, would call him still a *man*; or whoever should hear a *cat* or a *parrot* discourse, reason, and philosophize, would call or think it nothing but a *cat* or a *parrot*; and say, the one was a dull irrational *man*, and the other a very intelligent rational *parrot* (*Essay* 2.27.8).

According to this rather crude attempt at species taxonomy, the idea of man corresponds *not* to an entity that has reason and the ability to engage in discourse, but to one that has a certain bodily structure: "For I presume it is not the *idea* of a thinking or rational being alone that makes the *idea* of a *man* in most people's sense, but of a body so and so shaped, joined to it; and if that be the *idea* of a *man*, the same successive *body not shifted all at once* must, as well as the same immaterial spirit, go to the making of the same *man*" (*Essay* 2.27.8).

In order to substantiate the claim about the irreducibility of human corporeality for the idea of "man," Locke recounts a rather strange and anomalous narrative, one presumably drawn from his extensive library of travel literature.[26] The story is an anomaly not only because it departs so radically from the tenor of the argument,[27] but also because it seems to pose a pretty serious challenge to it: By recounting a narrative about a talking parrot, Locke himself begins to resemble the discoursing parrot that he so playfully invokes to make his point. He attempts to illustrate the point with the verbatim citation of a story, one so strange and fantastical that he must somehow disown its authority even as he affirms it. "I have taken care," Locke begins, "that the reader should have the story at large in the author's own words" (*Essay* 2.27.8).[28]

The author of the story, described by Locke as "an author of great note," is motivated by the same keenness of curiosity as Locke: "I [not Locke but Locke's author, the unnamed Sir William Temple] had a mind to know from his (Prince *Maurice's*) own mouth, the account of a common but much credited story, that I had heard so often from many others of an old *parrot* he had in *Brazil* during his government there, that spoke, and asked and answered common questions like a reasonable creature" (*Essay* 2.27.8). Locke's incredulity is registered in his explicit citation of the story, done presumably so as to distance himself from the claim to truth contained in the testimony. Like Locke, "the author of great note," we are told, who had heard so many particulars of the story, "by people hard to be discredited," took it upon himself to visit one "Prince Maurice" in Brazil in order to have the story verified. Also like Locke, the author's skepticism is expressed by the desire to hear the story at first-hand, "from prince Maurice's own mouth."

Prince Maurice, or so Locke's author claims, "had heard of such an old *parrot* when he came to *Brazil*; and though he believed nothing of it and 'twas a good way off, yet he had so much curiosity as to send for it." Having the parrot in his company, he begins to ask it questions. To the astonishment of its audience, the parrot responds to the questions in a coherent and concise manner:

> They ask'd it what he thought that Man was? pointing at the Prince. It answer'd, *Some general or other.* When they brought it close to him, he ask'd it, *D'où venez vous?* It answered, *De Marinnan.* The prince: *À qui êtes-vous?* The parrot: *À un Portugais.* Prince: *Que fais-tu là?* Parrot: *Je garde les poules.* The Prince laugh'd and said: *Vous gardez les poules?* The parrot answered, *Oui, moi, et je sais bien faire*; and made the Chuck four or five times that people use to make to chickens when they call them. (*Essay* 2.27.8)

As if the relay effect of this story and the appropriation and disappropriation of voices (through to the parrot's mimicry of chickens) that takes place within it were not enough to problematize the voice as the *proper* medium of subjective consciousness, the explicit act of translation also figures prominently in the remainder of the story. For the bird, we are informed, speaks "Brazilian" while Maurice does not (he gave the account to Temple in French). To ensure the value of the testimony, Maurice solicits the help of two translators, one a Dutchman who speaks "Brazilian," the other a Brazilian who speaks Dutch. Having heard the parrot's testimony, the two are isolated from one another and are made to quote the bird, "both of them agreed in telling him just the same thing that the *parrot* said."

Not Locke himself, but Locke's author, having validated the story of the bird-on-trial in Maurice's own words, who had also had the story validated, not by his own experience per se, but by the verbatim translation—another form of telephony—offered by two others, concludes his narration as follows: "I could not but tell this odd story, because it is so much out of the way, and from the first hand, and what may pass for a good one; for I dare say this Prince at least believed himself in all he told me, having ever passed for a very honest and pious man . . . it is not perhaps amiss to relieve or enliven a busy scene sometimes with such digressions whether to the purpose or no."

Locke uses this story to illustrate that the parrot, no matter how reasonable and eloquent, is nevertheless *not* a man and so does not disturb the boundaries that separate man and animal.[29] However, the story has a far greater impact on the *Essay*'s contentions regarding narration and identity than Locke officially grants to it. Indeed, one senses a certain amount of disingenuousness in the reluctance to acknowledge the story's most distinguishing and perhaps most disturbing feature: that the parrot *seems* to possess a narrative authority as sound as that of the humans who are called upon to attest to the story's truth. For, quite apart from the visible differences between parrots and humans, the fact that parrots are speaking machines poses an almost continuous threat to the humanness that Locke attempts to stabilize.

From the moment the storyteller—who is first Locke, then his author, then the prince, and finally the parrot's translators—appears in the guise of a witness and narrates the events as a faithful imitation, another witness is required to establish the reliability of the first and then another and another and so on, until we are caught in an infinite regress. The trustworthiness of the story can only be guaranteed by the narrator, yet the narrator can only be verified by a

mimetic authority—that is, quotations of quotations of quotations—
that can in no way be guaranteed or stopped. That the story is ostensibly *about* a parrot who can speak and who has both memory and
a sense of humor belies an even more outlandish possibility: that the
parrot in the story is merely one instance of a more all-encompassing
parrot-logic governing the story. This regress of narrative authority
suggests that mimesis is not enough to guarantee the truthfulness of
the narrated, empirical, and so supposedly historical event and that
furthermore, narrative authority attains its truthfulness only through
the mimetic authority that cannot, in a story that is mimetically told
as a historical occurrence, be guaranteed or stabilized.[30]

The circularity of this fable-telling—a story whose mimetic truth
cannot be verified except through its endless retelling, which itself
cannot be authorized except by the rigor of its mimetic repetition—
itself repeats itself, less surprisingly this time in Locke's section on
language. In keeping with Paul de Man's contention that examples
used to illustrate logical arguments have a "distressing way of lingering on with a life of their own,"[31] it is here that we again meet
the parrot as that which "speaks out of control"; that is, it speaks
without any sort of grounding in consciousness that would provide a
modicum of stability. This time, however, it is not the parrot that so
convincingly imitates man but rather man that displays the qualities
of the parrot.

After having generated a theory of the origin of ideas in Section
Two of the *Essay*, Locke states the unavoidable necessity of meditat-
ing upon language. "Upon a nearer approach," he writes, "I find that
there is so close a connexion [*sic*] between *ideas* and words, and our
abstract *ideas* and general words have so constant a relation one to
another, that it is impossible to speak clearly and distinctly of our
knowledge . . . without considering first the nature, use and signification of language" (*Essay* 2.33.19). From the outset, Locke frames
the discussion in anthropocentric terms. Language is, in other words,
God's gift to man.

However, no sooner has Locke made this assertion than he is
confronted with the burden of having to exclude animals from the
domain of language. Not surprisingly, his example is again that of
the parrot: "But this," he quickly adds, "was not enough to produce
language; for parrots, and several other birds, will be taught to make
articulate sounds distinct enough, which yet by no means are capable
of language" (*Essay* 2.33.19). In order to make good on this claim

and to distinguish what is proper to human language, Locke raises
the issue of the connection between ideas and words:

> Thus we may conceive how *words*, which were by nature so well
> adapted to that purpose, come to be made use of by men as the signs
> of their ideas; not by any natural connexion that there is between par-
> ticular articulate sounds and certain ideas, for then there would be
> but one language amongst all men; but by a voluntary imposition,
> whereby such a word is made arbitrarily the mark of such an idea. The
> use, then of words, is to be sensible marks of ideas; and the ideas they
> stand for are their proper and immediate signification. (*Essay* 3.2.1)

The relation between words and ideas is such that words give external
shape to ideas residing in the mind and so allow for communication
among men to take place. Words are "the marks of the ideas of the
speaker" (*Essay* 3.2.2), ideas that are "invisible and hidden from others," which "of themselves, can[not] be made to appear." Although
Locke repeatedly comes back to the relation of words to the entombed
world of ideas, his focus is not on how one might set about defining
such a relation but instead focuses on how the sociality of language
might be derived in light of the possibility, given its arbitrary system of signification, of its unruly multiplication. That words "signify . . . by a perfect arbitrary imposition," and that, "every man has
so inviolable a liberty to make words stand for what ideas he please,
that no one hath the power to make others have the same ideas in
their minds that he has, when they use the same words that he does"
(*Essay* 3.2.8), does not, for Locke, alter the propensity of reasonable
men to partake in a realm of shared ideas when they speak.[32]

The realm of shared ideas is the hidden source for words, a source
whose only access is itself provided by language. After having contended that words are the external marks of the (internal) ideas of the
speaker, Locke then attempts to account for the possibility of communication, one that is, for him, based on the a priori condition that words
used in speech reflect (although they are not *essentially* related) a shared
realm of ideas. That words mirror ideas will alone provide the stable
difference between man—the entity within which, as de Man reminds
us, "the proper, which is a linguistic notion, and essence, which exists
independently of linguistic mediation are said to converge" (EM 40)—
and all other animals that have the capacity to speak.

In attempting to ground this contention in what appears to be
a logical argument, Locke writes, "That then which words are the
marks of are the ideas of the speaker; nor can anyone apply them as

marks, immediately, to anything else but the ideas that he himself hath; for this would be to make them signs of his own conceptions, and yet apply them to other ideas; which would be to make them signs and not signs of his ideas at the same time, and so in effect to have no signification at all" (*Essay* 3.2.2). How, one might be tempted to ask, is such a formulation possible, given that it both suggests what one cannot do (in the logical sense of necessity), and then immediately admit to the possibility of what it forecloses? However one might read this passage, one thing is clear: The formulation is less a logical form of argument than it is one that obliquely admits the possibility of that which it has just foreclosed.

In any case, however possible it may or may not be to speak with no signification at all, the good sense of communal understanding prevails. To speak "otherwise," to have words be *"signs and not-signs"* at the same time would, Locke adamantly suggests, elicit nothing but verbal nonsense. Animals that are capable of forming sensible speech through the use of a vocal apparatus are thus excluded from the realm of language, as are various other kinds of babble: "Words being voluntary signs, they cannot be voluntary signs imposed by him on things he knows not. That would be to make them signs of nothing, sounds without signification" (*Essay* 3.2.2).

As undesirable as the proliferation of speech unanchored from consciousness or of words without corresponding ideas is, Locke cannot stop himself from considering it, a kind of preoccupation that alerts us to the possibility that there may be more to this senseless babble than Locke would care to admit. In the closing remarks to the section, he is led once again to consider the parrot. This time, however, it is not a question of disassociating human speech from that of the parrot; it is, rather, a reluctant admission of the parrot's ubiquity *within* the realm of human speech. Locke writes,

> Yet, because by familiar use from our cradles we come to learn certain articulate sounds very perfectly and have them readily on our tongues, and always at hand in our memories, but yet are not always careful to examine or settle their significations perfectly, it *often* happens that *men*, even when they would apply themselves to an attentive consideration, *do set their thoughts more on words than things.* Nay, because words are many of them learned before the *ideas* are known for which they stand: therefore some, not only children but men, speak several words no otherwise than parrots do, only because they have learned them, and have been accustomed to those sounds. (*Essay* 3.2.7, emphasis in original)

Having begun by limiting the "mindless" abuse of words to the domain of children, talking parrots, and a few men, Locke is forced to admit that this abuse is capable of reaching unsettlingly global proportions.

Indeed, he ends his investigation on "Of the Abuse of Words" by pinpointing its most general—and most insidious, because "less observed"—application. The target of his attack this time though is the very guardian of ideas himself, indeed the very thinker of consciousness: the philosopher-intellectual. "This abuse *taking words upon trust*," Locke contends, "has nowhere spread so far, nor with so ill effects, as amongst men of letters. The multiplication and obstinacy of disputes, which have so laid waste the intellectual world, is owing to nothing more than to this ill use of words" (*Essay* 2.10.22, emphasis added).[33] In other words, the very domain in which one would expect a modicum of clarity regarding the relation of words to ideas is the domain where one would do well to expect the worst. Using words without accompanying meaning, Locke says in no uncertain terms, "has nowhere spread so far" as in intellectual disputes. In fact, the "great variety of opinions in the volumes and variety of controversies the world is distracted with" can be attributed wholly to the fact that they "speak different languages" (*Essay* 2.10.22). The remedy for this proliferation of speech without the guardianship of ideas is deceptively clear: "I am apt to imagine that when any of them, quitting terms, think upon things, and know what they think, they think all the same" (*Essay* 2.10.22).

Although Locke's aim here is to highlight the use of words without ideas as a linguistic abuse that causes conflict and disagreement, and to generate a sense of how one might overcome its Babel-like effects, the logic of the argument inadvertently returns us to the undecidability exemplified in the episode of the parrot. For, the separation of ideas from words implies that humans use words to communicate their ideas: hence, it would only be through language that a consensus could ever be reached or a disagreement raised. But since language *substitutes* for ideas, how could one ever be sure of the authority of a statement, much less give one's consent to it, given that a consensus could only ever happen in language?

In contrast to Plato's elaboration of speech in the *Phaedrus* as that which never leaves its rightful owner, Locke's discussion of "voice" renders explicit the threat of repetition, of appropriation of that which is improper, of mimicry, and of mechanical imitation. The impropriety of this machine-like speaking, one that fails to reflect a consciousness that is at one with all its previous moments, is threatening precisely because of its capacity for verisimilitude: that is to say, it is threatening, not only because in it, voice fails to reflect ideas located in the mind by being more concentrated on words than ideas, but that such speech *appears* to reflect ideas, and that there is no way to distinguish between an agreement between words and ideas and the mere appearance of such an agreement.

As such, Locke's discussion of the proper use of language opens itself up *not* to the stabilization of language in terms of the ideas that it signifies but rather to the possibility of even more linguistic abuse. This applies not only to parrots, children, and childlike adults but also to those endowed with the greatest philosophical and narrative authority. Indeed, it applies even to those who have no intention to deceive: "Even those who apply themselves to a careful consideration" are, according to Locke, not immune from its effects. Language, read thus, is not so much a tool to communicate ideas as it is the very embodiment of impostership. What is more (and worse), one can be an impostor without having any idea of it at all.

What Locke has developed in these sections on language calls into question the claims that the text makes with regard to its own authority. In the development of the argument, Locke distinguishes his argument from the contaminating effects of what he diagnoses. That is to say, the argument is predicated upon the notion that the abuse of language is distinct, and distinguishable from the terms in which he formulates his argument and his diagnosis. How, though, can we ever be sure of escaping this distressing linguistic predicament, especially given that the language in which we elaborate on such abusive instances is also caught within linguistic and rhetorical structures, ones within which the predicament appears in the first instance? In other words, how are we to read these sections on voice and authority with respect to the larger philosophical claims in the *Essay* regarding the origin of ideas?

One could, with good reason, suggest that the *Essay* secures a philosophical authority for itself—in light of the radical problematization of authority and the potential for linguistic nonsense that it possesses—by attempting to ground the origin of ideas in an empirical event: what Locke calls "experience." After all, the whole treatise is framed by a desire to rid philosophy of much of the verbal nonsense around the innatist claim that ideas are present in—and, for Plato, forgotten by—the individual at birth. For Locke, even if the argument regarding innatist principles were "drawn from *universal consent*," such would not be sufficient to prove them innate (1.2.3). Rather, Locke suggests that an examination of the origin of ideas—one not shored up "with props and buttresses, leaning on borrowed or begged foundations" (1.4.26)—will serve to dispel much of the consent around innatism, given that, "one may perceive how, by degrees, afterwards, ideas come into the minds [of children], and that they get no more nor no other, than what experience and the observation of things that come in their way, furnish them with: which might be enough to satisfy us that they are not original characters stamped on the mind" (*Essay* 1.4.2).

In calling into question the claims made by innatism, Locke may be attempting to avoid the problematic exemplified by the fiction of the parrot; that is, in grounding the origin of ideas in empirical events (the experience of childhood and the development of the child into an adult), he may perhaps be attempting to bypass the narrative spiral that ensues from taking a quasi-fictional account, one whose origin is absent and unlocatable—in this case, innatism—to be empirically verifiable and true.

Empiricism attempts to find a way out of the predicament of absent and unrepresentable origins by asserting that all ideas are acquired through experience. "I know it is a received doctrine," writes Locke, "that men have native *ideas*, and original characters stamped upon their mind in their very first being. . . . [the critique of this position] will be much more easily admitted when I have shown whence the understanding may get all the *ideas* it has, and by what ways and degrees they may come into the mind; for which I shall appeal to everyone's own observation and experience" (*Essay* 2.1.1). The appeal of empiricism is first and foremost that it brings the origins of human knowledge—a self-constituting knowledge and one that constitutes the world—out of the ungrounded realms of myth and fiction and into the purview of man's own analytic capacity given to him by what is most properly *his*: the experience of his own life.[34]

As such, one burden of Locke's treatise is to give voice to these origins and moreover, to ground the constitution of "man" in a beginning that is as representable as an historical event might be. This quasi-historical dimension of the origin is thus extremely important both to the structure of the text as a whole and to the itinerary of "personhood" contained within it. For if Locke's "person" is determined through the appropriation of its origin through the faculty of memory, Locke's own preoccupation with origins suggests that the *Essay* itself attempts to perform an act of memory, one that not only grounds the origin of ideas in the two sources of experience, "sensation" and "reflection," but that also attempts to bring this origin of the understanding to consciousness in an appropriating act of memory. The account that Locke gives of these systemic origins and the role that memory plays within that account has a particularly important role to play in our understanding of memory's role in self-attestation and, in particular, to that which Locke's "person" attests when it speaks in the name of memory.

§

The confirmation in "Of Identity and Diversity" of memory as both the ground of the self and, more tenuously, as the self's most intimate possession is treated with more explicit ambiguity in the earlier sections of the treatise where Locke attempts to establish the main tenets of empirical philosophy. There, memory is conceived as a *problem*. By reading these two seemingly incompatible sections together—memory as a structural element of empirical philosophy along with the notion of memory as identity's most decisive and vivifying factor—we can gauge the ways in which the tensions of the role of memory in the constitution of identity play themselves out.

The experience of childhood and the relation of adult to child play central roles in the description of the role of memory within the system of empiricism that Locke is undertaking to develop. In fact, one could say that his abiding interest in childhood—both here and in other writings[35]—frames the discussion of the constitution of identity through memory by referring once again to the constitutive feature of childhood as both the origin of adulthood and human sociality *and* as the origin of ideas.

Although explicit reference to childhood is wanting in the descriptions of memory that inform personal identity in the *Essay*, this absence is conspicuous given that the entire framework of memory that Locke had developed in the earlier section "Of Ideas in General, and Their Original" (hereafter abbreviated as "Of Ideas") revolves around the proofs that he provides regarding the experience of childhood and in particular, regarding the relation of adult memory to childhood experience. In fact, its absence in the section that deals with identity, given its centrality for the earlier formulations, should alert us to a sense of its importance, however oblique. In "Of Ideas," the observation of childhood is the point of departure from which the experiential modes of "sensation" and "reflection," and the means by which ideas are brought to the understanding, attain clarity.

"He that attentively considers the state of a *child*," Locke writes in his ongoing attack on innatism, "at his first coming into the world will have little reason to think him stored with plenty of *ideas*, that are to be the matter of his future knowledge" (*Essay* 2.1.6). That the mind of the child is a "white page, void of all characters" offers Locke the opportunity to analyze the origin of certain sensate ideas, using his own powers of observation. In calling to account for the origins of "sensation" in experience, Locke observes that children are "usually employed and diverted in looking abroad." This preoccupation with sensation, Locke suggests, is a perfectly natural phenomenon, one that "whether care be taken about it or no," affects "all that are born into the world, being surrounded with bodies that perpetually and diversely affect them, variety of *ideas*, are imprinted on the minds of children" (*Essay* 2.1.6).

This preconscious sensation yields no memory of itself. That children do not remember their first impressions is explained by their undeveloped ability for reflection; that is, they do not yet have the ability to retain images and to reflect upon them—the true mark, for Locke, of an enlightened "person." At this stage sensation predominates, even before "the memory begins to keep a register of time and order" (*Essay* 2.1.6); this preconscious sensation is the foundation upon which the later-developed reflection on images already stored in the mind is built. Locke describes this constitutional amnesia in terms dictated by his ensuing discussion of memory in the treatise: "Though [sensations] pass there continually, yet, like floating visions, they make not deep impressions enough to leave in the mind clear, distinct, lasting ideas, till the understanding turns inward upon itself, reflects on its own operations, and makes them the object of its own contemplation" (*Essay* 1.2.8). Childhood, then, is the developmental stage at which the inability to store images in the mind corresponds to an overload of sensory stimuli. In time, these sensory stimuli will, the text confidently suggests, become the source of material for the mind's own reflection on its contents. This process of reflection is the desired outcome of human development: It will provide the groundwork for memory and for the ability of the self to reflect on the images stored as its own. "Men then come to be furnished with fewer or more simple ideas from without, according as the objects they converse with afford greater or less variety" (2.1.7).

Recently, critics have noted that the transition in question—from sensation of that which is external to reflection on that which is stored within—is not so much rigorously explicated as it is dramatically staged. From early childhood, wherein *"light* and *colours* are busy at hand everywhere, when the eye is but open; sounds and some tangible qualities fail not to solicit their proper senses, and *force an entrance to the mind"* (*Essay* 2.1.6) to the stage of developing memory, where the mind "comes by degrees to know the persons it daily converses with and *distinguishes them from strangers"* (*Essay* 2.1.21), the mind of sensation is likened to a vault or to a chamber hall, one that, by virtue of the door of the "open eye" or the solicited senses, admits entry to and domesticates foreigners.

Following the work of Ernest Tuveson, Cathy Caruth has commented at length on the importance of the rhetorical and fictional aspects of Locke's treatise. Concerning the passages just quoted, Caruth suggests that at the stage of sensation, "what seems at first a straightforward observation of sensory mechanisms becomes more like an anxious story of a precariously governed state," that it operates "on principles less like a 'natural philosophy' than a literary text," and that what is narrated in Locke's text is "an anxiety-ridden story in which the empirical world *solicits* or seduces and then forces itself upon an unsuspecting mind."[36]

Far from suggesting that Locke's text is merely fictional, Caruth ascribes a certain necessity to Locke's use of rhetorical figures at the stage of sensation. At the stage of sensation, the empirical world represents an almost constant threat to the mind; through the sheer magnitude of its intrusion, it overwhelms the mind and does not allow for memory to take a register of events. As such, the period of sheer sensation is literally a blind spot in the past for the adult who attempts to contemplate it in herself; it has no more empirical status in her memory than if it had never happened. Reflection in the adult seems, then, to be founded on the radical forgetfulness of the period of sensation, one that Locke himself cannot remember so must figuratively derive under the pretense of observing children—that is, by speculating on childhood—in the empirical world.

For Locke, the period of childhood corresponds to a period of sensory overload that, because of its excessive or overwhelming nature, leaves very few mental traces in the constitution of the individual. That childhood is so conceived, that is, as a period in the life of an individual that has trauma-like effects, suggests that the "child" is less an empirically verifiable entity—its status cannot, according to the terms of Locke's own argument, be empirically verified much less experienced—than it is a figure in the text, one whose characteristics and "experiences" tell a tale of foundations. That these "experiences" of the overwhelming period of sensation are not experiences strictly speaking, and that they can never be experienced firsthand suggests that the terms of the narration of one's self does not so much consist in a remembering of the experience of an origin as it does in a recovery from the origin that one could only ever "experience" as a blank.

Inasmuch as the nonexperience of this child threatens the development of Locke's system, it is little wonder that he attempts to put the child-figure of his empiricism safely behind him, just as he does the child that develops into an adult and of whose status the adult has little or no recollection. Thus, the goal of the section is to submit the differences between childhood amnesia (sensation and the threat of the empirical world) and adulthood memory (reflection and the mind as a self-enclosed region) to a teleology.[37] This narrative of human development tells of a triumphant overcoming of sensation to the contemplative world of reflection and self-inspection, an overcoming by means of which the understanding can reflect on its own contents without the looming threat of unwanted or unanticipated visitors. If the empirical validity of childhood—dictated, in the text, by the narration of the blind acceptance, insofar as the child's eye is too wide-open, of all sensations of the external world—allows Locke to explain childhood as the origin of the human understanding, its unavoidably figural status attests to a threat of oblivion that governs the course of the understanding's development of its reflective powers. The submission of his own descriptions to the reassurance offered by the historical development of the individual is just his attempt to recover from the threat posed by the blind origin.

The general anxiety informing this recovery is suggested by the text's subsequent trajectory. The more feverishly Locke attempts to rid himself of the specter of childhood and to relegate the unruly event of sensation safely to the past,[38] the more adamantly it seems to assert itself in the lives of adults. Reflection—the sober and controlled domain of adulthood—comes late for children, Locke asserts, because they are busy with the external world. The ability to contemplate comes later; it must wait "till they come to be of riper years, *and some scarce ever at all*" (*Essay* 2.1.8, emphasis added). If the ability to contemplate the regions of the mind is itself the domain of the adult, adulthood is however no guarantee: "Some," he admits, "have not any clear or perfect ideas of the greatest part of them all their lives" (*Essay* 2.2.8).

It is unlikely that Locke would include the empiricist in this category of childlike adulthood, given especially that the task that he has set for himself is to define the broad reach of the human understanding in purely empirical terms. Indeed, given the aims of the *Essay*, one would expect Locke's own reflection on reflection to exemplify the self contemplating the self in a hermetically sealed environment. However, in the less triumphant and less self-assured aspects of his discussion of memory, his own doctrine resembles just such an instance of the childlike adult, one who in attempting to observe the contents of the mind, cannot quite make out what he sees.

In the section "Of Retention," Locke submits memory to his survey and begins by more or less predictably defining memory as the "storehouse of our ideas," a mainstay of Aristotelian discourse on memory. Because the narrow mind of man is incapable of holding many ideas in mind at once, Locke further explains, "it was necessary to have a repository, to lay up those ideas which, at another time, it might have use of" (*Essay* 2.10.2). Despite the certainty of the deposits that are made, Locke expresses a palpable anxiety about the security of the investment. Indeed, despite the strength of his own contentions, Locke seems compelled to attest to memory's most ubiquitous nature: "But, our ideas being nothing but actual perceptions in the mind, which cease to be anything when there is no perception of them, this laying up of our ideas in the repository of the memory signifies no more but this, that the mind has a power in many cases to revive perceptions which it has once had, . . . in this sense it is that our ideas are said to be in our memories when indeed they are actually nowhere" (*Essay* 2.10.2). Memory serves as a repository for ideas, ideas that have ceased to be anything; it is a storehouse whose stores are nothing, stored nowhere. Strictly speaking, then, memory houses nothing and is nowhere. This atopical quality of memory presents problems for Locke from which he quickly, if spuriously, recovers: The mind, he contends in the same paragraph, "has a power in many cases to revive perceptions it has once had, with this additional perception annexed to them, that *it has had them before*" (*Essay* 2.10.2, emphasis in original).

Locke's doctrinal explanation of memory and in particular his attempt to distinguish memory from perception are undermined by the peculiar force of his own description. Unsurprisingly, he describes the weakness of memory as an episodic or accidental weakness of the memory of individuals and not as a weakness of the empiricism that is called to account for it. Memories though, particularly those of childhood, are encrypted alternatively as monuments, as "cautions for the future" (*Essay* 2.10.3) and as tombs (*Essay* 2.10.5), all of which suggest that the human understanding houses not the products of its own lively powers, but the dead to be revivified.

In his description of the inscribed quality of memory, Locke's tone takes a deeply lugubrious turn as if to remind his readers of the fragility of what is stored there. "There seems to be a constant decay of all our ideas, even of those which are struck deepest," he admits, "the print wears out, and at last there remains nothing to be seen. . . . [I]n some it retains the characters drawn on it like marble, in others like freestone, and in others little better than sand . . . we oftentimes find a disease quite strip the mind of all its ideas, and the flames of a fever in a few days calcine all those images to dust and confusion, which seemed to be as lasting as if engraved in marble" (*Essay* 2.10.5). Even marble, that most durable and permanent of engraving surfaces, is not immune to erosion and defacement. Old age and disease accelerate this process of defacement, a process that results in the complete erasure of what is inscribed upon the tomb of the mind. Again, we find ourselves confronted with the enigma of childhood: "Thus the ideas as well as children of our youth often die before us; and our minds represent to us those tombs to which we are approaching: where, though the brass and marble remain, yet the inscriptions are effaced by time, and the imagery moulders away. The pictures drawn in our minds are laid in fading colours, and if not sometimes refreshed, vanish and disappear" (*Essay* 2.10.5). The strange and morbid analogy offered here suggests that memories are like children, children subject to an early death. Once again, as in the famous case study immediately preceding this passage of the child who, in going blind, fails to retain the memory of color, Locke's reflection on memory circles around the subject of childhood, highlighting the ways in which it could be cut off—or cut short—from adulthood by the loss of vision or, even more decisively, by the loss of life.

In one sense, one could read these descriptions as a set of melancholy reflections on the progressive loss of memory that accompanies

aging. However, if we follow the figure of the child from its association with sensation and with the overwhelming intrusion of the
empirical world to its present incarnation as an abiding feature of the
reflective mind, then we are forced to reconsider the claims that the
text has made with respect to human development. In relation to that
teleological development from childhood to adulthood, what Locke
articulates here suggests that the phenomenon of forgotten childhood
can no longer be explained, and ultimately overcome, using the physiological and "empirical" fact of development into adulthood. For
we are now told that the child, which is a figure for the foreboding
possibility of amnesia and the threat posed by that amnesia to self-
enclosed reflection, persistently abides in the adult mind; even more
horrifically, it is a dead child that keeps silent and that, as corpse,
inhabits its most proper tomb.

To what property does the "child," read as both the ostensibly
empirical source of human identity and as that which poses its most
deadly threat, owe its excessive figurative power? It is significant here,
I think, to invoke what might seem to be the most obvious characteristic of the child: its speechlessness. According to the *Oxford English
Dictionary* "infant" is derived from the Latin term *infans*, which
means "unable to speak."[39] It also passes into the juridical realm as
the *terminus technicus* of "child" as that which is unable to exercise
sovereign power over itself. It is in light of this speechlessness that the
child is given a voice in Locke's text, in the form of the *Essay*'s own
philosophical authority. At one level, we might be tempted to say that
the subject emerges in language—namely, in a verbal act that mourns
the child that dies before it. The supposed anteriority of the child's
death opens up the possibility for the child to be made present in the
form of an unsubstantiated memory, speaking in a voice that is not
and could never be proper to it. As such, if we are to interpret this
structure as one in which the reflection constitutive of adulthood can
only be established on the condition of living *with* the death of this
child, then the task of reflection to establish a solid and stable identity—one that has all the moments of its own development within its
reach—involves not so much giving consciousness or observation the
full breadth of its own reach as it does the awakening of the dead and
the giving of voice to that which is, so to speak, born (and dies) silent.

This interpretation, as well-founded as it is, fails in two respects:
firstly, it requires that we turn the language of memory and, indeed,
language in general, into a property or tool of the self; and secondly,

it overlooks the double syntax of *before*—that is, "before" as the straightforward temporal index of "previously," "in the past," or "prior to" as well as the more speculative preposition of "demanding the attention of," "in the presence of," "ahead of" or "in front of." The difficulty of choosing between these two modes of *before* is, I think, central to working out the stakes of Locke's somber description of testimony, beyond the fiction it undoubtedly also inaugurates that the self's identity is given by a past that is wholly accessible to it. At odds with that fiction is the sense in which the phrase "the children of our youth often die *before* us" articulates a structure of testimony wherein the past and future—both dictated by *before*—are no longer rigorously distinguishable.[40]

If we do attempt to read the "before" of the phrase, "ideas as well as children of our youth die *before* us" in terms of this undecidability, what are we to make of its futurity? Indeed, a nagging suspicion remains concerning the remnants of the future contained in this passage, replete as it is with effaced tombs, dying children, and fading ideas. The sense notwithstanding that the figure of the child is, if nothing else, an incredibly vivid image of the future, how could such a morbid set of descriptions—ones revolving around a *dead* child—possibly serve as orientation toward the future?

It is, I think, in light of "before" as "in front of" that a more complex temporal dimension is brought to bear on the representation of experience in Locke's narrative of the self, beyond its itinerary of a quasi-historical narrative that incorporates experience, the silence of which is overcome by the narratives we generate about it. Though only barely articulated, Locke's formulation nonetheless does gesture toward a more speculative temporal structure wherein the self is literally confronted by the silent past—the past stands *before* it, in front or in advance of it—as its own future. So, far from simply giving itself over to the confident memorial discourse of the self, Locke's self does attest to its own finitude but in an entirely unexpected sense. In fact, the latter part of the phrase in question—"and our minds represent to us those tombs *to which we are approaching*"—all but confirms this dimension of futurity in Locke's description, when the self "experiences" its own finitude in the past to the precise extent that it cannot possibly be incorporated into the self's narrative and so must be relegated to the future. For finitude as such could never be known or experienced, for the deceptively simple reason that one can never experience one's own death, much less narrate it. As a strange kind of memento mori, then, the Lockean past does not simply disappear nor is it fully represented in the subject's narrative of itself; it simply abides, silently, as a reminder of the self's own unnarratable and, for that reason, ungraspable, future.

Indeed, in saying that the subject bears witness to that which is most silent and so most resistant to its appropriation through voice, it does not seem especially compelling to speak of a proxy. For the silent one—at one point, the "child"; at another, "sensation"—has no voice, no "story" to tell, one that could be otherwise transmitted, told to or by others. Locke's *Essay* tells us, then, if not exactly in the way it intended, that whoever bears testimony to their own past experiences does so by facing a certain resistance, a resistance those experiences put up to speaking. To be sure, the idea that it is difficult, if not impossible, to ground the self on the stories it tells of its own experience is to provoke the potentially endless displacement of narrative authority that we saw at work in Locke's story of the parrot. But this need not generate the sense that testimony is in need of moral improvement or of a more sober policing of its boundaries, as has been suggested.[41] Rather, it is precisely by virtue of this difficulty, as well as the inexhaustibility of past experience implied by it, that the *before* of the past is able to retain any futurity—and the "I" any sense of its own finitude—at all.

In brief, many of the difficulties and tensions of Lockean testimony to finite experience are borne on this *before*: it both inaugurates the impulse to generate narratives of the past in order to keep it safely before—that is, behind—us and, at the same time, it also generates a sense of how fragile the narrative authority is that might keep it there. As such, the truth contained in these passages is poorly served if it is thought to reside in how they procure a sense of the self's certitude by virtue of its making the past "speak." To the contrary: those past experiences retain their force by not *remaining* past, by not being fully narrated or articulated in a narrative of self. In Locke, then, the problem of narrating infancy stands for the difficulties of stabilizing experience in narrative form: "the children of our youth" dying before us both provokes the impulse to narrate at the same time as it marks it out as a potentially difficult and indeed, as an endless task. And it is in such moments of narrative insecurity that the past remains *before* us—that is, behind and in front of us, in and as the indeterminate and as yet unarticulated future.

In the next two chapters, we will have occasion to examine what is quite possibly modernity's fullest account of memory as a speculative relation to the past in Hegel's philosophy. For now though, we can at least point to the following: That if versions of Locke's legacy are to continue to provide the ground for personal and communal identities in the form of claims to subject-memory, what some of the less clearly articulated aspects of the *Essay* suggest is that to bear witness to past experience as the source for a positive and stabilized identity is, paradoxically perhaps, to invoke a foreignness that will not be incorporated or domesticated within the logic of a biographical narrative. To live in and with such an aporia is perhaps one of the things we should hear in Locke's discussion of testimony and experience; that to invoke testimony as the means by which the self can be definitely stabilized through its own memory is a great fiction, greater even than that of our uncanny resemblance to the talking parrot.

CHAPTER THREE

Mourning Memory

The "End" of Art or, Reading (in) the Spirit of Hegel

A mended sock is better than a torn one; not so with self-consciousness.
—G. W. F. Hegel

Despite the more complicated reading of Locke's *Essay* that I hope to
have generated in Chapter 2—especially in terms of the kinds of temporality that are generated when memory is understood to be mediated in and through language—it nonetheless remains the case that
a more conventional understanding of Locke's *Essay* prevails in discussions of memory and identity, ones that tend to see Locke as relegating language and sociality to positions of incidental or secondary
importance. When we disregard the complex forms of relation and
of temporality that considerations of language introduce into Locke's
theory, we are left with the familiar, yet still powerful, picture of a
self that is deeply disengaged from history and tradition, one that continues to underpin modern psychological accounts of the subject right
through to our time.

On the one hand, this putatively disengaged subject provides the
ground for a particularly modern sense of freedom: As Charles Taylor
writes in *Sources of the Self*, "many things have been declared author-
itatively true . . . which have no real title to the name. The rational,
self-responsible subject can break with them, suspend his adhesion
to them, and by submitting them to the test of their validity, remake
or replace them."[1] According to Taylor, the ideal of freedom or independence from forms of unquestioned authority—as well as the commitment to questioning forms of "innate doctrines" that this disengagement demands—as it is articulated in Locke's *Essay* accounts in
large part for its tremendous and continuing influence: It "helps to
explain why we think of ourselves as 'selves' today." Further, Taylor

argues that this notion of freedom is uniquely modern since, unlike the ancients who also called for a stop to living in unreflecting habit by returning to an objective order, the modern self is called upon to separate itself from itself through self-objectification and this, he says, "is an operation that can only be carried out in the first-person perspective": "It calls on me to be aware of *my* activity of thinking or *my* processes of habituation, so as to disengage from them and objectify them" (*Sources* 175).

As Taylor also notes, though, the flipside to this ideal of freedom that emerges in modernity through an articulation of the self is its almost total alienation from the world, against which it defines itself. However, precisely because the self's ungroundedness or "extra-worldliness" provides the ground of its independence and freedom—that is, it is distinct from and ultimately superior to all other things—it also introduces a paradox into the itinerary of the self, as Taylor notes in his chapter on Locke: "The philosophy of disengagement and objectification has helped to create a picture of the human being . . . from which the last vestiges of subjectivity seem to have been expelled. It is a picture of the human being from a completely third-person stance." And, finally, "radical objectivity is only intelligible and accessible through radical subjectivity" (*Sources* 176).

The contention that philosophies of the self—of which Taylor sees Locke's as inaugural and exemplary—almost inevitably result in a deep division between the first- and third-person perspectives also has implications for the conception of the modern self as a remembering self. For, if one of the conditions of "self"'-accounting is that the self is able to appropriate the past as its own—and not as a given past, say, in the form of history or tradition—then according to Taylor, the act of narrating one's own past, and overcoming the division from it, would itself give way to an even more vexing sense of the past's impropriety; that is, the foreignness of the past would not emerge *despite* the fact of the past's appearing in its most highly subjective expression, but rather *because* of that very act of appropriation.

While the *Essay's* official statements and formulations certainly do not foresee the very division that it would help to inaugurate—much less recognize it as its own or actively seek to overcome it—the self-splitting does get acted out in the more explicitly literary moments of the text. In a significant sense, the tone of the *Essay* is more anxious than most commentators are willing to admit; in fact, on many levels it reads more like an allegory of discontinuity than it does a

celebration of a new and free "I," opening all age-old dogma and presupposition to the force of its own interrogation and disavowal.

Still, though, the question remains: if the Lockean project is said
to have located the possibility of knowledge and ultimately of human
freedom from dogmatic authority in the life and in the memory of the
self-contained individual, what can we make of the human remains
of such a project, especially in light of what Taylor sees as its logical outcome: the "severe outlook" given by "a picture of the human
being from a completely third-person perspective," wherein all traces
of subjectivity and individuality have been erased?

This question constitutes the backdrop to the work that follows,
beginning with Hegel's critique of Locke in the *Lectures on the History
of Philosophy*. Regarded from the perspective of the history of philosophy, it may seem nothing short of reckless to compare the philosophy of Locke with that of Hegel, given their seemingly unbridgeable
differences in historical context, orientation, and method. However,
more than any other thinker in the modern philosophical tradition,
it was Hegel who sought to rectify the divisions that Taylor suggests
are created by a Lockean stance of radical subjectivity, and to offer an
account of spirit that did not simply ignore these painful divisions—
as Hegel will suggest is the case for Locke—but rather that moved
through them as part of its own memorial movement.

In that sense, Hegel's critique of Locke can help set the stage for
an understanding of what is at stake in his own articulation of memory. Given that the aim of his critique is to foreground what Locke's
philosophy has itself forgotten—Hegel's description is of a "philosophy . . . humbled in the forgetting of its own activity [*solches
Philosophieren ist . . . demütig mit Vergessen seiner Tätigkeit*]"[2]—he
also implies that the *proper* way to do philosophy is to perform an
act of memory. In a way, then, Hegel's aim is not so much to help the
modern subject to remember as it is to remember the modern subject from a philosophical perspective that has moved beyond it. In
the sense that Hegel wrested memory away from its expression of
subjective consciousness, it could indeed be argued that the resulting
notion of memory is complicit with and contributes to the process of
its de-humanization. However, given that the most deeply subjective
accounts of memory yield all manner of bizarrely inhuman elements,
Hegel's critique might be able to lend more subtle clarity to what is
at stake in the contention that memory is not only, or not simply,
human.

§

From (practically) the outset, then, we may as well state the obvious: The prospect of discovering affinities between Lockean empiricism and Hegel's speculative philosophy does not look especially promising. For, while Kant had famously commended Hume's empiricism for awakening him from his dogmatic slumber, the same can hardly be said of Hegel's reception of Locke's *Essay*. Indeed, the very first lines of Hegel's treatment of Lockean empiricism in the *Lectures on the History of Philosophy* suggest that Hegel is preparing to awaken self-professed Lockeans—of which, according to Hegel, there were many (295, 298/312–13)—from their own dogmatic slumber. The tone of the exposition's opening lines stops just short of contempt: "that the notion has objective actuality for consciousness is indeed a necessary element in the totality. But as this reflection appears in Locke, signifying as it does that we obtain truth by abstracting from experience and sensuous perception, it is utterly false [*der trivialste, schlechteste Gedanke*]. Instead of being a moment, it is made the essence of truth" (295/342). But "stop short" it nonetheless does, if only just. In fact, the account of Locke that follows this damning initial assessment has a pendent feel: It oscillates between the need to expose the sheer nonsense of Locke's notion of truth (Hegel will repeatedly call it *seicht* and *oberflächlich*, or "shallow," "superficial") and alternatively, the equally pressing need to commend the *Essay* for having initiated something important: "Thus Locke has striven to satisfy a true necessity in that he attempted to show where the universal ideas come in, on what they are founded and how they are verified" (298/348, translation modified); "thus the course adopted by Locke is quite a correct one [*ist . . . ganz richtig*]" (300/349).

In particular, Hegel's praise for Locke's initiative focuses on the latter's critique of innate ideas: "Locke combats the so-called innate ideas . . . ie. the universal, absolutely existent ideas which at the same time are represented as pertaining to mind in a natural way . . . which we have and are present and exist in consciousness as such" (300/350). "The expression 'innate ideas,'" Hegel continues, "was at that time normal, and these innate principles have sometimes been foolishly spoken of" (301/350).

It is not that Locke made the wrong intervention; indeed, his rejection of innate ideas as well as a rejection of the practice of relying on oracular (*orakelmäßige*) axioms, statements, and definitions, as Hegel repeatedly insists throughout the course of his exposition, was the right one to make. It is just that Locke threw out the baby—what is essential to thought (*was in dem Wesen des Denkens liegt*)—with the bathwater of these so-called innate ideas.

Hegel's critique focuses on two main points: The first is that Locke's treatment of thinking as an activity of finite individual consciousness is one-sided, and the second involves the undialectical nature of the claims Locke makes regarding the origin of universals. These criticisms are mutually reinforcing: Hegel sees their convergence in Locke's assertion that all knowledge, including that of universals, is accessible to finite consciousness through its own experience and through its own activity of thinking. Effecting a preliminary contrast with Spinoza, Hegel suggests that the main thing for Locke was "the sensuous and the finite, the immediate present and existent," which he made into "the main and fundamental matter" (296/343). As such, the real limitation of Locke's theory is that "the finite is thus not grasped as absolute negativity, ie. in its infinity [*als absolute Negativität in seiner Unendlichkeit aufgefaßt*]" (296–97/344).

Indeed, according to Hegel, Locke is so adamant about the finitude of all knowledge—and thus even the finitude of universals; they too are temporal, happen in time, etc.—that there can be no admission of difference or division within experience between the particulars of individual existence and universals: "When thought and the universal are synonymous with what is set before us, the question of the relation between the two [i.e., between the 'universal' and 'what is set before us'] which have been separated by thought is destitute of interest and is incomprehensible. How does thought overcome the difficulties which it itself has begotten [*erzeugt*]? Here with Locke none at all have been begotten or awakened. Before thought can overcome anything, pain and disunion must first be awakened" (312/350, translation modified). If pain is to be felt anywhere, one would think that it would be felt in experience. According to this passage though, Lockean experience is painless, at least at the level of the relation or discrepancy—temporal or otherwise—between particulars and universals, since they are presented in his theory as already unified within finite consciousness. By prematurely asserting the unity of universals with the particulars of experience, as Hegel makes clear here and elsewhere, Locke has not only failed to understand experience; he has also failed to understand the nature of thought. For Locke, he writes, "thought itself is not the essence of the soul, rather it is one of the latter's powers and manifestations [*Äußerungen*]" (305/352).

Mimicking Locke's gesture, in Hegel's demonstration of the temporality of Lockean universals, an appeal is made to common understanding: "Every person undoubtedly knows that when his consciousness develops empirically, he commences from feelings, from quite concrete conditions, and that it is only later on [*später der Zeit nach*] that general conceptions come in. . . . Space, for example, comes to consciousness later than the spatial, the species later [*später als*] than the individual" (299/349) and, further on: "Universal ideas are later, they are first formed from the particular" (352).

Indeed, when Hegel goes on to describe how the individual consciousness proceeds from the particulars of its own experience to the knowledge of universals as the product of its own thinking activity, it is to the temporal dimension of delay or deferral that he sarcastically draws attention: "The work of the mind now consists in bringing forth from several simple so-called ideas [those procured through sensation and reflection] a number of new ones, by means of its working upon this material through comparing, distinguishing, and contrasting it, and finally through separation or abstraction, whereby the universal conceptions . . . take their rise" (305/357). The example Hegel uses is Locke's own: "For example, we form the general conception of space [*die allgemeine Vorstellung von Raume*] from the perception of the distance [*der Entfernung*] of bodies by means of sight and feeling. Or in other words, we perceive a definite space, abstract from it, and then we have the conception of space generally; the perception of distances gives us conceptions of space. This however is no deduction, but only a setting aside [*ein Weglassen*] of other determinations" (306/358). And finally, to highlight the arbitrary and absurd nature of subjective consciousness creating universals by virtue of what it chooses to omit, Hegel writes, "the *Entfernung* [a reference both to the 'distance' from the second to last sentence and to the 'omission' or 'setting aside' from the last sentence] is itself really space; the understanding thus determines space from space" (306/358).

This contention, that universals are on a continuum with the particulars of human experience, yields the idea of time as temporal succession. Here too, Hegel's exposition remains very close to the letter of Book 2 of Locke's *Essay*: "Similarly we reach the notion of time through the unbroken succession of conceptions during our waking moments, i.e., from determinate time we perceive time in general.

Conceptions follow one another in a continual succession; if we set
aside the particular element that is present, we thereby receive the
conception of time" (306/358). Locke's theory is grounded in the contention that there is no essential difference between the time of the
experience of particulars and the time of universal ideas: Finite consciousness comes to its knowledge of universal ideas, not *at* the same
time as the particulars of finite experience (Hegel points to the delay
or deferral of their acquisition), but *in* the same time, or in the same
temporal modality of succession. When universal ideas are said to be
the product of a thinking consciousness that abstracts from the particulars of their own experience, universal ideas are set on a par with
those particulars and thus like them, become temporal and finite. In
having set universal ideas on a temporal continuum with the particulars of experience, Hegel suggests, Locke's theory of subjective experience has robbed consciousness—and so too, experience—of the tension between finitude and infinitude that thinking spirit is in the business of producing.

    In Hegel's estimation, Locke has failed in his attempt to prove
that universal ideas are finite. The Lockean act of deriving universal ideas from finite particulars avoids the task of thinking the relation, at times painful, between the infinite and the finite: The so-
called derivation or abstraction (*Ableitung*) of the universal is made
by simply replacing one word with another that has the form of universality. "A determination is brought into notice which is contained
in a concrete relationship; hence the understanding on the one hand
abstracts and on the other establishes conclusions. The basis of this
philosophy is merely to be found in the translation [*Übersetzung*] of
the determinate to the form of universality, but it was just this fundamental essence, that we had to explain [*von dem zu sagen wäre,
was es sei*]. As to this Locke confesses of space, for example, that he
does not know what it really is" (307/359). That Hegel disparagingly
calls Locke's derivation of universals from particulars a "translation"
might be enlisted as support for the familiar argument that the task of
thought—to know what infinitude and universal ideas are—is beyond
human language. But Hegel's claim here is more modest. In fact, it is
wholly in keeping with Locke's own repeated warning against the use
of words without meaning that Hegel censures this so-called translation as a translation in the worst sense of the word: By simply giving
the linguistic form of universality to particular experiences, it generates no insights at all, either about universality or about its relation

to the temporal parameters of finitude. The point for Hegel is neither that all translation is bad nor that language corrupts infinity (as it would be for Plato or for that matter, for Leibniz); rather, he suggests that a more appropriate language would effect the translation of the particular to the universal and would be able "to say" (*von dem zu sagen wäre*) something about what the latter is, without reiterating that it is immediately available in the time of the present or that it is infinitely unknowable.

As tedious—he repeatedly describes it as *langweilig* or boring—as Hegel may find Locke's *Essay* though, he finds it hard to dismiss. At the close of his critique, he voices concerns about its almost limitless capacity for translation into Hegel's own day and into practically every area of human knowledge: Not only has Lockean philosophy, he writes (not without a touch of irony), "become the universal [*allgemeine*] method of thinking which is called philosophy" (312/363, translation modified), its "reasoning," which "starts from the present mind [or spirit: *geht vom gegenwärtige Geiste aus*], from what is one's own interior or exterior," has become "the preferred method of observation and knowledge in England and indeed in all of Europe" (312/363). Insinuating that Lockean philosophy has perhaps enjoyed more of a future than is its due, he sums up: "The sciences in general [*Wissenschaften im allgemeinen*] . . . have to ascribe their origin to this movement" (312–13/363)

Returning to some of the statements with which we began, let us summarize the two main points of Hegel's argument: The first point concerns the status of acquiring knowledge of universals and the second involves the claims the argument makes about temporality. Against Locke's assertion that all knowledge—including that of universals—is acquired in the finite time of succession, Hegel seems to want to accord another temporal parameter to the knowledge of universals, one that may not be directly accessible to experience but that nonetheless belongs to the activity of thinking.

It would be a mistake, however, to suggest that he is simply pitting the particular against the universal, or the finite against the infinite (and establishing such a distinction in order to privilege the latter over the former). For he does praise Locke's initiative of asking where these universals come from, and even offers hints throughout the course of the exposition to suggest that the notions of experience and finitude are not, in themselves, bad starting points. He is also explicit on the point that the finite and the infinite do not occupy discrete realms when he takes Locke to task for having failed to register "the finite . . . as absolute negativity in *its* [that is, *finitude's*] infinitude" (344). As such, the infinite for Hegel is accessible to the finite world not through subjective experience as it is understood by Locke and others, but through thought. In other words, Hegel is gesturing toward another understanding of finitude, one that thinking forces into a kind of painful confrontation with the infinite itself. If thinking is to restore this painful division within the finite itself, what then of the temporality of this division or of its overcoming?

In light of his having drawn attention to Lockean time as finite temporal succession and in light also of the claim that expressions of finitude themselves harbor the infinite, Hegel seems compelled to articulate finitude's aspect of infinitude not in terms ostensibly more befitting of the infinite but in those very same terms, not, that is, in terms that are diametrically opposed to temporal succession—say, a brute timelessness or otherworldly eternity—but in terms that actively seek to recover the aspect of infinity *within* temporal succession itself.

In these formulations, it is easy to detect strains of Hegel's own philosophical project, here acting as a bulwark against the preoccupation with finitude that he saw characterizing the modern age: to submit the painful divisions of finitude and infinitude to an exhaustive dialectical examination and to bear witness to spirit overcoming the ruptures engendered by that divisive relation as it comes to recognize itself in the *temporal succession of history* itself. Indeed, in light of what he saw as the very real possibility of a future for finitude that limited it to its expression of an individual lifetime, a framework that only constrains and constricts its philosophical expression—he contends in no uncertain terms that "das individuelle Leben wird immer gleichgültiger"[3]—one could say that he sought to give the time of finitude another future, one in which the temporal succession ostensibly marking out and giving boundaries to finite life is recognized by spirit as the site of its own infinitude.

But in saying that Hegel sought to give the time of finitude *another* future other than the one expressed by the far-reaching popularity of Lockean empiricism, are we not reintroducing the question of temporality precisely where it should not be expected? Indeed, many of his modern commentators, including both Kojève and Heidegger, suggest that there can be no more question of temporality for Hegel's spirit, given that historical succession culminates in and is completed as spirit recognizes its own infinitude. *After* that moment of recognition, how could there still be any question of time or of a future? Precisely on the point of Hegel's lack of futurity, Heidegger writes, "Hegel occasionally speaks about having been, but never about the future. This accords with his view of the past as the decisive character of time: It is a fading away, something transitory and always bygone."[4] Much the same point is again made in the context of his analysis of the *Self-consciousness* section of the *Phenomenology*: "For Hegel the former time, *the past,* constitutes the essence of time. . . . Hegel's explication of the genuine concept of being—is nothing less than leaving time behind on the road to spirit, which is eternal."[5] Indeed, the notorious final lines of the *Phenomenology* do little to dispel the sense of the future's emptiness:

> Time is the concept itself that *is there* and which presents itself to consciousness as empty intuition; for this reason Spirit necessarily appears in time, and it appears in time just as long as it has not *grasped* its pure concept, ie. has not annulled [*tilgt*] time. It is the *outer*, intuited pure self which is *not grasped* by the self, the merely intuited concept; when this latter grasps itself it sublates [*aufhebt*] its time-form, comprehends this intuiting, and is a comprehended and comprehending intuiting. Time, therefore, appears as the destiny and necessity of spirit that is not yet complete within itself.[6]

Spirit, having had to appear in time, has as its final task to gather its shapes within itself and to recognize itself as itself. This process of return, unsurprisingly, is affected by memory: "The realm of spirits which is formed in this way in the outer world constitutes a succession in Time [*eine Aufeinanderfolge*] in which one spirit relieved another of its charge and each took over the empire of the world from its predecessor. . . . The *goal*, Absolute Knowing, or Spirit that knows itself as Spirit, has for its path the recollection of the Spirits as they are in themselves and as they accomplish the organization of their realm" (*Phen* 493). The sense in these passages that a certain regime of time—that of temporal succession—comes to a close as Absolute Knowing circles back on its own development is, I think, irrefutable. Donald Verene, in his close reading of these lines, has underscored memory's return as the means by which time in general is mastered: "Recollection (*Er-innerung*)," he writes, "is a denial of time. When we rethink the course of spirit, we cancel its time. We are masters of its time. Philosophical knowing is always a denial of time on behalf of the whole."[7] But, in saying that Hegel's memory exhausts time, are we—as Hegel's readers—really prepared to say without qualification that this applies to all time, and *for* all (the) time(s)? Might we not rather feel inclined to get drawn back into the circle to discern other times to which these statements might not apply?

The status of time indeed remains difficult to decipher, even in these lines where it is suspended between an outright annulment or erasure (*tilgen*) and a sublation-preservation (*aufheben*). Derrida has also commented on these passages, in terms of the linearity that circles back on itself in the time of speculation: "Everything that is, all time, precomprehends itself, strictly, in the circle of *Sa* [*savoir absolu*], which always comes back to the circle, presupposes its beginning, and only reaches that beginning at the end."[8]

Though, far from adopting Heidegger's complaint in *Being and Time* that Hegel simply reiterated the vulgar definition of time by giving it its fullest and most complete expression,[9] Derrida rehearses this remarkable scene of temporal completion in order to ask the question—replete with Hegelian nuances—of what might remain of time in Hegel: "Does time remain, and if it does remain, does it remain in *Sa*?" (*Glas* 227). Strikingly, by rereading this scene wherein temporal succession reaches the point of its teleological circling-back, Derrida gestures toward a sense in which this culmination nonetheless does not exhaust the question of spirit's temporality.

Obviously though, if there remains any possibility of a future, its meaning cannot be restricted to the ordinary connotation of an ordered relation among moments, that of the "future" as a tense. In other words, it cannot be articulated as another moment in a succession or series—in the mode of "that which is to come"—for this would be tantamount to redeploying the logic of historical linearity that has ostensibly come to an end.[10] That is to say: If we contend that a new kind of time—a new time and a new future—arrives on the scene *after* Hegel's memory has done away with temporal succession, that contention itself would be drawn back into the teleological circle, making escape from it seem even more implausible than the prospect of having to remain within its narrow confines.[11] Thus, if time has any bearing on the Hegelian corpus other than that of the chronology of historical succession, it is to his explicitly historical-philosophical writings that we must turn—with an eye, namely, to other "suspended" temporal modalities inhering within them.[12]

§

The thinking regarding time, that is, the thinking that knows how to grap-
ple with its own temporality and finitude, is thinking that accepts "seeing"
neither the past nor the future. It is thinking that thinks about—but as the
places of its own mystery—its birth and its death, because no one can see
oneself being born or dying.

—Sylviane Agacinski

To readers of the *Phenomenology of Spirit* (1807) and the
Encyclopedia (1830), it has become something of a truism that
Hegel attached enormous significance to memory. Less obvious, perhaps, is the role memory plays in his extended treatment of art in
the *Aesthetics* (1830). The relation—between art and memory—has
remained obscure, not least because of the comparatively little critical attention it has received in the secondary literature.[13] And indeed,
due to the variety of ways in which art and memory are formulated
both in association with and independently of each other, any definitive assessment of this relation would prove difficult, if not impossible, to achieve. Much of the floundering of attempts to discern the
contours of the relation between memory and art or, in perhaps a
more pressing way, to make out the relevance of that relation for an
understanding of our own modernity's memory, has taken place on
the rock of what has been dubbed Hegel's "notorious thesis on the
'end' or 'death' of art."[14]

It is accurate, I think, to describe Hegel's "thesis" as notorious if by
using the word we mean to describe a kind of knowledge or a statement that has attained its privileged status less through the exactitude
of its reference and more by virtue of its public circulation.[15] Less dramatic, perhaps, is Hegel's own contention in the general introduction
to the *Aesthetics* that "art, considered in its highest determination
[*nach der Seite ihrer höchsten Bestimmung*], is and remains for us a
thing of the past" (*Aesth* 11/25).[16]

Even a qualification of the statement does not entirely rid it of its
strangeness, though. It is, after all, a peculiar gesture to inaugurate
what would become a series of lectures delivered over many years
and amounting to over one thousand pages of posthumously published text by pronouncing the "pastness"—even if only "in its highest determination"—of its object.[17] Why devote so much theoretical
rigor and philosophical energy to the project of art, when its highest
point had already been reached and presumably, surpassed?

According to a historicizing line of reception, the force of the statement lies in its consignment of art to a historical past, the former eminence of its project having been supplanted by spirit's other emergent enterprises. This position is adopted by Berel Lang who, in discussing the unprecedented pressures that were placed on the exigencies of representation and memory by the Holocaust, uses the Hegelian "end of art" thesis to support the claim that art's social relevance vis-à-vis the past has itself passed. Rather, the task of transmitting the past in our day falls to the discipline of history, or to those artistic endeavors that "assume the event of the Holocaust as a historical given."[18] Lang writes:

> At the center of [Hegel's] thesis is the claim that art, like the genres within it, is as a whole a historical phenomenon, causally contingent—having once come into existence and so also with the prospect of passing away. Indeed, for both Hegel and 170 years later, for Danto art *has* passed away, displaced by the movement of mind or consciousness that has since "progressed" to other projects. It is not, however, the claim of that actual end but the assertion in these accounts of art's contingency that shows, through the contrast it points out, the idolatry—that is, the assumed immortality—of art that is being rejected.[19]

Alternatively, Stephen Houlgate has argued that the lectures point to the loss of art's ideal moment in Classical Greece in order to stave off the "definitive end of art" and furthermore, to ensure that art and artistic production remain concerns of and for the present.[20] But this interpretation is at odds with the statement's own insistence on its historical relevance: not only "is" the art of the classical Ideal a thing of the past (*ein Vergangenes*), but it "remains" so "for us." The passage's use of the present tense in "remains" (*bleibt*), along with the self-referentiality of the "us" make it plausible to suggest that what is being discussed here is the historical moment of the statement itself; presumably, Hegel is referring to himself, to his students and to their own epoch. As such, despite its ambiguity, the passage is not so much making a claim about the historical future or the historical past as it is suggesting that something about the past-ness of the art of the classical Ideal abides, or remains. Art's ideal moment has passed, writes Hegel, and other "spiritual aims" and modes of comprehension are *"no longer* so akin and friendly to sense as to be capable of appropriate adoption in this medium" (*Aesth* 10).

Further along in the same passage, Hegel articulates these "spiritual aims" as belonging to his own time; that is, they belong to the development of reason and reflection that is proper to "the spirit of our world today." However, even as he establishes the fairly clear-cut temporal distinction between the (Greek) past of art and his own modern philosophical present, he also blurs the line between philosophy and art or between conceptual and sensual presentation that is necessary for the claim of a historical or epochal disjunction. Immediately following these lines, he writes the following: "The Christian view of truth is of this [reflective] kind, and above all, the spirit of our world today . . . appears [*erscheint der Geist unserer heutigen Welt*] as beyond the stage at which art is the supreme mode of our knowledge of the Absolute. . . . Thought and reflection have spread their wings above fine art" (*Aesth* 10/24). Even if we disregard the beautiful and indeed artistic figures in the passage, Hegel's more sober and straightforward claim is that, although his modern epoch bears witness to the excessiveness of spirit with respect to artistic representations, the spirit of the world, "today," is nonetheless bound by the exigency of having to *appear* as beyond the stage of art. Indeed, to appear as beyond art means that thought—a nonsensuous mode of truth, if there ever were one—must *appear*, even if that appearance brings it into closer proximity to art than is suggested by a decisive overcoming.

However counterintuitive this formulation seems, the notion that truth must take on appearance is not at odds with Hegel's own view of things. Very early in the *Aesthetics* in fact, Hegel makes the claim that appearance is in no way inimical to truth but rather is central to it: "Appearance itself is essential to essence" he writes, "Truth would not be truth if it did not show itself and appear" (*Aesth* 8). Either this privileging of modes of presentation for truth comes as something of an embarrassment for a philosophy that aims to think in a mode adequate to the concept (and for which appearance has traditionally posed such difficulties), or Hegel is attempting to say something more complicated about the passage—historical or otherwise—between art and thought than simply that art is historical and that, given enough time, it too passes away. It is quite possible that, beyond making the claim that art is historical, Hegel's lectures are also pointing to the ways in which art's pastness lingers in philosophy, and that what *is* past *remains* in that philosophical explanation as the expression of its lingering. In other words, Hegel's claim regarding art's pastness may well be as much *about* how history comes to appear as it is itself a historical claim.

Of interest to the discussion of art's ambiguous pastness is the relation that it might have to the possibility of philosophizing or even of thinking about art. Although seldom invoked in disputes over Hegel's purported assertion of art's redundancy for modernity, Hegel is resolute on this point: He suggests that it is not *despite* art's being "of the past" for us but rather *because* of it that the philosophy of art has attained its great significance and art, its unprecedented importance. The "truth and life" that art once embodied have since gone elsewhere; art has "been transferred into our ideas instead of maintaining its earlier necessity in reality and occupying its *higher* place" (11, emphasis added).

That this distinction of *higher* admits of no comparison or relativization is something that Hegel had already confirmed in the context of an earlier admission of the unwieldiness of the term "higher." In the discussion of the distinction between the beauty of art and that of nature, Hegel acknowledges that "'higher' is a quite vague expression that describes natural and artistic beauty as still standing side by side in the space of imagination and differing only quantitatively and therefore externally" (2). However, "what is *higher* about the spirit and its artistic beauty is not something merely relative in comparison with nature" (ibid.). If art once had its *higher* place in reality, this moment has passed. The implication is a familiar one: modern philosophy, in submitting art to its "regulating activity" thereby stands in a position superior to it, a superior position moreover that admits of no comparison.

This conclusion, however neatly it fits the conventional schema of art's being overcome first by religion and then by thought (a trajectory also famously followed in the *Phenomenology of Spirit*), is not precisely what Hegel says. In the period of modernity that Hegel considers his own, art is not simply for enjoyment nor is it simply or nonreflectively created; specific to modernity is the judgment and thought that art affords. As such, "the philosophy of art is therefore a greater need *in our day* than it was in days when art by itself as art yielded full satisfaction. Art invites us to intellectual consideration, and that not for the purpose of creating art again, but for knowing philosophically what art is" (*Aesth* 11). If the philosophy of art is responsible for our understanding of what art in fact is, then art too ought to be grateful, for "it is this reawakening (of philosophy) alone that aesthetics proper, as a science, has really to thank for its genuine origin, and art for its *higher* estimation" (*Aesth* 56, emphasis added).

What kind of topsy-turvy world is being presented here, wherein art's loss of its *higher* position and its subsequent allocation to a *lower* position in thought—wingèd thought has, after all, flown *above* art—belies, in fact, its *higher* estimation? This formulation, wherein *lower* seems to get mixed up in the estimation of the *higher* domain of thought, substantially complicates the relation between the philosophy of art and its objects, beyond that of an assertion of the autonomy of the regulating activity of thought in terms of its own reflective powers or, what amounts to the same thing, in terms of the celebration of thought's own emergent sovereignty on the basis of the subordination of its objects of reflection. In particular, it challenges what has become the familiar interpretation of Hegel's strategy as the "overcoming" of a previously active form of spirit by recuperating it in any straightforward way.

"The beauty of art," Hegel contends at the very outset of the study, "is beauty *born of the spirit and born again* [*aus dem Geiste geborene und wiedergeborene*]" (*Aesth* 2/14, emphasis in original). Although this statement does not belong to those often cited regarding the end of art, its suggestion of the double origin of art's beauty certainly makes it a likely candidate. For, since the formulation suggests that the beauty of art is determined by a double origin, it also seems to presuppose an end since obviously, only what has died can be reborn. However, Hegel remains strangely silent on the topic of death at this very place in the text where one seems logically and structurally inevitable. How are we to understand this exclusion from Hegel's formulation of a rebirth that is not based on a death but rather on the withholding of one? Furthermore, in relation to what (not-quite dead) object can beauty be said to arise?

Eva Geulen has submitted to scrutiny the ways in which this double origin might possibly be conceived.[21] Beginning with the relation of art's beauty to that of nature and then moving on to that of art to reality, she argues that on both these counts, Hegel's exposition accounts for how the beauty of art is born or begotten of spirit but not, finally, why it is born and reborn—born not once but twice. Regarding the former, Geulen argues that since Hegel understood artistic beauty to be of a higher order than the beauty of natural objects,[22] it alone designates the proper domain of spirit: "Everything beautiful is truly beautiful," Hegel writes, "only as sharing in this higher sphere and

generated [*erzeugt*] by it" (2). Alone bearing the seal of spiritual pro-
ductivity (*EA* 20), art is *conceived* (in every possible sense) by spirit.
It is, then, the prodigy, the very offspring, of spirit.

With regard to the relation of art to the actual world, in response
to the widespread attitude that sees art as harsh deception in comparison to the empirical world, Hegel contends that art brings the
mere sensuousness of the empirical world—the even "harsher deception"—to a mode of appearance necessary for the communication of
truth. Art, in other words, transforms the actuality of "this bad transitory world" (9) by raising it to the level of "a higher actuality, born
of the spirit" (*Aesth* 9). The ability of art to give birth to actuality as
artwork is attributed to the power of art's spiritual origin, through
which mere sensuality rises to the level of spiritual appearance.

Hegel's articulation of the relation of art to actuality thus appears
to be able to account for the double birth, for its emphasis on the
transience that governs "the capriciousness of situations, events, characters, etc." (9) suggests that it is within the character of "what happens" to come to an end. And this, it must do: For Hegel it is only by
shedding its transience that reality is ultimately born of spirit. Though
here too, as Geulen notes, Hegel uses the term "born" of spirit, not
"reborn" to describe the process by which a higher actuality comes
into being (*EA* 20).

Since both of these relations are effectively illustrated by a (one-
time) "spiritual birth," Geulen turns more directly to the question
of the double birth in order to argue that the birth and *rebirth* of the
beauty of art signals its two-fold relation to spirit, in accordance with
which spirit not only begets art but, equally importantly, art itself
provides spirit with a medium in which it can recognize itself (*EA* 21).
At this moment of recognition, where the beauty of art is both recognized—the word Hegel uses in this context is *wiedererkannt*—and
reborn [*wiedergeborenen*], the question is no longer what art and its
artworks were or what they should be (either in relation to nature or
to reality); rather, the beauty of art is reborn as philosophical insight
into the beautiful. The supplementary "rebirth" marks the passage of
art into its philosophical treatment. Rebirth means, then, that art's
beauty has turned into knowledge and that this passage—from art to
knowledge—secures art's spiritual origin.

Geulen's discussion helps to make sense of why it is only when art
has moved into the sphere of philosophy that it takes on the position to which it is indebted for its *higher* estimation. In one sense, the

orthodox commitments of this interpretation are quite clear: what passes away in and as art is raised to a higher level when it enters spirit's truer realm of thought. However, given that there is no break or rupture between birth and rebirth right where one seems indispensable, the consequences of the absence of such a formulation for the relation between art and philosophy are fairly unconventional. I quote Geulen at length:

> If "born and reborn" expresses the double-sidedness of artistic beauty as the work of art on the one hand and its philosophical concept on the other, then the qualitative breach between art and philosophy, between the "beautiful" and that "higher" dimension, disappears. This differentiation loses its organizing power when the path from spirit-born art to its rebirth in philosophy passes through its death. The copula "and" in the phrase "born and reborn" dispenses with sublation, or at least silences it and consequently obscures the difference between philosophy and art. (*EA* 21)

When "born and born again" expresses the force of artistic beauty as the work of art on the one hand and as philosophy on the other, any rigorous distinction between art and philosophy and thus between "beautiful" and "higher" has been formally, if not effectively, eliminated. That there is no mention of death between these two moments of spirit's relation to art and that nothing must come to an end in order for art to be reborn suggests that there is no secure differentiation, no clear dialectic of overcoming, and therefore no unambiguously progressive logic governing the relation between the beautiful art-work and philosophy's speculation on it.

Whatever Hegel's own reasons for elaborating the relation in this way, the result may be that his own philosophical reflections risk participating in the beauty of the art that forms the subject matter of the study. From the philosophical treatment of art there should really be no more expectation of beauty (beauty's highest region is that of art and thus presumably not philosophy), but Hegel's enigmatic withholding of an end suggests that whatever it is that informs the beauty of art could very well have migrated into the philosophical aesthetic. The philosophy of art, then, rather than strictly or exclusively providing insight into what constitutes beauty, is perhaps no longer entirely distinct from the objects that it observes in beauty's constitution.

Among other things, Geulen's reading of the double birth of artistic beauty allows her to advance another interpretation of Hegel's pronouncement of art's end—when art is assessed by philosophy as beautiful, it has always already passed, is already a 'has-been': "If art is taken to be beautiful—and for Hegel this is only the case where beauty has been philosophically recognized—this beauty is part of the past" (*EA* 22). Art can only be beautiful insofar as it has been reborn as recognized. In other words, beautiful art is already "of the past" to such an extent that there is no room left for an end between its birth and its rebirth. Thus, the beauty of art appears at the very beginning of the *Aesthetics* as without end, but this is because it appears there as always already past: It has no need of an end, precisely because it has already passed. The end of art, then, does not so much lead from art to philosophy in the sense of philosophy's break with and eventual overcoming of art (as the orthodox reading would have it), but rather the end of art continually drifts somewhere between art and philosophy. Simply put, in these lines Hegel is *connecting* art and thought across time even as he is also chronologically and historically dividing them between the various times and the various historical developments of art on the one hand, and the time of philosophy, on the other.

That art's beauty is always already of the past means that beauty only ever appears in the present as something other than art. Beauty is awoken in the present in the form of philosophical knowledge. But precisely because of this reawakening not as art but as reflection on it, art in the present is always only no-longer beautiful. If beauty for Hegel is contemporary anywhere, it is only as "reborn" in philosophy or religion. This pastness of art implies that in the course of philosophy's self-empowerment as art's judge, whose decisive act it supposedly was to relegate art to the past, philosophy could have infected itself with beauty and might consequently have to concede a place to a rebirth of art that is passed and always passing, but still abides in philosophy as reflection on art and as artistic reflection. Philosophy is not entirely immune to the fate of art: Whatever happens in or to art could, ostensibly, also happen to philosophy.

(A corollary to Hegel's articulation of the rather volatile and by no means entirely governable boundary between art and thought is, quite simply, that art in modernity is no longer "thoughtless"; that is, art is not, and cannot be, autonomous from thought or from philosophical articulation. One consequence of art's lack of autonomy in modernity is a renewed attention to thought's own reliance on figurative language, such as has been rigorously explored by Derrida, Nancy, de Man, and others.

The flipside of this modern constellation, although less often explicitly thematized, is also significant: The very possibility that thought becomes aware of its own dependence on structures of representation implies also that art in the modern period becomes conscious of its own conceptual procedures, and of its own thoughtfulness.[23] In other words, it is only when art's social function ceases to be a simple or unproblematic reflection of pregiven social or communal norms, is art able to investigate, explore, or problematize its own relation to historical normativity as such. To say that art reflects on its own participation in pastness is to say that art can respond, critically and consciously, to the very question of historical and communal transmission. It is also to say that modern art, no less than modern philosophy although perhaps less explicitly, does not simply reflect a series of norms as they are inherited from the authorities of the past; rather, it has the ability to theorize and reflect on "pastness" as such.[24])

Hegel's radical point would somehow be lost if we were to too hastily invoke art's pastness either as testimony to its lack of relevance for the present, or as a call to resuscitate beautiful art in order that it mend a damaged or fractured relation to the past. For the insight that art's beauty is passed does not so much draw attention to the sequential temporality of the "then" and "now" of the historical narrative that is otherwise so prominent in the *Aesthetics*, as it constitutes the very possibility of thinking about art. In other words, in this very first determination of the beauty of art, beautiful art is "of the past" in a sense that allows for no recuperation precisely because the status of its pastness is originary—it is the condition of recognition that constitutes art's beauty in the first instance. "Born and born again" does not refer, then, to two distinct historical periods or epochs in which art is variously esteemed (although one could certainly be forgiven for having that impression): Rather, the double birth of art is required in order that "we moderns" be able to think about art at all.

For Hegel, then, no recuperation of the beauty of art as a vehicle that fuses past and present, or that marries the sensible world with the ideal world of representation is possible in the present, even though to locate the supreme moment of art in the past is somehow to call that recuperative or nostalgic impulse into being, whether the form of its return be as art theory, philosophy, or history.[25] It is precisely this tension—the condition of modernity being to put the past safely into a space of nonrecuperation while at the same time and in the same gesture, registering in that act of deposition the loss of an untroubled relation to tradition—that is operative in Hegel's text, beyond the familiar and not entirely unwarranted accusation that his formulations on art suffer from the nostalgia for the Classical art of the Greeks that was so widespread in his epoch.

In pursuit of what remains of this radical pastness with respect to art, let us pick up the thread of the argument as it pertains to the *Aesthetics*. Having determined that the modern invocation of "pastness" in terms of art's beauty is not exclusively a historical-referential invocation, that it is not precisely a historical "fact," but is something belonging to the structure of modern philosophical recognition, what status can we then accord to the more explicitly referential—i.e., historically and geographically delimited—character of Hegel's contention that "art, considered *on the side of its highest determination*, is and remains a thing of the past"? As we shall see, it is in Classical art that art's capacity to refer, and more specifically to refer to the past, reaches its zenith in the instantiation of Greek art as a memorial form, perhaps as the memorial art-form par excellence.

§

In the corpus of Hegel's works, wherever there is evidence of an inward movement, what de Man has translated as the "inner gathering and preserving of experience," memory or recollection (*Erinnerung*) is at work.[26] For Hegel, memory is in no way a deadening archival impulse, one that neutralizes the past by storing its accumulation of riches or disasters: It is the actualization and the fulfilment of the living urge that abides within that archive, its "ensouling [*Beseelung*]" (88/122), that requires the moment of spirit's recognition of itself in that material in order to be ensured continued life.

As we saw at the beginning of this chapter, when in the final lines of the *Phenomenology of Spirit* we read that spirit, at the end of its long journey, is confronted with the task of abandoning its outer existence, it is so that it can recognize itself as the culmination of the Becoming of the different shapes of spirit as they have preceded its present form. This procedure of inwardizing is memory (*Er-innerung*): "its existential shape is given over to recollection." Although spirit feels itself to be utterly alone, without precedent, and although it looks at history as something foreign and alien to it, recollection is in fact already at work: "a new world, and a new shape of Spirit. In the immediacy of this new existence the Spirit has to start afresh to bring itself to maturity as if, for it, all that preceded were lost and it had learned nothing from the experience of the earlier Spirits [*der früheren Geister*]. But recollection, the inwardizing, of that experience, has preserved it and is the inner being, and in fact the higher form of the substance" (*Phen* 492).

Likewise, in the *Aesthetics* recollection is the means by which the transition from the Classical period of art—what Hegel in the *Phenomenology* calls "Kunstreligion" or "Art-religion," mitigating somewhat its transition to the "Revealed Religion" of Christianity— to the religion of Christianity and its art is performed. Although the ideal of art in which the "content has been perfectly revealed in artistic shapes" had already been reached in Greece, the end of art *as* the passage to religion is prepared by the insufficiency of these former shapes and by their consequent consummation in religion: "the Absolute has shifted from the objectivity of art into the *inwardness* of the subject" (*Aesth* 103). The objectivity of art's shapes is, within the religious community, "consumed and digested . . . [so that] the objective content has become a possession of mind and feeling" (104).[27] The revealed religion of Christianity is, thus, a form of remembered, interiorized art, wherein the emphasis is not on abolishing all claims to appearance but rather on preserving art's ethos and, in particular, on preserving its ability to make the divine appear, albeit in the more highly interiorized and subjectified space of religious devotion. In very general terms, then, memory owes its substantial place within the larger scheme of Hegel's speculative philosophy to spirit, whose general and trans-historical nature it is to proceed inward.

This "memorial movement"—the movement *inward*—enables the (historical) passage *from* art as the space where the divine is revealed in sensuous form to religion whereby the spirit that art pressed into sensuous form is preserved in and as the Christian religion. That memory here is both a force of movement and change on the one hand, and of preservation and continuity on the other, is clear. However clear it may be that memory enables the development of a historical narrative that tells a story both of change and continuity though, what remains unclear in this explanation is how memory is itself enabled, beyond the somewhat unsatisfying assertion that it simply belongs to the nature of spirit to generate such narratives about itself.

An examination of the more unassuming role that memory plays *within* art may, I think, help to lend precision to how memory generates these art historical narratives and how, simultaneously, it is able to generate philosophical knowledge about what art is. Of special interest in this regard are the arguments that Hegel makes for the centrality of memory in the creation of the work of art itself. There, Hegel suggests that art is wholly indebted to memory, since memory offers to art the universality shorn of contingent particularity that on its own, in "always simultaneously touching on the accidental" (12), art might lack:

> The past . . . belongs only to memory [*Erinnerung*], and memory automatically succeeds in clothing characters, events, and actions in the garment of universality [*das Einhüllen . . . in das Gewand der Allgemeinheit*], whereby the particular external and accidental details are obscured. To the actual existence of an action or a character there belong many insignificant interposing circumstances and conditions, manifold single happenings and deeds, while *in memory's picture [in dem Bilde der Erinnerung]* all these casual details are obliterated. In this liberation [*In dieser Befreiung*] from the accidents of the external world the artist in his mode of artistic composition has a freer hand with the particular and individual features if the deeds, histories, and characters belong to ancient times. (*Aesth* 189–90/248–249)

The temporal divide installed by the artist's drawing on memory, far from being an unfortunate by-product of an imperfect representational system, is precisely the condition upon which beautiful art can be made. In other words, it produces a perspective amenable to the ethos of beautiful art. Its very beauty, the passage suggests, rests on what is afforded by memory's temporal delay; that is, through it the artist is furnished with a detached relation to the material on which he works that helps to obscure contingent details and thus also helps the form of the artwork to embody what is truly spiritual and truly universal. In no uncertain terms, drawing from the past, as Hegel suggests elsewhere, "brings about automatically, owing to our memory, that generalization of material with which art cannot dispense" (*Aesth* 264).

The temporal divide that Hegel establishes as the primary condition for the production of beautiful art is analogous to the relation that he had already established earlier on in the text between art and everyday objects. There too, it is by virtue of art's *coming after* that it possesses the ability to rid objects of their transient nature: "Through this ideality," Hegel writes,

> art at the same time *exalts* these otherwise worthless objects which, despite their insignificant content, it fixes and makes ends in themselves. . . . The same result art achieves in respect of time, and here

too is ideal. What in nature slips past, art ties down to permanence: a quickly vanishing smile, a sudden roguish expression in the mouth, a glance, a fleeting ray of light, as well as spiritual traits in human life, incidents and events that come and go, are there and are then forgotten—anything and everything art wrests from momentary existence, and in this respect too conquers nature. (163)

If art draws on memory, then, it is with the aim of memorializing the objects it portrays. Infused with spirit, art's renderings make its objects permanent and enduring. Thus, the relation between memory and art is two-fold: Memory is both the means by which the timeless universality of artistic portrayals is ensured, and the product of that universalization. Because memory is the source of art, art in turn becomes a source for memory.[28] In each case, Hegel's high esteem for both art and memory lies in their ability to rescue objects from decay and disappearance, to exalt them, and to preserve them from fleetingness. Regarding this ability to protect objects from their own transience, Hegel makes two central claims: The first is the claim that memory and art are constituted by the belatedness of temporal delay and of time passing, and the second involves the more complicated assertion that this temporal delay is the very source of art's "timelessness."

There is certainly a magisterial quality to the conviction with which this evaluation of memory as art (and, conversely, art as memory) is elaborated. Its most official voice states that the past is simply the unqualified possession of memory and that memory's impulse is unerringly to universalize the material of the past and to rescue it from transience. However, the peculiarities of the passage's rhetorical formulation warrant a closer look.

On the one hand, it is unsurprising that an argument that concerns the universalizing work of memory focuses on its capacity to obscure the "particular external and accidental details" of the past. Indeed, in its own way, the paragraph raises the philosophical and aesthetic issue that opens up—the tensions of which, to some degree, motivate the whole of the *Aesthetics*—between the history of art and the knowledge that *that* history can yield about its objects. While art presses spirit through and out of its forms, it yields a certain narrative about where spirit is and what has become of it. Tracing art in this way yields (its) history.

But that is not all that the *Aesthetics* manages to show. For this narrative of spirit pressing its way through its recognizable (historical) stages and forms is also the analytic argument of the lectures about what art *is*. In fact, the former is the expression of the latter. But, if the very fact of the changes in art's historical appearance are predicated on temporal dispersal—its movement can only be determined by virtue of time's passage and the changes in perspective afforded by it—then the narrative form of art's philosophical study can be understood to represent a recuperation from time's dispersal. Through this recuperation, the theory or philosophy of art appears in an ideal temporal register, beyond that temporal divide that made it possible— recall that the necessity of "knowing what art is" was also recounted in temporal mode, that "*ours*" is not a time for making art, as it was *when* art afforded full satisfaction. At the level of its enunciation, then, it is only when art theory presents itself as having overcome temporal appearance that it can yield a conceptual argument about what art is. It is also only in this way that Hegel's art theory and indeed, theory in general, could ever make the claim of being *outside* (its own) *time*.[29]

It is, however, well known that the requirements of history and those of theory, especially in our day, are not always easily reconciled. The tension between them, at times demonstrated by the divergence of their paths, often rests on the claim of philosophy's timelessness, in contrast to history's temporal commitment: to change, contingency, difference, temporal heterogeneity, and the like. What makes Hegel of special interest in this regard is how rigorously he attempted to do justice to both the demands of history and those of philosophical knowledge, by making philosophy accountable to its own historicity and, importantly, by making it account for the passage of time as an essential part of its own knowledge.

In our particular case though, the ways in which Hegel seeks to shore up temporal dispersion as the condition for a possible universalization surely complicates things. To be sure: In the formulations we are looking at, memory is not only the means by which art takes on its spiritual task of universalizing the transient but at the level of the argument itself, it is also the means by which "knowing what art is" is effected. On that basis alone, one might be tempted to argue simply that Hegel's own memory is also at work here, rendering history as well as its chronological structure infinite.

Returning to the quotation about the reliance of art on memory, the one that we left hanging: Its main suggestion is that memory furnishes the artist with genuinely spiritual content by offering up the past in its most highly universalized form. Engaging material from a belated perspective grants this putatively universalistic perspective. What is, however, less expected from the formulation—but what I think complicates substantially its perspective on "timelessness"—are both the figurations of clothing and attire that are employed in its presentation of universality and the ways that this act of universalistic obscuring is not represented as "automatic" at all but rather, in a vague and not easily discernable way, as the outcome of a kind of bodily struggle.

The use of the figure of clothing to illustrate the role that memory plays in art is counterintuitive, to say the least. In fact, nothing could seem less adequate to a philosophical presentation of how universality appears in sensuous material than the image of something being dressed up in clothing, a trope that more surely evokes visions of calculated disguise and disfigurement—hiding a "true" nature—than it does the spiritual disclosure or revelation of what is eternally and not transiently true. At the very least, this presentation of memory as that which dresses up the naked body of the past ("characters, events, etc") in the "garment" of universality flies in the face of a more conventional understanding of clothing as itself a figure for transience and detachability.

In this respect, the figure of clothing is a most unlikely candidate for the presentation of a force that evacuates all that is "external and accidental" in the presentation of the past. Nonetheless, the centrality and the force of the formulation suggest that it is less a poorly chosen metaphor for the art-object giving shape to a timeless truth, as it seems to generate the sense of a veiled desire to articulate another kind of transience, one that is perhaps not easily assimilable into the historical narrative but that nonetheless becomes legible—and persists—in the material of the past.[30]

Even supposing that our impulse were to neutralize the figure of clothing in its presentation here by ascribing to it the value of rhetorical flourish, the rest of the passage somehow demands that its implications nonetheless be carried through. And certainly, other questions arise: What, for example, of the body that is to be dressed in this garb of universality? It is not at all clear why or even how it is that manifold and singular events, histories, deeds, and characters would find their most adequate expression in a body, one in need of (universalist) adornment. How is this transition or translation (from deed, say, to body) affected, and moreover what kind of a body could aspire to such robes?

As counter-intuitive as all of this may sound, the passage's appeal to corporeality does have a precedent within the context of Hegel's lectures. In fact, earlier in the text's development of the classical ideal of art, quite explicit clues are given to suggest that Hegel's theoretical formulation regarding the (bodily) relation among memory, art, and universality has taken much of its impetus from the body that is found in the art of the classical ideal. Human in form, it makes its ideal and godly appearance in Greek robes.[31] In fact, if we turn to Hegel's argument for the supremacy of Greek art-form, it is there that we find a similar bodily configuration, employed to describe spirit's most perfect sensuous appearance. Spirit, as it turns out, becomes materially and artistically visible when it takes on the form of a human body: "In classical art the peculiarity of the content consists in its being itself the concrete Idea, and as such the concretely spiritual, for it is the spiritual alone that is the truly inner. . . . This shape, which the idea as spiritual—indeed as individually determinate spirituality—assumes when it is to *proceed out into a temporal manifestation* [*in zeitliche Erscheinung*], is the human form" (*Aesth* 78, emphasis added).

Spirit becomes visible by taking on the appearance of the human body; spirit's corporeality is thus the means by which the relation between humans and gods—in the mode of their sensual identification—is established and upon which the various dynamics and tensions of ancient Greek art will be played out: "Of course, personification and anthropomorphism have often been maligned as a degradation of the spiritual," Hegel writes, "but in so far as art's task is to bring the spiritual before our eyes in a sensuous manner, it must get involved in this anthropomorphism, since spirit appears sensuously in a satisfying way only in its body [*in seinem Leib*]. . . . [T]he human form [is] the one and only sensuous appearance appropriate to spirit" (*Aesth* 78).

What is striking here is not so much the anthropomorphism that is being defended against its critics as it is the singling out of its movement into "temporal manifestation" as the basis for its defense. The notion of divine corporeal visibility is certainly complicated when Hegel ties that corporeality to its ability to move, and to move "*out into*" a realm of temporal appearance. Were this not the case, Hegel goes on to suggest, spirit would remain artistically unrepresentable and thus also philosophically unknowable; this unrepresentability would have, moreover, the *absence* of a temporal dimension as one

of its consequences: "As purely absolute and eternal, [spirit] can pro-
claim and express itself only as spirituality" (*Aesth* 79). While it is
evident that spirit attains its ideal sensuous presentation in the human
body, what is less evident is why Hegel claims here that the body is
already *its* body. Resistant to the notion that spirit prefigures—or
comes *before*—its sensuous presentation, Hegel describes the relation
between spiritual content and sensuous presentation in such a way
that can only be consistent in terms of a circularity: That the body
is already there, as spirit's *own* body, before the artistic actualization of the two in the anthropomorphism of Greek art suggests something of a telos *and* a beginning. The body is not a medium foreign
to spirit into which spirit compresses itself; it is not, in other words,
an attribute. The harmony of the interpenetration of spirit and body
resides in its being one of mutual formation: Spirit becomes formed in
the human figure that, for its part, is spiritually informed as "exemplary individuality." That said though, no sooner has Hegel defined
the artistic form of spirit as a sensuous human body, than he is faced
with the burden of limiting and circumscribing its temporality.

Of course, this further qualification is not particularly surprising.
To the extent that the characteristic of temporality is given special
emphasis in the Greek gods' making their appearance in the human
body, Hegel must also keep a tight rein on its potential unruliness.
Timothy Bahti has analyzed this itinerary in terms of the ways that it
complicates the notion of *containment*. Not only is (inner) spirit contained in the (outer) body, Bahti argues, spirit must also work to contain and limit the body by ridding it of the transience that it was the
hallmark of that very bodiliness to inaugurate. Bahti writes that the
"'temporal appearance' that qualified spirit in the shape of the body
is now recalled as its 'accidental finitude,' but it is precisely this that
must be suppressed or removed."[32]

Taking the suppression of that bodiliness as his cue, Bahti's detailed
reading of Hegel's argument yields the observation that the means
by which the argument attempts to prune the body of its temporal
finitude only serves to entrench its bodily commitment even further.
When, for example, Hegel argues that the body is necessary for the
expression of spirit, he qualifies spirit so that the latter does not end
up "towering beyond and above this expression" of the former (*Aesth*
78). The suggestion that spirit not "tower above" the sensuous is a
spatial and, ultimately, bodily metaphor. According to Bahti's reading, it is an indication of bodily excess: It "suggests more body than

spirit can fill, or more *of* the body than spirit's meaningfulness can inform" (AH 109).

If we apply Bahti's insight to the context of the paragraph on memory with which we began, what becomes immediately apparent is how Hegel's own claim for the universality of memory is itself governed by figures of the body and its adornment, figures that substantially complicate, if not compromise, the claim to universality. Put otherwise, if the human body in ancient Greece is what organizes the perfect union of sensuousness and spirit *in* the Greek pantheon of exemplary individuals, it is also that which determines its reappearance in Hegel's own philosophizing on art. The figurative constellation of corporeality of Hegel's own formulation is one that it has borrowed from art.

Thus, Hegel's reflections here are not so much *on* art as *of* art, duplicating and rereading the very structures that he sees as operative in the emergence of art itself. One consequence of this structure of duplication is that, at both the level of artistic production and that of its theorization, the strength of the distinction between timeless universality and the transience of contingent particularity is called into question by their both being rendered legible by the same figural context, that of corporeal visibility.

On the one hand, the implication is that contingent particularities are *like* bodies whose "unreadable" nakedness is to be "obscured" and "obliterated" by memory's tendency to universalize. On the other hand though, this process of universalization is not so much represented as an "overcoming" of that body's temporality as it is also figured as an aspect of temporal appearance and as a site or dimension of the bodily. The suggestion that universality participates in this bodiliness makes it possible to read in both of these formulations a contest between various temporal possibilities or indeed, a multiplication of time, rather than simply as the automatic ascendancy of timelessness over transience.

The language of the passage suggests, in fact, that the ascendancy of memory's universalized version of pastness is anything but guaranteed. Although the universality of memory is clearly privileged over the accidental particularities of what happens, the passage also suggests that the latter are not so insignificant that they pose no risk; they *can* in fact intervene (*vermittelnde*) and possibly compromise a more highly spiritualized presentation of the past. That this formulation is presented in a negative mode—that is, that the "particular and accidental *do not* shine through [*nicht hindurchscheinen*]"—suggests that perhaps they *do* pose exactly the threat that is here being denied them.

Thus, what is presented as the ascendancy of timelessness over transience seems decidedly less assured than what is afforded by Hegel's claim that the process is simply an "automatic" one. The language of the rest of the passage—that the artist's hand must be subject to a liberation (*Befreiung*) from the accidents of the external world, and that transient details must be "obliterated" (*verlöscht*)—suggests that the tendency of memory to universalize the particular is not quite as secure as it seems, but is rather predicated upon an annulment or an erasure of certain aspects of that body. Despite the assurance of the claim that memory rids the past of all of its spiritless unsightliness, then, its language of destruction and erasure—and this, in the context of human bodies—nonetheless gives off a disquieting aura of risk and loss.

§

At the beginning of the extended treatment of classical art (in the second part of the *Aesthetics*), Hegel reiterates what he has already claimed regarding the anthropomorphism of ancient Greek art, saying that the "concrete individuality and its adequate external appearance" of classical art makes its objective appearance "purified from the defect of finitude" (*Aesth* 432). This description is immediately followed by a discussion of how Greek art contrasts with earlier forms of what he calls "symbolic art," suggesting that this purification from temporality constitutes one of the major differences between the two. The sentence reads: "From this point of view [that is, the view from which classical art is seen as purified of finitude], it is obvious at once that the classical mode of representation cannot, by its very nature, be any longer of a *symbolic* kind, in the stricter sense of the word" (*Aesth* 432).[33]

Less than two pages later, another contrast between the classical and symbolic art forms is effected but this time the description focuses on the perfect adequacy of corporeal expression for spirit in the classical ideal: "Of course in the human form there are dead and ugly things," Hegel writes, "while this is the case, it is precisely the business of art to expunge the difference between the spiritual and the purely natural and to make the external bodily presence into a shape, beautiful, through and through developed, ensouled and spiritually living" (*Aesth* 434). The formulation's explicit and perhaps even overly insistent rejection of what is dead and ugly suggests that the classical ideal is defined in terms of this ridding, so as to become the perfect means of expressing spirit. And again, this is what marks its radical difference from symbolic art: "It follows that in this [classical art's] mode of representation nothing symbolical remains in regard to the external shape, and every mere search, pressure, confusion, and distortion is cast away" (*Aesth* 434).

If what is symbolical elicits visions of dead and ugly elements, failed expressions of spirit, and a falling asunder of the two sides of body and spirit, the solace of classical art lies in its unification of meaning and expression. Spirit can identify itself with the body so perfectly, in fact, that one need not look further than the body itself for the presence of spirit: "When the spirit has grasped itself as spirit, it is explicitly complete and clear, and so too its connection with the shape adequate to it on the external side is something absolutely complete and given, which does not first need to be brought into existence by way of a linkage produced by imagination in contrast to what is present" (*Aesth* 434). In the anthropomorphism of Greek art, then, all that is spiritual is there to be seen, present to the form insofar as the latter perfectly expresses the former, "the inner side" having been "brought into an adequate identity with the outer" (*Aesth* 435). The ideal, in becoming embodied, gives its spiritual form to the singular subject, which for its part, sculpts the ideal into its form. Unsurprisingly, this is precisely the opposite of the situation of symbolic art, wherein spirit is always *somewhere* on the nether-side of sensuous appearance. Given the claim that in symbolic art, its "troubled quest" yields a relation to the spiritual that is probably distorted anyway, the relation of the two sides is at all points described as agitated and restless. It is one over which the threat of its falling apart always looms.

After having thus established the relation between classical and symbolic art as one of practically complete alterity, it seems that Hegel has prematurely resolved rather too much of the tension—and hence, any sense of development—between them. At the end of the introduction, a corrective is added to the contention that classical art simply rejects, or "casts away" symbolic art, through a specification of their relation in more structural-historical terms. Through this correction, Hegel substantially complicates their relation by granting to symbolic art the status of beginning what *would become* the classical ideal. The claim begins by noting "the first point to which we must direct our attention"—namely, the *sequential* or chronological nature of their relation: The classical art form, although ideal, should not be regarded "as the direct commencement or *beginning* of art, but on the contrary, as a *result*" (*Aesth* 441). The origin of Greek art is, he writes, to be found in the "symbolic modes of representation which are [the classical art-form's] presupposition" (*Aesth* 441).

The implication is that art had already begun before it reached its zenith; the germ of its potential beauty, unrealized, lies in a past that it cannot simply leave behind (as was previously implied), but that classical art must make its own as part of its own beauty. This passage suggests, though here still in preview, that classical art is not simply unified with itself, but it must also reckon with its being *no-longer* symbolic.

Hegel expresses the imperative that classical art's mode of representation cannot achieve the pinnacle of beauty simply by leaving behind the deadlier, uglier, or more finite aspects of symbolic art. Rather, classical art must relate to its own *proper* past of symbolic art in the negative mode of having *overcome* it—that is, as a relation of "no-longer." The freedom of the classical ideal depends upon its inheritance of the past in and as symbolic art that, as such, is subsumed in Hegel's narrative as the origin of the classical art form: "Now just as the essence of freedom consists in being what it is through its own resources, so what at first appeared as mere presuppositions and conditions of art's origin outside the classical sphere must fall into [*hin-einfallen*] that sphere's own territory, so that the actual appearance of the true content and genuine shape may be produced by overcoming what is negative and inappropriate for the ideal" (*Aesth* 441–442/ Vol. 14, 31–32). Art that is truly permeated with spirit cannot just start anywhere; nor can it just begin with itself. It must start from the *elsewhere* that is its own origin. Of necessity, says Hegel, for only in this manner is spirit truly freed from that which no longer satisfies spirit's expression and that in its inadequacy, could stand to pose only hindrance for spirit's recognition of itself. The freedom and independence of spirit's expression in the human body is predicated, then, on the question of dependence: The ideal must work to gain its freedom by first considering itself dependent on former failures. By relegating these former shapes—now presumably dead or at least inactive, so that they just passively "fall into" the classical sphere—to a position of inferiority and moreover, by showing itself to have overcome this inferior shape, spirit arrives at its ideal artistic expression.

What, for Hegel, constitutes the memory of Greek art is not simply a reproduction of the past, but rather its recuperation and transformation in and as artistic production. The imperative that art demonstrate a mastery over the past as part of itself also implies that art carries within itself the impulse to generate narratives about its own historical emergence. So Hegel contends, variously, that "the relation of the Greek spirit to these presuppositions is essentially a relation of formation [*Bilden*] and, first of all, of negative transformation [*des negativen Umbildens*]. . . . Therefore poetical composition does not exclude the reception of material from elsewhere but only points to its essential transformation" (*Aesth* 444); that the gods in the religion of Antiquity once belonged "to a tradition" that has been "transformed by art" (*Aesth* 477); that "*tradition* comes first, the starting-point which provides ingredients but does not yet bring with them the proper content and the genuine form" (*Aesth* 478). It is, finally, only by using what "confronted them in the material of the tradition" and by "consuming everything murky, natural, impure, foreign, and extravagant" that remains in that material, that the artist can "*seek* or *invent* [*finden oder erfinden*] the corresponding external appearance" for the "properly spiritual"—that is, as the Divine in human form (*Aesth* 479, emphasis in original).

These statements suggest that the artist's imaginative capacity to wed his own creative impulse—evidenced by the "external appearance" of the ideal human form that the artist gives to the work—with the "remembered" past of spirit, is thus one of ancient Greek art's most significant characteristics. The kind of harmony between the past and the present that Hegel understands to be operative in classical art would, though, be ill-rendered by an assumption that ancient Greek art simply and naively transmits the past, in the form of adherence to tradition or to traditional norms. For a traditional attitude is what Greek art seeks to overcome. It is precisely through wresting itself away from the past in the form of strict adherence to traditional norms, that the art of Greek religion is able to evince itself as self-conscious knowledge about itself. As such, the relation to tradition, as what in the *Phenomenology of Spirit* Hegel calls the pre-Hellenic "contented acceptance of custom and its firm trust therein" (*Phen* 425), is the *background* of classical art, not its *ground*.

From the viewpoint of classical art, then, the object to be overcome is a nature that has already been spiritualized as tradition and that guarantees the relation of the past to the present as being one of nondifference. Basing its own emergence on the overcoming of the simple givenness of traditional norms and "hallowed custom," classical art does not have to contend with "nature as such" but with its artistic precedent, with "a nature," that is, "already itself permeated by spiritual meanings, that is to say, the symbolic form of art" (*Aesth* 443).

Although these pronouncements and the assurance with which they are given historical and artistic substantiation in the following section ("The Process of Shaping the Classical Art-Form") make it sound as if there is no loss, destruction, or death in art's process of shaping its own narrative history, one formulation in particular that lies closer to the assertions of classical art being no-longer symbolic—both with regard to its position in the text as well as to its modality—lends a slightly more difficult and ominous tone to the discussion.

The episode to which I am referring develops out of Hegel's assertion that classical art must demonstrate its status as *no-longer* symbolic art, and that it must demonstrate this as part of its own ideal and unified beauty. Specifically, it is drawn out within the context of his argument for the privileging of the human form for the expression of spirit. While defending the privileged position of anthropomorphism against those who see in it a merely accidental and faulty trait of art, he suggests that whatever the deficiency of classical art, "so little does the deficiency lie in the anthropomorphic as such that on the contrary it is steadily to be maintained that classical art is anthropomorphic enough for art, but not enough [*zuwenig*] for higher religion. Christianity has pushed anthropomorphism much further" (*Aesth* 435).

This refrain is, of course, familiar to readers of Hegel: Christianity both historically and formally overcomes classical art as the expression of spirit. Here though, the interest of the passage lies in how it is organized around the trope of anthropomorphism, and the implications that arise when anthropomorphism becomes the force of history's organization—that is, when it is seen as the best way to organize the history of spirit's quest after itself. Insofar as the trope of anthropomorphism offers Hegel a neat way to offer the whole trajectory in toto, it also places special emphasis on the in-between status of the gods of classical art: Not only are they *no longer* the gods of symbolic art but equally importantly, they are *not yet* the god of Christianity. One consequence of giving classical art the status of *no-longer* symbolic art and *not-yet* Christianity is that the classical

art-form is constituted both by its emergence from the (now) dead—
merely external, ornamental, etc.—forms of symbolic art and by the
immanence of its future passing away into Christianity.

As Hegel elaborates on why anthropomorphism is so significant to
the development of Christianity, its implications begin to loom larger.
According to Christian doctrine, he explains, god is not "an individual merely humanly shaped but *an actual single individual*" whose
earthly providence is to progress "into the temporal and complete
externality of immediate and natural existence" (*Aesth* 435). In this
worldly experience, the divine does not simply appear in the form of
a finite human as is the case with the Greeks: The Christian god actually *is* a finite human. Thus exposed to all the vicissitudes of human
existence, it is also fully temporalized: The Christian god "experiences the feeling, consciousness, and pain [*Schmerz*, not 'grief' as the
Knox translation has it] of disunion," the precondition, to be sure,
for his infinite reconciliation: "Whereas in classical art while the sensuous is not killed and dead, it is also not resurrected from death to
absolute spirit" (*Aesth* 436).

On the one hand, the historical formation of classical art is suspended between a *no-longer* and a *not-yet*, an idiom of differentiation
that enables and motivates Hegel's historical narrative. On the other
hand, while the past proffers no threats or struggles in this form—as
the foundation of classical art, it is in fact highly edifying—there is a
certain forebodingness to the suggestion that classical art's sensuousness is determined not only by reference to the past but also by what
the future has in store, in the *not-yet* of the radically humanized God:
Not yet dead, killed, or canceled, the sensuousness of the Greek gods
is also not yet raised, or lifted up into the realm of eternal survival.

It seems crucial, at this stage, to underscore the temporal register in which this chronicle of a death foretold is articulated, a register—Hegel's own—whose futurity enables the various scenes of art's
history to unfold as scenes in which spirit is pressed out into expression. But that is not all it enables. In fact, it is exemplary of a more
general complexity inherent to the time of reading Hegel, wherein
the linear movement of the historical narrative is rendered substantially more complicated by the introduction of a teleological circularity: by a sense, indeed, that the outcome has already arrived. The
process that unfolds is both prospective—ie. unfolds in linear fashion—and at the same time, it is retrospective. This means, in other
words, that reading Hegel amounts to being in two times at once, for

these two moments do not belong to the same temporal order. As a result, the reader is drawn into a sense of expectation that is irreducibly two-fold: On the one hand, we follow the movement of the narrative according to which the future has not yet arrived and—but the possibility of this *and* is in question—we recognize that the future is already there, in the past.

One way of expressing the double temporality that is articulated by these two perspectives might be "the future of the past," provided that the phrase's genitive grammar is taken into account. On the one hand, Hegel recalls the future of Christianity to the past of the Greek gods and so announces to the past a posteriori its future. In return though—this is "the other hand"—the Greek gods also appear as the future of the Christian god, just as much as the Christian god appears as the mode of explanation that will ensure the Greek gods a future.

Our particular instance of this "future of the past," wherein the scene of classical art (at this stage, even before its full treatment) is forced into a confrontation with a murder that awaits it, is itself an instantiation of these competing temporal orders. Catherine Malabou, whose work we have already mentioned in passing, has argued that Hegel's understanding of the import of Christianity—"the central point," Hegel writes in the *Philosophy of Religion*, "around which everything turns [*um den es sich dreht*]"[34]—itself turns on the temporal revolution inaugurated by it. She writes: "The great revolution in time effected by Christianity is the paradoxical inauguration of a non-recurring time. The time which makes history *turn* is the time which itself does not turn or return: a linear time radically distinct from teleological time. The reason for this is that the Incarnation only happens *once,* and in a *unique individual*" (*FH* 116). Christ is a god who is also a particular individual with a determinate history and a definite end. This means that he does not simply enter into a preexisting temporality but more radically, that he creates a new kind of time: "By dying, Christ reveals to the Western world a new relation between spirit and finitude, in which death is the *limitation*, the end of a linear series of moments linked one to the other" (*FH* 120). Were this not the case, Malabou argues, the Revelation would reveal nothing at all and there would be no way of distinguishing the life of Christ from that of any other exemplary individual, Greek or otherwise.

Writing the transition from the Greek art-world to that of the Christian era cannot simply involve Hegel in crafting a conventional history of the formal changes that have occurred in spiritual expression.

If Malabou is correct in her assessment of Hegel's Christianity as the turning-point of history itself, then the task of achieving a certain unity between these two radically different epochs must also involve bringing their radically divergent notions of time together: The modern notion of linearity must be paired off with the circular movement of the Greeks.

The Christian crucifixion, somehow already being present to the Greek moment, gives off the sense of something death-like that threatens the scene of classical art a little closer to home, at the very heart of its "anthropomorphic enough for art but not enough for religion." What is it about anthropomorphism that flirts so dangerously with death? Moreover, how are we supposed to read the status of the death promised by the future of Christianity, beyond that it simply comes to pass historically, after classical art?

Greek art's sensuousness cannot die: This is the preliminary determination that accounts for why spirit must pass beyond the religion of art of ancient Greece and into the romantic art of Christianity. The negativity of the expression, and the form of denial contained by it—that is, its *not* dying—presents us with a paradox: In preview, the art of ancient Greece art passes, and remains something past, "falls to its ruin," precisely because it cannot do so. It is not able to pass away. That this is marked as a flaw, or a failure—a failure, that is, to die—means that this failure itself must belong to the structure of the classical art-form itself, if classical art is to pass away of its own devices, as Hegel repeatedly suggests is the case. How is this fatal and seemingly incurable flaw implicit to Greek art registered in the historical narrative though?

On the one hand, we might want to suggest that the inability to die is subsumed into the historical narrative, whereby sensuousness will eventually, historically, be able to die. But this historical explanation does not completely rob the negativity of the expression here of its strangeness; its form, indeed, of denial. If the immortality of the Greek gods is what guarantees their historical and geographic localization—indeed, guarantees that they take their place in the historical narrative of spirit's journey—then how is this historical passage articulated within ancient Greek art itself, especially when its anthropomorphism does not display any of the finitude or temporality that would constitute the possibility of its death? How does this *withheld* death, one that cannot exactly be seen or witnessed as an aspect of Greek art's visible phenomenality, become inscribed within

Hegel's theoretical account of the passage of the Greek sculptural art-form?

As Hegel prepares the way for a full articulation of the classical ideal, these questions do not arise within the itinerary of the lectures. Indeed, despite the argument's flirtation with deadness, murder, and not quite-so-historical passing away, it is by virtue of the *not-yet* that Hegel is able to reassert its harmonious beauty. The argument immediately proceeds to reestablish the classical ideal as the art-form that has "only the untroubled harmony of determinate free individuality" as its element, "this peace in that real existence, this happiness, this satisfaction and greatness in itself, this eternal serenity and bliss which even in misfortune and pain [*Unglück und Schmerz*] do not lose their assured self-repose" (436).

As was mentioned earlier, after Hegel affirms the supremacy of the Greek art-form that has no affiliation—*not yet*—with death, Hegel's subsequent task in the following section of the treatment is to situate this harmonious picture in terms of what came before it: "The chief deed of the *Greek* gods is to engender and frame themselves out of the past" (444). What Hegel's explicit formulation yields in his description of this past is hardly reconcilable, though, with the historical "not-yet" that we have just encountered. We are told that this freedom from death and finitude that is the hallmark of classical art is, in fact, the result of a struggle with and from the past. What he tells us precedes the art of the Greeks is summarily treated as the following: "Since the gods are supposed to exist as spiritual individuals in bodily shape, this involves that, on the one side, instead of contemplating its own essence in what is merely living and animal, the spirit regards the living being as unworthy of it, as its misfortune and death [*sein Unglück und seinen Tode*], and, on the other side, overcomes the elemental in nature and its own confused representation therein" (444). In characterizing the past of the classical ideal in this way, the passage explicitly invokes a confrontation with and overcoming of death and finitude, the very same one that has just been denied for the Greek classical ideal less than ten pages earlier. To be sure, it is a struggle that Hegel locates, perhaps safely, in the historical past, one whose outcome includes the classical spirit-body cleansed of all finitude and the struggle with death. But what is to be gleaned from the paradoxical contention that the gods of Greek art here achieve their own singular corporeal perfection, a corporeal perfection that is at the same time also a reminder of a past struggle with misfortune and death?

When Hegel poses the question, presumably to the students in his over-filled lecture-hall, "Whence comes the *material [der Stoffe]* for this mode of appearance of the gods as individuals, how do they progress in their particularization?" (*Aesth* 491), he reasserts what he has already said, which is that their "primary abundant source is supplied by the symbolical nature religions" (ibid). In the brief account of the ways in which the symbolic forms give rise to the foundation for the Greek ideal that follows it, Hegel suggests that "the remains *[die Reste]* of symbolic meanings peep through *[hindurchblicken]*": "having lost their symbolic character," their appearance in the Greek ideal occurs as "purely external events" (492/Vol 14, 95), and so "for us, remain without meaning *[für uns ohne Sinn bleiben]*" (*Aesth* 493/ Vol. 14, 97).

This passage more or less directly follows the itinerary of the section prior to it ("Shaping the Classical Art-Form"), one that offers a dazzling array of historical and mythological examples to support the contention that the Greek ideal arises from what came before it. At the conclusion of that section Hegel summarizes, "Even if, therefore, something symbolical is still retained in the ideal figures of the spiritual gods, nonetheless it is not apparent in its earlier meaning, and the indication as such of nature, earlier constitutive of the essential content, remains in the background as only a relic *[als Rest,* or remnant] and something particular and external which now *[nun]* from time to time *[hin und wieder]*, on account of its accidental character looks bizarre *[bizarr aussieht]* because the earlier meaning no longer dwells in it" (475/Vol. 14, 73). What comes from the past, then, having lost its immediate validity, is neither fully absent nor is it taken up in the present of the new context. To be sure, it no longer appears in the fullness of its earlier meaning; in being denied a context that would give it meaning, it simply abides—*nun*—as an object, one that takes on its strange countenance—"looks bizarre"—by virtue of the fact that its nonpresence/nonabsence no longer yields meaning for the Ideal.

What of the temporality contained in this passage by the "*nun . . . hin und wieder*"? Of course, we could see it as referring to the "present" of the Greek gods' artistic portrayal, the moment when they came into being and relegated their symbolic presuppositions to a position of inferiority and exteriority. This interpretation would suggest that Hegel's own text is to be read as "of a piece" with the moment in the historical trajectory that it is reading, identifying its own descriptive and analytic moment—and its attendant difficulties—with the Greek historical moment in which symbolic forms no longer govern spiritual life. According to this straightforward historical reading, the moment of Hegel's speculation would be effaced as in any way temporally distinct from that of the object that it attempts to historically locate and philosophically describe.

But given that we have already gestured toward how inadequate it is to read Hegel in this manner, another reading of the *nun* or "now" moment could, alternatively, give priority to the historical moment of Hegel's lectures themselves—the moment shared by him and his students at the University of Berlin. This reading would bear witness to a temporal difference between the "then" of the classical ideal and the "now" of its historical future, that of the philosophical and historical exposition that discovers the symbolic remnant in the ideal at the very moment when the attempt is being made to account for them.

But, how is the addition to the "now" of "from time to time" or, alternatively, "now and then" to be read in the context of either of these possibilities? True, I think, to the rigor with which many years earlier, in the *Phenomenology of Spirit*, Hegel had read the vicissitudes of attempting to derive the historical singularity of a moment through deictic markers like "now" and "then"[35]—to which we could *now* add the even more complicated "now and then"—the temporality here, as the time in which the symbolic takes on a bizarre appearance, should itself be marked as radically undecidable. In accordance with Hegel's own suggestion that the structure of the symbolic has the potential to "look bizarre" at any time, this propensity of the symbolic to abide in strange and senseless form does not so much confirm a historical, narrative unfolding as it disturbs the assurance with which that narrative chronology unfolds.

This reading suggests that the bizarreness of the symbolic remains itself *remains*, and in a more unsettling way perhaps than the philosopher would care to admit. It is unsettling, primarily because it does not simply pose problems for interpretation at a particular and historically locatable moment, ones that, given enough time and enough interpretation, would finally be over and done with. The contention, therefore, that the possible threat of the symbolic elements' bizarreness (namely, their resistance to interpretation) occurs "from time to time" is not and cannot be a historical proposition: Rather, it suggests that the time in which its strangeness could arise is *anytime*. And, by exposing the logic of narrative succession to what resists its own framework of temporal organization, those bizarre-looking elements

could expose historical contentions to those elements that their narratives can neither recognize nor explain. This temporal undecidability would, to be sure, include Hegel's own time (and in particular, it
would account for the troubles he had in generating a stable set of
meanings for the symbolic form), but it cannot for all that be limited
to it.

The complex temporality inaugurated by the bizarreness of an
object voided of substantial and contextual meaning is inherent to
the difficulties of pairing a narrative history with its philosophical
knowledge. If the precondition for the former is precisely the removal
of the object from its native context in order to make of it a moment
in a historical narrative, then the strangeness of the object arises, not
so much as a condition to which the historical narrative responds
(although that might well be the self-understanding of history) but
rather, as a consequence of that very process.[36] For Hegel does say,
quite explicitly, that only when the objects no longer govern within
their native or organic context do their residual elements begin to
look bizarre and remain perniciously senseless.

The strangeness of the symbolic arises and remains, then, just as
Hegel witnesses it "peeping through" in instantiations of the Greek
ideal, when he attempts to know that ideal, to remember its past, and
to generate out of that remembrance a key artistic moment in spirit's
history. The look of bizarreness is, then, latent to the very structure
of knowing the art of the past. It is not a bizarreness for which the
(historical) structure of knowing art offers compensation; it is, and
remains, part of that knowing itself.

Directly on the heels of this temporally enigmatic formulation,
Hegel delivers his concluding remarks, which are themselves an
attempt to put an end to all of the temporal and interpretive enig-
mas—indeed, all of the bizarreness—he has just raised. He continues the section, and concludes it by specifying what remains of these
symbolic elements in the Ideal and by relating them, once again, to
its corporeality. "Further," he writes, "since the inner essence of these
gods is the spiritual and the human, what is external about them now
becomes a *human* accident and weakness" (*Aesth* 475). The paradox
of the formulation is suggested by the way in which "the human"—in
the form of weakness and accidents of body—is both central to spirit's full expression and, at the same time, operates as so many signs of
human accidents and frailties, ones presumably that do not generate
meaning and so are to be ignored as no longer central.

These elements belong to what, several lines later he calls "mortality [*Vergänglichkeit*, or 'transience'],," as it is to be contrasted with the immortality of the Greek gods: "With the degradation of [the now bizarre-looking symbolic forms of the previous passage], and with the re-acceptance of these within the higher independence of spiritual individuality permeated by and permeating nature, *we have left behind us* the proper presupposition of the essence of classical art, namely its necessary origin in history" (*Aesth* 475, emphasis added). The gods of classical art have conquered the old ones and in so doing, the passage suggests, have also conquered what is transient about them, in order to display the immortality [*Unvergänglichkeit*] that is their true domain. "For mortality [*Vergänglichkeit*]"—this is Hegel's final comment on the matter— "in general lies in an inadequacy between the Concept and its existence" (*Aesth* 475).

Despite the interpretive difficulties, everything seems to depend upon the possibility of locating those symbolic elements that abide in the ideal and more specifically, upon the possibility of distinguishing the former corporeality from the latter's. But, who is the "we" of the passage, the "we" who has "left behind us" the historical origin? Once again, it is presumably Hegel himself, as well as his students who are there to witness the overcoming of the past—the *Vergangenheit*—of Greek art, so that they too can partake of the full determination of its independence and freedom—its *Unvergänglichkeit*—that follows in the next section. They—Hegel's students—are there to witness the philosopher wresting the Greek ideal away from any remnants of a past body that might remain tethered to it, of a body that might nonetheless look bizarre from time to time and one that may, at any time, give way to interpretive difficulties.

If, as Hegel observes, the bizarreness of the symbolic arises from time to time, we might also expect it to make an appearance in his treatment of Greek art, especially given the extent to which the Greek ideal tarries with bodiliness. For, despite the confidence of the contention—the one we just read—that the gods, in conquering and subsuming what remains of the past, display only what is immortal and intransient, the fact is that for Hegel these gods are not abstract in their universality but are concrete and individual. They are representable in the extreme; they take on sensuous existence in the form of human, bodily shape. So, it is to the tension that arises *within* the Ideal that we will now direct our attention, and attempt to decipher the ways in which the past abides a little less comfortably, perhaps, than a simple "leaving behind" would have it.

§

In the middle section of the full treatment of the classical form of art, after having established its traditional origin, the argument then proceeds to give an account of what arises out of this encounter with traditional forms. "*The New Gods of the Classical Ideal*" begins, then, by asking the question "of what sort are the new gods of Greek art" (*Aesth* 481)? The first point Hegel makes has to do with the source of our esteem for the Greek art-form: It lies in its "concentrated individuality" that it has accomplished by "pulling itself together out of the variety of appendages, single actions and events into the one focus of its simple unity with itself" (*Aesth* 481). In so doing, the Greek gods have withdrawn from the "unrest of the finite [*Unruhe des Endlichen*]" and thus rest secure "on an eternal and clear foundation" (*Aesth* 481/Vol. 14, 82). Unlike the symbolic out of which the perfection of the ideal arose, the gods' appearance as eternal is not "entangled with something other than and external to them" (*Aesth* 482).

Although eternal, of intrinsic worth and not muddied by any uneasy relation to an external "outside," the gods are not, Hegel insists, to be considered a "pure abstraction of spiritual universalities and therefore so called universal ideals." To the contrary: These gods are individuals and so achieve a determinant existence through their artistic portrayal. This determinate existence is brought about by what Hegel calls "character": "Without character no individuality comes on the scene. . . . The manifold aspects and traits which enter on account of this particularity constitute, when reduced to simple unity, the *character* of the gods" (*Aesth* 482).

Not the gods of natural religion, which imperfectly manifest their worldly presence in some transient object (abstract particularity); yet also not an abstract universal ideal that fails to become visible because it cannot enter the world (pure universality): Each Greek god "hovers in the very middle between pure universality and equally abstract particularity" (*Aesth* 482). In the character of the gods is expressed his or her divinity. Moreover, this character does not simply appear as an idea of spirit but rather, in being beautiful, it is also fully visible: "By being beauty in classical art, the inherently determinate divine character . . . appears also externally in its bodily form, i.e. in a shape visible to the eye as well as to the spirit" (*Aesth* 482).

Still in the mode of a back-and-forth movement of what the Greek gods are and, just as importantly, what they are not or are no longer, Hegel continues by asserting that, "classical beauty must not be called '*sublime*'" (*Aesth* 482). This point is as much a historical contention for Hegel as it constitutes an aspect of the argument's structural development. In terms of the structural claim, the language of the classical ideal must be distanced from that of sublimity; that is, it must be distanced from the temptation to *call* the Greek gods "sublime" [*den Ausdruck gewähren*], chiefly because this language, this word, elicits "the look of the sublime [*den Anblick des Erhabenen*]" (*Aesth* 482–3/ Vol. 14, 83): the look of "the abstract universal," namely, "which never coincides with itself in anything determinate."

In certain respects, the language of sublimity stands for what is most troublesome about the interpretation of the symbolic, here at its very limit of representability. Constituted by a lack of correspondence between the divine and *anything* determinate or sensuous, sublime excess is articulated as the most extreme form of the inadequacy between the idea and its material existence or appearance. This is what constitutes the determination of the symbolic. Sublime language is symbolic art's most extreme and also final form, because art that is to be historically classified as sublime has accepted the very inadequacy that the more thoroughly and steadfastly symbolic forms could not stop striving to overcome.

Briefly, to recall the extended treatment of the sublime: It is precisely the division of the divine from the phenomenal world that marked out the impossibility of its being portrayed visually: "Such a way of looking at things can, on this account, be expressed artistically only in poetry, not in the visual arts which bring to our vision only as existent and static the determinate and individual thing" (*Aesth* 366). Likewise, in his discussion of the sublime status of Hebrew poetry, "visual art cannot appear here, where it is impossible to sketch any adequate picture of God; only the poetry of ideas, *expressed in words*, can" (*Aesth* 372, emphasis added).

There is of course much to be said about the status of the sublime for Hegel's *Aesthetics* and its privileging of language over imagery for its worldly expression. For our present purposes, let us hone in on one point: For Hegel's *Aesthetics*, the sublime historically and structurally *falls within* the realm of the development of symbolic art as its most restricted and final moment and thereby, also *falls short of* the beauty of the Greek gods. Within a sublime notion of the divine, it is literally impossible to visualize divinity, much less to know it by virtue of its visibility.

As such, the use of the term "the look of the sublime"—*den Anblick*—in this context is surely an ironic one; the term is made, in Hegel's hands, to play on its affinity with *den Ausdruck*, the expression or the word, "sublime." The very language of invisibility that sustains and develops the earlier specification of sublime art—what he has developed more fully as the "purely spiritual and imageless, contrasted with the mundane and the natural, is spirit completely wrested from nature and sense and released from existence in the finite" (*Aesth* 371)—is recalled but this time, simply in and as a word.

The irony, of course, lies in pairing the word "sublime"—which signifies what we cannot see or look at—with the notion "of looking at" something sublime. In the terms of the sensuous expression that the argument is in the process of developing, it is precisely the *lack* of visual expression for sublime notions of the divine that disqualifies its language as suitable for expressing whatever is lofty or divine about the classical ideal. Within this play on the resonance of the terms *den Anblick* and *den Ausdruck* though, there is perhaps also something more serious to be gleaned from its implicit suggestion that language has the capacity to signify negativity, in the mode of harboring or carrying what it does not make visible and what is, in itself, not visible. In the context of the analysis whose development we are following, this is also to suggest perhaps that what one cannot see, or that which fails to produce knowledge in the form of visual sensuous presentation is nonetheless there, to be read, in and as a word.

Ironic therefore, but not in any simple sense. In fact, if we continue our reading of the section, we find that the disqualification of the word for a description of what goes on in the classical ideal is itself disqualified, or at least partially qualified within the determination of the classical ideal's relation between embodiment and spirit. Contrary to what the argument has developed up to this point, Hegel indeed describes the classical ideal, not as purely or simply beautiful but rather, as "classical *beautiful* sublimity" (*Aesth* 483). What could possibly account for the sublime's reentry into the argument, precisely as it is fine-tuning the notion of spirit's embodiment, given that the basis for its unsuitability was the sublime's negative attitude "to every embodiment" (*Aesth* 483)?

Before proceeding to this paradoxical formulation, let us continue to follow the development from where we left it. There we saw the Greek gods' "infinite security and peace, untroubled bliss, and untrammelled freedom" articulated in opposition to the sublime since classical beauty "unfolds the inner only in the medium of external appearance" (*Aesth* 483). The beautiful harmony of the gods, unlike the sublime unity of the abstract god, is there to be seen. What one sees in the art of the classical ideal "must be withdrawn from all finitude, everything transient, all preoccupation with what is purely sensuous . . . only flawless externality, from which every trait of weakness and relativity has been obliterated and every tiny spot of capricious particularity extinguished, corresponds to the spiritual inwardness which is to immerse itself in it and therein attain an embodiment" (*Aesth* 483).

Timothy Bahti has drawn attention to this passage in terms of the energy of erasure or effacement that it employs. In Bahti's reading, the body as it is described here is not so much recognizably human as it is the very opposite of anything organically human-looking. Hegel's language is striking here; it suggests, Bahti writes, "an excessively clean surface, or tabula rasa . . . a surface or scene about to be (re)-marked" (*AH* 115). Diverging from the more explicit of Hegel's claims, Bahti's suggestion is that this body is not simply there to be seen or described; rather, it is there to be rewritten or reinscribed.

While I share Bahti's impulse to "read" this body as a text rather than to take it as an anthropomorphic given, my intention thus far has been to draw attention to the body as it is indeed to be rewritten and re-marked here, but as a site of memory—that is, as a body sufficiently voided of all temporality so that it can form the ideal mode of spirit's appearance in a way that it never could in its purportedly now-passed and deficient (because thoroughly temporal) form. Moreover, if rereading and rewriting the past is precisely what is implied by Hegel's art of memory,[37] a question that I have been attempting to raise is the following: What relation to temporality is installed in and through this process of rewriting and rereading, one that is not entirely subsumed within or expressed by the more official development of the historical and visual emergence of the human body and then, of its passing away? To what temporal dimension(s) does Hegel's rewriting of this body bear witness, aside from or perhaps even within the well-known conclusion that Hegel's notion of art yields its history?

§

It is with this question in mind that we direct our attention to the passages in which the contention is made that the classical ideal is "sublime beauty." To recommence (for the final time) then, and to recap: It is not as if on the one side lies spirit's corporeality and on the other its spiritual content. The two are mutually penetrating, such that the gods' determinacy of character is also reflected back into their universality. In this, Hegel suggests, lie their "self-repose and self-security in its opposite" (*Aesth* 483):

> Therefore in the concrete individuality of the gods as it is conceived in the properly classical Ideal we see all the same this nobility and this loftiness of spirit in which, despite spirit's entire absorption in the bodily and sensuous shape, there is revealed to us its distance from all the deficiency of the finite. Pure inwardness and abstract liberation from every kind of determinacy would lead to sublimity; but since the classical Ideal issues in an existence which is only its own, i.e. the existence of spirit itself, the sublimity of the Ideal too is fused into beauty and has passed over into it, as it were immediately. For the shapes of the gods this necessitates the expression of loftiness, of classical *beautiful* sublimity. An immortal seriousness, an unchangeable peace is enthroned on the brow of the gods and is suffused over their whole shape. (*Aesth* 483)

This complicated formulation contends, once again, that ancient Greek sculpture is far from having any deficiencies of finitude, but that it nonetheless finds spirit's perfect sensuous form in human embodiment. Spirit has been entirely absorbed into bodily shape, but this absorption is not such that, through it, the gods lose their loftiness or their height (*Hoheit*). Insofar as the loftiness is preserved, maintained, and brought to visibility in the human body, the balance is precarious indeed: Their sublimity or *Hoheit* has fused with the beauty of their (bodily) expression. In other words, their being pressed into bodily and artistic expression does not, at this point, mean that they have lost any of their divinity.

It does, however, mean that Hegel's own terms have to be subject to a compression, in order to maintain the singularity of this bodily constellation, one that is unified and beautifully harmonized with its own sublime spiritual heights. The gods of the classical ideal are *sublimely* beautiful, then, to the extent that their corporeality perfectly evinces their excessive loftiness, rather than simply or arbitrarily represents it. But they are also *beautifully* sublime, to the extent that their loftiness is particular and determinate by virtue its artistic (bodily) shape. To this, we may as well also add that they are past-present. This "past-presence" of ancient Greek art is not simply because "sublimity" lies in the historical past of symbolic art and "beauty" in the present of the ancient Greeks, but also because what comes from the past—extreme and therefore nonsensuous loftiness, for which Hegel has just warned against the use of the word "sublime"—remains in the ideal, strangely enough, as part of its articulation.

At this point, Hegel is forced to concede a degree of restlessness to the gods' constitution. Indeed, all is not as quiet, stable, and peaceful for the gods of sculpture as has been repeatedly suggested. Rather, "the gods appear as raised above their own corporeality, and thus there arises a divergence between their blessed loftiness, which is a spiritual inwardness, and their beauty, which is external and corporeal." Spirit as it is figured here is both immersed in its bodily shape and yet also "raised above" it, suggesting something of a *spatial* excess of spirit that no human body is quite big enough to contain. At the very end of the paragraph in question, Hegel concludes in enigmatic, proto-Christian terms, "It is like the wandering of an immortal god amongst mortal men" (*Aesth* 484). Mortal-immortal, the gods of ancient Greek sculpture are no longer precisely serene or unchanging. Even as sculpture in fact, they are beginning to seem restless: As so many objective representations of spirit, they are, internally at least, on the move.

As Hegel attempts to lend precision to this formulation, he sustains the notion of a "divergence" between their loftiness and their corporeality and at the same time, complicates the perspective on it. At all times, hovering in the background of these formulations is once again the question of the Greek art-form as itself the product of an emergence—and in particular, the divergence that is its consequence: Greek art, it is recalled, has already overcome the kinds of divisions and nonharmonious forms of expressing spirit that had preceded it. The divisions and separations that informed Hegel's descriptions of those earlier symbolic forms—and the at-times disparaging comments he makes about them—reappear here, but this time they are central and integral to the sculptures of Greek art themselves. No longer are the divisions ones that could potentially lead to their overcoming; rather, they are of a piece with, and interior to, the work of art itself. As Hegel qualifies the immediately preceding claim of the identity of the body with its spiritual being, he returns to the sense of an inner departure from this unity: "But since the above-mentioned divergence is present," he recalls, "yet without appearing as a difference and separation between inner spirituality and its external shape [as it was in symbolic art], the negative inherent in it is on this account immanent in this undivided *whole* and expressed therein itself" (484).

As the argument is made to focus on the idea of a unity in division, or of a division implicit to harmonious unity, the perspective on it is made more complicated by the introduction of a witness to its internal division. The argument almost loses its academic tenor as it itself seems to become vulnerable to the effects of this inner division: "Within the loftiness of the spirit this [inner division] is the breath and scent of mourning [*der Hauch und Duft der Trauer*] which gifted men have felt in the ancient pictures of the gods even in their consummate beauty and loveliness" (*Aesth* 484–5).[38] As Hegel introduces the notion of mourning into his description of the divisions internal to the gods, he also departs from his own aesthetic argument. For this rather sudden "appearance" of mourning in the argument is not, strictly speaking, an artistic appearance: It is one that "gifted men" can inhale or smell, but not one they can see. By virtue of what invisible, or nonvisual trait of ancient Greek art, then, is this ghostly mourning registered, one to which Hegel, as himself a "gifted man," no doubt sees himself as responding?

When he turns away from the gifted men who feel the "breath and scent of mourning" and back to the gods once again in the next and final paragraph of the section, it is to defend and uphold their "warmth and life" against yet another outside perspective on it: The conventional, and exemplarily modern propensity to accuse their universality of "frigidity" and lifelessness (likewise, the descriptions of their repose as "rigid, cold and dead" on the following page also belong to this perspective). And, by claiming that this attitude toward the gods is solely a consequence of "our modern fervour in the sphere of the finite [*Innigkeit im Endlichen*]" (*Aesth* 485/Vol. 14, 86), Hegel is establishing a rather deadly parallel: By setting up the Greek gods' infinitude as a counterpoint to the finitude of the moderns, Hegel implies that it is not the Greek gods who are dead and lifeless but rather, the critics themselves who, in pronouncing them so, are at risk of falling victim, via their deadening judgment, to their own finitude.

One can, I think, read this final paragraph as a philosophical attempt to sustain and validate a certain response to "mourning" against what is set up as its diametrical opposite, which is the simple pronouncement of the deadness of the Greek gods. Through the contrast of the two possible reactions to the repose of the gods—one whose attention is directed toward "mourning" and the other whose pronouncement of a death somehow discloses, by disavowing, its own deadness—the implication is that the scholar who is attuned to mourning somehow secures life (his own, perhaps?) as the reward for his attention.

The emanation of life that Hegel so praises in the sculptures of the Greek gods is opposed to the deadliness of too-great an attention to finitude, and is signified by the Greek gods' overcoming of all that is temporal and transient: "The blissful peace mirrored in their body is essentially an abstraction from the particular, an indifference to the transient, a sacrifice of the external, a renunciation neither sorrowful nor painful, yet all the same a renunciation of the earthly and evanescent" (*Aesth* 485). The "renunciation" of this passage is, on the one hand, one that leaves no visible traces of pain or sorrow in the bodily form that the gods adopt. However, the text emphasizes the renunciation and insists upon it as exerting some kind of force within the sculptures themselves, as a loss that is nonetheless there to be dealt with.

The sentence that we have just interrupted midstream concludes by elaborating on this strange force, as the gods' own containment of the dead: "yet all the same a renunciation [*doch ein Entsagen*] of the earthly and evanescent, just as their spiritual serenity in its depth looks far away beyond death, the grave, loss, and temporality [*Tod, Grab, Verlust, Zeitlichkeit*], and, precisely because it is deep, contains the negative in itself" (*Aesth* 485/Vol. 14, 86). Precisely because the gods have overcome the temporal tendency to pass, they have also renounced its transience by "looking far away beyond" the more deadly consequences of time's passage. Yet, by virtue of that renunciation—*doch*—they have come to find that transience, but this time they find that it is *in* them. What has, all along, been thematized and narrated as the gods' struggle with and victory over what passes, is here settled in a mode of interiorized resignation or acquiescence to it.

Just as the gods are deep enough to house the dead, so too is a "we"—presumably a reference back to the "gifted men" and not to the critics who pronounce on the "frigidity" of the gods—deep enough to feel it. Although Hegel insists on the gods here as discrete and "*regarded* in themselves," he nonetheless once again seeks recourse to the perspective of an other, not in the mode of one seeing, but rather, as one who feels the growing contrast within the gods: "the more that seriousness and spiritual freedom appear in the shapes of the gods, so much the more can we feel a contrast between (a) this loftiness and (b) determinacy and bodily form. The blessed gods mourn as it were over their blessedness or their bodily form" (*Aesth* 485). As the contrast internal to the gods reaches its extreme, another contrast arises between the gods who are mourning their internal deficiency and the "we" who is feeling the contrast. This latter contrast does not so much duplicate the radical internal division that is the putative source of the gods' mourning, as it hints at a correspondence or similarity: that which arises between the gods' mourning and the "we feeling" that we have already seen at play in the "gifted men" who feel the mourning of the previous passage.

There is an undeniably dramatic, séance-like quality to this scene: As the gods mourn over the discrepancy internal to them, the "we" also mourns as it breathes in the air or the scent expelled by the dying. When the dying gods and the breathing scholars are brought together into a space of encounter, it is almost as if a secret is passed between kindred spirits. Indeed, any sense of temporal distance or of historical succession between the "gods mourning" and the "we feeling" has been eliminated; the scholar is present at the scene of Greek art's death and, as he hovers over the dying body of the gods, readies himself to receive the spirit as it leaves that body, by breathing deeply. But when the scholars are breathing in the last breaths of spirit as it separates and departs from the gods' body, the scholar and the gods are joined in this spiritually uncanny death ritual, precisely, at the body: The dying and expiring of the gods, who express this dying through the breath of mourning, is what the scholar senses, feels, indeed breathes into himself.

Hegel would surely be the last to contend that his own corporeality is of a piece with his scholarly expression of spirit. He is not a Greek god, and his task is not to resurrect or to reproduce this entanglement of spirituality with corporeality as a form of spirituality to whose ultimate contradiction the gods' mourning testifies. All the same, by breathing in the last of the gods, his task is also not that of simply taking leave of this body, now bereft of the spirit that he has inhaled. For true to Hegel's precise wording, noted above, the spirit that leaves the body or that rises above it, still contains the transitoriness, the fragility, and the mortality of the body that spirit in its elevated form both cancels *and* preserves.

As Hegel turns away from the death scene that he has just invoked, what his immediate claim suggests is that the body has not simply disappeared, but is one for which another modality of response—another way of registering it—must be found. "We read in their formation [*man liest in ihrer Gestaltung*]," he writes, "the fate that awaits them, and its development, as the actual emergence of that contradiction between loftiness and particularity, between spirituality and sensuous existence, drags classical art itself to its ruin" (*Aesth* 485, translation slightly modified).

What began as a celebration of Greek memory and its propensity to bring universal spirit to sensuous presentation becomes a scene of mourning over the absence of undisturbed unity that it had hoped to establish. In turn, the scene of the gods of Greek sculpture mourning itself turns into another kind of scene, wherein *"we read in their formation the fate that awaits them."* At stake here is, once again, the dual movement of anticipatory progression and retrospection in the renouncement of embodiment and the increasing interiority of spirit that will have marked the passage from Greek art to the future of Christianity and its romantic art, as well as to the prose of philosophy. If this narrative progression from the past to the present is (as we noted at the outset of our discussion) repeatedly signified elsewhere as an interiorization or *Erinnerung*, then why is the response to the gods' mourning not signified as such here but rather, as a task of reading? How does reading come to be a valid mode of philosophically approaching the past, where the spirit detaches from the body? To make of its body, now bereft of spirit, historical knowledge, no doubt, but why is the act of reading figured as the historical/philosophical mode of memory?

That a fitting response to Greek art, after its mourning has been imbibed, would be one of reading suggests first of all that its body has, somewhere along the way, become a text, one that philosophers who look to the past for meaning must learn to read. The visual embodiment of the gods that "one sees" in sculpture turns into a scene where something must be read—namely, the text claims, their fate as the future that is already inscribed within their formation. But here too, the future is both already there and *not-yet* there. In fact, we need not wait for Heidegger to articulate the dimension of "sending" (*schicken, Geschick*) and historicity (*Geschichtlichkeit*) implied in fate (*Schicksal*):[39] Here fate is already tied to an idiom of waiting, separation, and emergence, all of which complicate its more fatalistic sense as simply a forgone conclusion.

In the section devoted to the explication of the "fate" awaiting classical art, this mourning is again invoked, not as an aspect of its sensuous visibility but as "a trait" that both necessitated the historical development of spirit through its visible forms and that also prefigured or predicted the failure of that visibility: "Yet, they [the gods in their blessed repose] retain something lifeless [*etwas Lebloses*], an aloofness from feeling, and that tranquil trait of mourning which we have already touched on. It is this mourning which already constitutes their fate because it shows that something higher stands above them" (*Aesth* 503/Vol. 14, 108). When the constitution of the Greek gods is described as retaining "something lifeless," this can only mean that they have contained and preserved something dead from the past whose presence, although unseen and therefore unrecognizable, nonetheless abides there.

To the extent that the sculpture of the classical ideal has internalized the past, the passage also suggests that it harbors in itself "something dead." Unlike the earlier formulations wherein a degree of dismissive impatience was detected regarding the status of the symbolic elements that were retained from the past but that "for us remain without sense," it is precisely here that Hegel gives them a sense, and that is to have been there all along, dictating the fate of the gods that "we" are to read in their formation. That they must be read is, I think, exactly of a piece with both the contention that they are dead, and that they "remain senseless" and bizarre looking.

§

What is it about these dead things abiding in and retained by the ideal that thwarts and troubles a visual imagination, but that nonetheless allows "us" to read them? The transition from seeing to reading that is affected here—where a visualized and sensuous body takes on the attributes of a text, one that "has retained something dead"—is certainly abrupt and conspicuous at this point of the text's development. However, it itself prefigures the account that Hegel will provide for the transition to the language of romantic poetry in its full determination.

As is well known from Hegel's estimation of poetry, it is in poetry's language that spirit ultimately loses shape and sensuous embodiment. At the beginning of the transition from music to poetry, Hegel makes the contention that it is by virtue of the "art of speech" that poetry can "more perfectly unfold the totality of an event, a successive series [*eine Reihenfolge ... vollständiger ... zu entfalten befähigt ist*]" than any other of the arts (*Aesth* 960/224). This specification, while here still in preview, aligns whatever it is that poetry's language does with an ability to narrate and contain change as succession (*Reihenfolge*). As such, we are given a glimpse here that narrative as such and, by implication, Hegel's own narrative may very well be partaking of what poetry does.

In the course of the short introduction to the full determination of poetry, as materiality is being left behind, "objectivity exchanges its previously external reality for an internal one, and it acquires an existence only within consciousness itself, as something spiritually presented and intuited" (*Aesth* 964). Spirit becomes objective to itself on what Hegel calls "its own ground," "it has speech [*das sprachliche Element*] only as a means of communication or as an external reality out of which, as out of a mere sign, it has withdrawn into itself from the very start" (*Aesth* 964/Vol. 15, 229). Where poetry is concerned, it is a matter of indifference "whether we read it or hear it read"; the point is that poetry is a text that, just like the "fate of the gods that awaits them," is not so much to be seen but is, rather, to be read.

Speech, so asserts the above citation, is the means by which spirit can be communicated. By going out into the "mere sign," language provides an almost instant pathway back into spirit, a means of reentry that presumably leaves no trace of spirit ever having left itself, and therefore no dead body. This is what is specific to poetry, Hegel claims in the ensuing development, that although "its results are to be made known to the spirit only by communication in language," it does not labor under the duress of "towering heavy masses, bronze, marble, wood, colours, and notes" (*Aesth* 966) as do the other arts. By virtue of poetry's having "cut itself free from this importance of the material," it becomes the "*universal* art" (*Aesth* 967).

Poetry is the universal art because its foundation is that of the "universal imagination" itself, the basis and ground, Hegel suggests, of all the particular art-forms. To this contention, an objection might be raised: Poetry too has its genres and a history; it is one art among others, and Hegel is about to expound on it at length, both in terms of its artistic features and in terms of its various historical developments. Nonetheless, Hegel has anticipated this objection and despite it, continues to insist on poetry's claim to universality. In particular, his defense of the claim specifies and locates its universality in terms

of its "having been there" all along, latently, from the very beginning
of art:

> This is the point that we reached at the close of our treatment of the
> particular art-forms. Their culmination [*deren letzten Standpunkt*]
> we looked for in art's making itself independent of the mode of rep-
> resentation peculiar to *one* of the art-forms and in its standing above
> the whole of these particular forms. The possibility of such a develop-
> ment in every direction lies from the very beginning, amongst the spe-
> cific arts, in the essence of poetry alone, and it is therefore actualised
> in the course of poetic production partly through the actual exploita-
> tion of every particular form, partly through liberation from impris-
> onment in any exclusive type and character of treatment and subject-
> matter, whether symbolic, classical, or romantic. (*Aesth* 967)

This passage suggests not only that poetry was there, *avant la
lettre*, from the very beginning; it also suggests that, by virtue of
poetry's lifting itself out of every dependence on external, sensuous
material, it is not only at the origin of art, but it is also responsible
for the "possibility of such a development" as it occurs at each historical stage and in each of its "particular forms." As such, poetry
is also responsible for the entire philosophical, historical development both as Hegel has narrated it and as we, his readers, have read
it. The narration of art's historical development, and through it, a
coming to know art as that which gives new forms to the past of
spirit, corresponds exactly to what poetic language has been push-
ing art to do all along: to move spirit's memory through the successive stages of the historical forms and material through which
it became visible or audible, and back into spirit itself. The only
way to know this philosophically, Hegel suggests, is to register the
extent to which poetry's struggle for totality entailed "a cancellation [and preservation—*ein Aufheben*] of a restriction to the particular" (*Aesth* 968/234).

In the claim that poetry and the philosophy of art are closely
linked, Hegel develops Kant's contention in the *Critique of Judgment*
that poetry is the most philosophical of all the arts,[40] and intensifies
the relation between the two modes of discourse with the suggestion
that philosophy is itself somehow poetic: "Only as a result of considering the series of the arts in this way [as the successive historical
struggle for liberation from and the containment of material] does
poetry appear as that particular art in which art itself begins at the
same time to dissolve and acquire in the eyes of philosophy its point

of transition to religious pictorial thinking as such, as well as to the prose of scholarly thought" (968).

If philosophy is akin to poetry's spiritual inwardness insofar as both express spirit unburdened with materiality, and that both use language as the pathway for spirit to return to itself, what is on "this side" of spirit's triumphant home-coming? How does spirit and its historical trajectory become intelligible to it, now that it is practically void of all material presentation? To be sure, the development of the argument forecloses the possibility that philosophy and poetry remain dependent on visual, sensuous material but that does not mean that they are true only in their inaccessibility: "Poetry . . . reduces the opposite of heavy spatial matter, namely sound, to a *meaningless sign* instead of making it, as architecture makes its material, into a meaningful symbol" (*Aesth* 968, emphasis added). As it turns out, the sign, meaningless in itself, is the mode whose materiality spirit overcomes in order to return to itself.

Distinguishing the sign from the symbol, Hegel writes: "In the *mere sign* the connection which meaning and its expression have with one another is only a purely arbitrary linkage" (*Aesth* 304), an arbitrariness that disqualifies it for consideration in the arts: "We may not take account of it in reference to art, since art as such consists precisely in the kinship, relation, and concrete interpenetration of meaning and shape" (*Aesth* 304). What is initially excluded from consideration as and in art is thus explained, at the end, both as art's organizing force, and as the force by which the narration of its historical development (as well as the philosophical knowing that that narration generates) was ever possible in the first place.

What kind of insights are generated by the proposal that the memory of spirit find its most appropriate and most quintessentially modern expression in language, given that the linguistic sign might very well mark the return of spirit to itself with an inexpressible materiality, marking perhaps the impossibility of ultimately embodying or recuperating the past? For Hegel suggests that in poetry, "the fusion of spiritual inwardness with external existence" is destroyed and that as such, poetry "runs the risk of losing itself in a transition from the region of sense into that of the spirit" (*Aesth* 968). If poetry is the most idealized—and hence, universalized—mode of spirit's communication, it is because its barely material medium of the meaningless sign (*bedeutungslose Zeichen*) makes no pretence to presenting spirit in a visible form adequate to it and thus secures for spirit its most adequate space in the interiorized space of religious devotion or in the space of philosophical, historical reflection. In the contention that art's culmination finds itself right there at the beginning—indeed, even before the beginning, *elsewhere*—of art proper, Hegel is also suggesting that the senseless marks and objects of the unruly symbolic "remains" (*die Reste*) are formalized, in the end, as letters and words.

The sense of this development is that poetic language, for Hegel, comes to be the most compelling means of communicating modernity's memory of spirit. And that privilege is granted by virtue of how poetic language formalizes the past's irrecuperability; in other words, the sign's meaningless mark—and the final disjunction between spirit and sense that it marks—formalizes the *elsewhere* from where, Hegel insists, material from the past always erupts. What we need to take note of, though, is the relation that this formalization of exile or homelessness has to the element of surprise that Hegel had suggested was both immanent in the Greek relation to its not-fully mastered past, and immanent also in the philosophical explanation. There, we saw an element of surprise that remained as the enigmatic, bizarre persistence of the past within the very narrative prospect of making spirit comprehensible and recognizable. But if language has formalized the eruption of "meaninglessness" and has taken that eruption as its own ground, then it also seems to have formalized (and so mastered) the undecidability of the surprise that was promised by what remained of symbolic art. For what is a surprise if it is formalized: Does the process of its formalization neutralize it to the point of a "has-been"? Is the Hegelian surprise, in short, not so surprising after all? What, then, is left of Hegel's time?

In short, what remains of time is the time of memory itself, which Hegel presents as *reading the past*. For as I have been attempting to show, reading—and what does one read, if not language?—is a perfect literalization of the time of Hegel's approach to the past. This does not mean however that spirit has found its lasting and eternal place in the exile of language, and that we simply read and reread the same story over and over again (although to be sure, this story itself has become well-worn). Rather, reading the past for Hegel means to be exposed to more than one time at once. For is it not true that in reading, we attend to how the plot, argument or doctrine unfolds a not-yet articulated future, all the while aware that the text is already complete, its future having already arrived long before we started reading? And furthermore, that every moment of reading is marked by the impossibility of being in both of those times at once? That one cannot subsume the time of reading into one unique and self-same time means that any moment in which reading takes place will not be able to see the other moment, without experiencing an interruption or eruption of time.

While so many commentators have sought to emphasize that the end of time arrives in Hegel's philosophy, a rejoinder might be provided by emphasizing how Hegel, at his most legible, writes a history with the injunction to read it, and to read it in such a way as to provoke the sense that time is always in excess of itself. If for Hegel, it is true that all dominant forms and figures have already arrived, it is also true that their time is in no way fixed or settled. In fact, Hegel's memory announces that the future itself depends on the way the past is read, on the way those forms and figures are put back into play, and on the way that the past is mobilized to open up new perspectives.

Although Hegel does suggest that the question of sensual presentation is all but eliminated from spirit in language, his contention that poetry "runs the risk of losing itself in transition" from the meaningless sign into the realm of spirit, seems to ascribe more force to the power of inscription than might otherwise be suggested by language as a transparent medium. In fact, the overarching sense of these passages is that the risk of poetic language involves being exposed to time's openings. Language is the source of this "risk of getting lost in transition," not between finite linear time and its infinitizing presentation, but *within* time—a risk, then, to which the practices of reading the past must be exposed. Reading Hegel's memory as a rehashed version of eternalizing the finite is, in some sense, what results when this risk is refused.

CHAPTER FOUR

Speculating on the Past, the Impact of the Present

Hegel and His Time(s)

We must hold to the conviction that it is in the nature of truth to prevail when its time has come, and that it appears only when this time has come, and therefore never appears prematurely nor finds a public not ripe to receive it. . . . But from this we must distinguish the more gradual effect which . . . gives some writers an audience only after a time.

—G. F. W. Hegel

For Hegel, this end of history is marked by the coming of Science in the form of a Book.

—Alexandre Kojève

To argue for a rigorous reading of the "end" of historical time in Hegel is, in some sense, the condition for thinking the experience of narrative time in a mode other than that of the simple linearity of continuous progression. In Chapter 3, we demonstrated how Hegel's complex mode of narrating the pastness of "art in its highest determination" generates an understanding of past and future that goes beyond the notion of two distinct moments on a temporal continuum and conceives narrative temporality in terms of how an aspect of futurity is at work in it, not as a horizon of expectation but as a force of disruption within the experience of reading narratives whose "object" has ostensibly passed. By complicating the familiar notion (and the familiar experience) of narrative time, Hegel demands too that we bracket the familiar ways of thinking about the future as such: Hegel's future—both *of* his philosophy as well as *in* his philosophy—seems so difficult to locate in part because it is neither preprogrammed by the past nor can it be tied to an idiom of unprecedented novelty.

One implication of this understanding is that the future will only continue to be unpredictable or surprising to the extent that "reading the past" attends to the surprises and unforeseeable occurrences that it experiences and, furthermore, that it allows itself to be surprised. In Chapter 3, I argued that not least among those surprises might be the experience of reading in two irreconcilable temporal registers at once.

On the one hand, this temporality that we articulated through a notion of "reading the past" implies that any surprises history has in store for the future will emerge through and *as* the very act of remobilization: The fact that it is even possible to remobilize the past implies that its time is not given or fixed but is marked by a certain volatility. One might say that various forms of the past will demonstrate their own, perhaps surprising, future precisely by virtue of being put back into play. However, one might also be compelled to argue that the very act of remobilization itself must be underpinned or compelled by a lingering element of surprise inhabiting the presentation of the past, one to which a narrative logic, even of the more complex kind proposed by Hegel, can perhaps do only limited justice.

In fact, although our reading might well undermine the assumption that Hegel worked exclusively within the modality of successive time, could Heidegger's criticism of Hegel—that he "leveled down" time[1]— not be leveled at us? Could it not be argued, namely, that we too have leveled down the temporality of the past precisely by limiting it to *two times*, that of the successive unfolding and circular completion of narrative time? For if, as we are now suggesting, it is not only the future's substantive content that depends on how the past get remobilized but also its unpredictability and openness, have we not followed Hegel here in robbing history of the capacity to surprise, precisely by neglecting the question or the dimension of surprise itself?

These questions frame what I would like to pursue more fully here: the extent to which our interpretation of Hegel's *Aesthetics* might bear on his philosophical understanding of history as such. There is nothing obvious about this, especially when we consider the differences of the "objects" involved. While the philosophical consideration of an art object in the *Lectures on Aesthetics* involved ridding that object of its concrete shape so as to recover it in thought, it is not immediately apparent how historical events would be open to the same process. In fact, the means by which history becomes meaningful might seem to depend upon the reverse procedure: The infinite details making up any one moment of human history, what Hegel refers to in the *Logic* as the "unstable manifoldness" [*bestandlose Mannigfaltigkeit*] of existence[2] are, when considered in themselves, so varied as to have virtually no shape at all or what is perhaps the same thing, too many different shapes. One might say that they are given coherent form and shape for the very first time in historical narrative and that in this respect, events and their narration belong to two distinct and incompatible orders.

Pausing to reflect on the complexities of the word "history," Hegel will have already questioned the validity of this understanding. In the *Introduction to the Philosophy of History*, he writes:

> *History* combines in our language the objective as well as the subjective side and means the *historia rerum gestarum* as well as the *res gestae* itself; it is that which has happened [*das Geschehene*] no less than it is historiography [*Geschichtserzählung*]. We must consider the coincidence of these two meanings as of a higher kind than a merely external accident [*bloss äusserliche Zufälligkeit*, or "a purely external contingency"]: it should thus be maintained that historiography appears simultaneously [*gleichzeitig*] with properly historical acts and events; there is an inner common base driving both of them forward.[3]

Historical narration, this passage contends, is not an arbitrary or belated intervention imposing a shape on historical events that is otherwise alien to them. Their unity *in a word* is no mere coincidence (or, no pure accident). At one level, this doubling of the word "history" implies that historical narration is the most fitting discursive mode for historical events because, by unifying the massive changes that have occurred throughout the course of history, it alone is able to do justice to the sheer passage of long stretches of time.[4]

At another level though, the passage's claim for the simultaneity of the historical act and its narration is the site of another doubling: It is as much a historical claim as it is a logical or linguistic one. In other words, the logic underpinning the simultaneity of the two sides—that "what happens" and its narration occur together—is matched by the claim of their historical simultaneity, which is, they both appear (*erscheinen*) at the same time *in history*.

If the logical unity between historical events and their narrative inscription bears the trace of their simultaneous appearance in history, Hegel was also well aware that every story (*Geschichte* or *Erzählung* in German) must have its dénouement. Thus, it is not particularly surprising that the *Introduction to the Philosophy of History* reiterates the claim made at the conclusion of the *Phenomenology of Spirit*—that the linear conception of historical time is brought to an end as spirit digests the entire course of world history as *its* own development. In these later Berlin lectures, Hegel describes his own epoch as "absolutely [*schlechthin*] the end of History" (*IPH* 103); having attained "the ultimate goal of history [*das Ziel der Weltgeschichte*]" (*IPH* 110/141), he calls it "*the last stage* of History [das *letzte Stadium der Geschichte*]."[5] In light of these unequivocal claims, what is perhaps surprising is how Hegel complicates their perspective and their meaning by drawing attention, on at least two occasions, to the prospect of the future. The first involves the famous contrast Hegel posits between *Amerika* as "the land of the future" (*das Land der Zukunft*) and the "historic arsenal"[6] of Napoleon's *vieille Europe* (*PhH* 87/114); the second occurs in his discussion of the French Revolution, whose "knot" or problem—the constant, because constitutive, production of suspicion and paranoia—will be a task for the future to solve (*PhH* 452/535).

While it is easy to imagine how these admissions of the future could be marshaled as support for the claim that Hegel's attempt to stop history dead in its tracks has, even by his own admission, failed, I would argue that they challenge the standard perception of the modalities of closure operative in Hegel's philosophical history. In particular, the matter-of-fact tone with which Hegel points to the future—as if for him, it were self-evident that things will still happen—raises the question of what status to accord futurity right at the level of Hegel's philosophical thinking about history, not beyond it but *within* it; that is, how to position Hegel's exposition of historical narrative in relation to "what happens."[7] The most cursory inspection of these two particular cases suffices to show that they both express futurity in the mode of *departure* and, in so doing, do not so much undermine the claim that a particular understanding of history has come to an end, as they act to confirm it: Their force, namely, seems to lie in how whatever happens in the future will do so at a remove from the standard bearings of European thought, including the widely held understanding of history as an inexorable historical progression. On the one hand America's future, Hegel writes, will depend upon how it can "separate itself from the ground [*von dem Boden auszuscheiden*] upon which the world's history has taken place until now" (*IPH* 90/114) and on the other hand, the future of the French Revolution is literally cast as the return of history's "unfinished business."

It is, I think, noteworthy that these cases articulate two very different versions of the future—the one, a future that departs or separates; the other, an uncanny return from the past—as if Hegel were articulating the "new time" of modernity[8] as an opening-out of time or as a plurality of times. Nonetheless, what is immediately apparent about both of these futures is that neither is cast in the mode of prediction or anticipation—America is the new world about which Hegel is reluctant to speculate, except to say that its geographical remoteness can be translated into a vague sense of emergent novelty ("The World is divided into *Old* and *New*," he writes [*PhH* 80]); the future of the French Revolution is, scandalously, the site of an unresolved past, whose unworked dimensions Hegel detects in a lingering sense of suspicion and paranoia.

Although these references clearly contradict Heidegger's assertion that Hegel "never [speaks] about the future," Hegel's reluctance to make clear pronouncements on it has done little to dissuade readers from maligning it as a sign of Hegel's indifference toward anything but the past. It is just such a dim view that Kojève, for instance, gives in his assessment that "understanding or Knowledge of the Past is what, when it is integrated into the Present, transforms this Present into an historical present, that is, into a present that realizes a progress in relation to its Past."[9] By virtue of the suggestion that the present is the "moment" whose only knowledge of itself is gained through its relation to the past—it comes to know itself, in other words, as another step "in the right direction" on the historical path of progress—Kojève sees Hegel as having drained the present of all vitality: Its edifice is the past and it is solely a function, a passive outcome or necessary stage, of that edifying foundation.

More recently, Joshua Foa Dienstag has voiced similar concerns regarding what he sees as the absence of the present, or at least its deeply impoverished status, in Hegel's philosophy. For Dienstag, Hegel's predilection for a totalizing presentation of history effectively forecloses thinking about the present or the future. In tying the "end of history" thesis to the question of the role of narrative in politics, Dienstag too suggests that the Hegelian present is exhausted by its relation to the past: The present, which Dienstag describes as the moment in Hegel that "can be said to *own* the past,"[10] is identified "as the final episode of historical time [and] implies that his story is complete as it stands, and that history is at an end" (144). All Hegel can offer to the present, Dienstag argues, is "the remembrance of life in an ever-repeating picture show," one marked by little short of an unbearable ennui: "Hegel leaves us with nothing to do in the house our predecessors have built and that he has unveiled" (177).

Nietzsche, in his own inimitable way, will have already set the example. "Inside Hegelian heads," he writes, "God has already climbed up through all the dialectically possible stages of its process of becoming, up to the point of that self-revelation so that for Hegel the apex and culmination of the world process coincided with his own existence in Berlin. Indeed, he might even have said that everything that came after him could actually be regarded as only a musical coda of the world-historical rondo—or, more precisely, as superfluous."[11] Or Heinrich Heine who, only half in jest, will have named the serpent of the Garden of Eden as the first true Hegelian: *Die kleine Privatdozentin*, he calls it, "already delivered the entire Hegelian philosophy six thousand years before Hegel's birth."[12] Following these gestures, must we return to Hegel only to turn him against himself, applying to his notion of history what he says about *habit*—that activity without opposition for which only formal duration is left—that it is "like a watch wound up and going by itself?" (*IPH* 78).

Tempting though it might be, it is nonetheless difficult to leave it at that. A preliminary doubt, though admittedly a not very philosophical one: How to square the notion that Hegel conceived the present as a foregone conclusion or, alternatively, as the remembrance of the same sequence of history—maddeningly and predictably played over and over again in the mode of "automatic repeat"—with his almost obsessive preoccupation with his *own* present? The intense interest he took in the massive political and social upheavals of his time is well known: It is what caused him to implore his colleagues to join him in reading daily newspapers as their "morning prayer."[13] But no less could we cite his early injunction to philosophize in one's own idiom[14] or alternatively, his maxim that it is impossible to escape one's own time[15]—a maxim that Nietzsche would implicitly challenge with his own "unfashionable" or "untimely" observations[16]—to suggest that not only is the present at work in Hegel's texts but perhaps its unyielding force must be given a fuller account.

If for Hegel there is no flight from the present, then it is not surprising that he would conceive speculating on the future as an attempt to mitigate or soften its impact. It is just such an escape attempt that he questions when, in a remark made in the *Encyclopedia* (1830), he examines the everyday use of the word *speculation*. He writes,

> The term *speculation* tends to be used in ordinary life in a very vague, and at the same time, secondary sense—as for instance, when people talk about a matrimonial or commercial speculation. All that

it is taken to mean here is that, on the one hand, *what is immedi-ately present must be transcended*, and, on the other, that whatever the content of these speculations may be, although it is initially only something subjective, it ought not to remain so, but is to be realized or translated into objectivity (emphasis added).[17]

The difference between philosophical speculation and its more every-day usage, this passage implies, is that the former produces no images of the future, either on the basis of prognosis (commerce) or wishful thinking (marriage). A statement made early on in the *Introduction to the Philosophy of History*—and one repeated throughout—suggests that Hegel also sees a version of the common understanding of specu-lation at work in the naïve youthfulness of idealism that was so preva-lent in his time: "Nothing is more common today than the complaint that the *ideals* raised by fantasy are not being realized, that these glorious dreams are being destroyed by cold actuality . . . They can only be subjective, after all . . . Poets such as Schiller have presented these ideals in very moving and emotional ways, with the feeling of deep sorrow at the fact that they may never be realized" (*IPH* 38). For Hegel, the "should" or *Sollen* (12/37) of idealistic longing is trapped in the endless temporality of the "not yet"; its perennial imperative is dictated by a vision of the world as it "ought to be," one whose ideals—existing "who knows where" (*IPH* 12)—bear no relation to reality.[18] If Hegel ever dreamed, then, it was clearly not of the future. In this respect, he might very well belong among those iconoclasts who, Nietzsche charges, "would destroy the images of the future."[19] And indeed, what can the future possibly mean in the context of no projection, no anticipation or ideal, and no image?

What I would most like to avoid in this chapter is a reading that, contrary to Hegel's own injunction, makes him leap over his own time. If there is a "timely" relevance to be discerned in his think-ing about history, then, it shall be articulated in terms of what role "timeliness" plays in that thinking. In other words, before any pro-nouncements can be made regarding its ongoing relevance, Hegel's notion of "timeliness" must be set in the context of its own history (according to its doubled meaning, which would imply at once its his-torical "moment" as well as the force of that moment within his phil-osophical consideration of history). And is this fundamental lesson of Hegelianism not enough to contest the view that "timeliness" just is what it is, that it is a trans-historical property of time, a temporal essence? More to the point, might it not also suggest that the temporal modality in which a particular understanding of "timeliness" makes itself most sharply felt—that is, the historical time of a linear succession of "nows"—could also be finite and so historical?

Precisely in this respect though, Hegel's critics must be given their due, for he is not entirely innocent of the readings his work has generated. After all, even if the modalities of past, present, and future in Hegel's philosophical history are to be thought in the wake of the organizing principle of linear historical time, the process by which their various shapes are differentiated from one another must still be conceivable, if not in terms dictated by a narrative or linear temporality: In other words, the present must still be thought both in relation to the past, about which of course Hegel has much to say, as well as to the future, about which he will have said next to nothing.

At a glance, the prospects do not look especially hopeful: The fact that Hegel's systematic attempt to read World History could yield no knowledge about the future—that, in the end, it does not prognosticate—and that it does not even reserve a place for the future in terms of the temporal openness of a "to be continued" is used to support the argument that philosophical knowing and spiritual fulfillment *require* that there be no more future, that it be foreclosed. In the absence of a future "to come," what else is to be done but to cast a melancholy gaze on the past? The standard reading of the future's systematic foreclosure involves a clear case of Hegelian reversibility: Because the culmination of history in Absolute Knowing bids farewell to the future and consequently has no bearings to offer the future, history itself will have had to conclude that Hegel has no future. This is what ultimately leads Dienstag to summarize that "the ambition [to reconcile history with thought] may prove to be self-defeating, as Hegel's effort was."[20]

Rather than countering this argument in order to ensure some kind of future for Hegel (by assuring that there is a future in Hegel), I will focus mainly on the ways in which the modality of the present is articulated in *Introduction to the Philosophy of History* in order to complicate the sense of what is at stake when, at history's conclusion, the supposedly timeless realm of spirit's present (what Hegel describes as "not passed and not not yet, but rather it is essentially now [*nicht vorbei und nicht noch nicht, sondern wesentlich jetzt*]" [*IPH* 82/105]) is tied to the in/externalization of its history. Augmenting my sense of this complexity through readings of other texts, I will argue that Hegel's dense presentation of spirit as it presents the successive stages of history to itself as its own meaningful development demands consideration of what transformation has taken place at the level of spirit's own mode of appearing, and of the implications this transformation might have for an ongoing relation to the past.

HISTORY'S EXAMPLE

The introduction to the lectures on the philosophy of history begins with a discussion of the different approaches to history. It is a tripartite exposition, one involving "Original history," "Reflective History" and finally, "Philosophic History." "Original history" is the method that, according to Hegel, the historians of Ancient Greece used to "translate [*übersetzen*] what is externally present into the realm of mental representation" (*IPH* 3/11) in order to place those fleeting actions, events, and situations in the immortalizing "Temple of Memory [*Tempel der Mnemosyne*]" (*IPH* 4). This method is characterized primarily by the contemporaneity of act and its immortalization in history. The original historian is a witness, then, describing "more or less what he has seen, or at least lived through" (*IPH* 4).

If the witnessing-function of the historian implies that his mode of vision or seeing is governed by an identity or sameness of the historian's time with that of the action he chronicles ("the spirit of the author and of the actions he tells of, are *one and the same*"), nonetheless Hegel's description does not appeal to an unmediated or direct transparency. To the contrary, he freely admits that it is not possible for one person to have seen everything of his own time; that is why "these immediate [*unmittelbare*] historians rely on the reports and accounts of others" (*IPH* 3). So while there is no question, at this point, of a temporal difference between past and present—the historian is writing about what occurs in *his own* time—the historian must at all points draw on the written and oral testimonies of others: The supposedly "immediate" relation he has to the events of his own time is not really very immediate at all or rather, it is so only as a consequence of a shared language.

Language acts as a force of unity for original history: On the one hand, the language of the historian "translates" the events of history and "so binds together what is fleetingly swept along" (*IPH* 4/12) and on the other hand, Hegel argues that the events themselves are already emphatically linguistic. Speeches, reports, and accounts are the historian's most important source.[21]

As such, the passage from event to discourse—or, as Hegel would no doubt delight in saying, from *history* to *history*—is not so much affected as a translation of something *outside* language to its expression *in* language, as it is a kind of translation *within* language. Hegel's insistence on this point implies that the very notion of contemporaneity—that the spirit of the historian and the spirit of the time are, in fact, *one and the same*—is articulated together with language; their sameness could even be said to be a function or an effect of language, one that loses nothing in translation. "What the history-writer lets speak," he writes, "is not a borrowed consciousness [*geliehenes Bewußtsein*] but rather the very culture of the one speaking" (*IPH* 5/13, translation modified).

Hegel sees this privileged mode of translation exemplified in the way that Thucydides has committed the speeches of Pericles to Mnemosyne's realm of immortality. While Thucydides does not cite Pericles's speeches—they are not reproduced verbatim—his representation is faithful both to their voice (they are delivered in the first-person) as well as to their spirit, their register or tone.[22] Although "they were surely not spoken as they are represented," Hegel writes, nonetheless they are "not foreign [*fremd*] to Pericles" (*IPH* 5/13).

The reflective method of history, predominant in modern times, is primarily characterized by a rift within spirit or, more precisely, between spirits: "It is history whose presentation goes beyond the present in spirit, and does not refer to the historian's own time" (*IPH* 6). The historian approaches and elaborates the historical material "with *his* spirit [*mit seinem Geist*]—this being different from the spirit contained in the content." Because the reflective historian is at a temporal remove from his material—its time does not correspond to his own—his work is almost necessarily open to the charge of anachronism: "The spirit that speaks through the author is different from the spirit of the times for which he speaks" (*IPH* 6). No matter what the historian does, in some sense, the rift is insurmountable. Either the tone (*Ton*) of his writing is that of his own time, making his material "speak" in the tone of a language foreign to it or it is adjusted in accordance with the time he describes and so takes on a "wooden, pedantic appearance" (*IPH* 7).

Another strategy adopted by reflective historians to overcome the temporal division between past and present is to relate various events, however remote, directly to the present. This is the "pragmatic" type of reflective history, one that "negates [or 'sublates'] the past and makes the event present [*Dies hebt die Vergangenheit auf und macht die Begebenheit gegenwärtig*]" (*IPH* 7, translation modified). Abstract though their presentations might be, they "bring the accounts of the past to life in our present-day world [*zu heutigem Leben*]" (*IPH* 7). Within this category of history, Hegel includes the use of historical examples for instruction, otherwise known as the *historia magistra vitae*, the topos according to which history is supposed to be the great teacher of life. While history of this kind may be suitable for the moral education of children, Hegel argues, "it is also true that the destinies of nations and states—with their interests, situations, and complexities—are a different field of knowledge." He continues,

> Rulers, statesmen, and nations are told that they ought to learn from the experience of history. Yet what experience and history teach us is this, that nations and governments have never learned anything from history, nor acted in accordance with the lessons to be derived from it. . . . In the crush [*Gedränge*] of world events, there is no help to be had from general principles, nor from the memory of similar conditions in former times—for a pale memory [*fable Erinnerung*] has no force [*hat keine Kraft*] against the vitality and freedom of the present. (*IPH* 8/17)

The implications of this statement for a conception of historical time are as striking as is the strangely politicized dynamic of its sudden emergence. Nothing short of a revolution is afoot here; the reference to the French Revolution immediately following these lines—in which the "oft recurring appeal [*wiederkehrende Berufung*]" (*IPH* 8/17) of its agents to Greek and Roman examples (*Beispiele*) are belittled as *schal*, or trite—confirms the political investment of the passage at the same time as the passage's temporal revolution seems to outstrip the political revolution in exemplary force.

For it is precisely against the notion of history as a massive compendium of exempla worthy of emulation and repetition that Hegel is directing his revolutionary rhetoric. According to the conception of time Hegel is articulating here, events happen once and once only; no repetition or return of them is possible. History cannot possibly offer examples or formulae suitable for the present because the conditions within which politics occurs are never comparable with those of the past: "Each era [*Jede Zeit*] has such particular circumstances, such individual situations, that decisions can only be made from within the era itself" (*IPH* 8/17).

It would be difficult to overestimate the extent of the changes in historical sensibility that made a statement such as this possible. The idea of a unique present unmoored from history, one that derives no lessons or bearings out of the past, is itself not unique to Hegel; rather, it is a feature that would come to be expressed—unevenly but persistently—throughout modernity. In general terms, prior to the modern period the idiom of *historia magistra vitae*, coined by Cicero in accordance with the Greek notion of history as a storehouse of exemplary models for the betterment of later generations, had survived more or less intact as the dominant understanding of history's function for the present. Predicated as it was on repeatability, it could only hold sway so long as social, cultural, and political conditions were perceived to be fundamentally the same: It was an ethos that, for more than two thousand years, had established links between the past and the prospective future in the form of historical examples of statesmanship, war, governance, moral behavior and the like.[23] According to this understanding of history, conduct that was demanded by circumstances in the present was more or less prescribed or dictated by past events, bound to the present by a continuous and relatively homogeneous space of experience.

Although the notion of exemplary history would, in certain respects, continue to inform the eighteenth-century historical imagination,[24] its authority as an organizing principle would ultimately be undermined by the massive social and political transformations that were to characterize the subsequent period: The most basic condition that was required for it to be effective, the constancy of human experience, could no longer be assumed or taken for granted. What could remain of history's meaningfulness once the forcible political events of the period, in particular those of the French Revolution, had outstripped all previous history of its exemplary force—that is, once its storehouse of individual histories could no longer act as so many templates for action?

Hegel's act of "translating" the revolutionary rhetoric of upheaval and overthrow into a statement about time means that his notion of the historical present is one that does not derive its vitality and life from a barely remembered past, but from what the *Phenomenology* calls *"free contingent happening"* (*Phen* 492). Moreover, the temporal revolution seems to supercede and even usurp the political revolution, since it forecloses the possibility of (temporal) restoration.[25] Over and against the historical specificity of any one particular revolution, the revolution proposed by Hegel is tantamount to a temporal *révolution en permanence*, wherein *every* epoch or era is unique and unrepeatable, their freedom standing opposed to the dim authority of history.[26] To understand what is at stake in this conception of time for an emergent understanding of history (itself brought about in no small measure by a philosophical investment in the revolutionary tenor of the late eighteenth and early nineteenth centuries), it might be helpful to turn briefly to Hannah Arendt's discussion of the temporality of revolution and in particular, of the strange form of return inhabiting it.

Arendt begins by pointing out that the first political usage of the term "revolution" was borrowed from astronomy, wherein it designated the cyclical and lawfully revolving movement of the stars. When it was metaphorically applied to the realm of politics, she argues, it signified the eternal recurrence of a few known forms of governance, whose irresistible force seemed as immutable and fixed as that of a preordained celestial pattern. Entirely absent from this conception of "revolution," then, are the notions of rupture, novelty, and freedom that would come to characterize its modern use. "Nothing," she writes, "could be farther removed from the original meaning of the word 'revolution' than the idea of which all revolutionary actors have been possessed and obsessed, namely, that they are agents in a process which spells out the definite end of an old order and brings about the birth of a new world."[27] As radical a transformation as this is of the word's meaning, modern revolutionary discourse would retain one aspect of its older usage and would even make it the primary focus: that of the irresistibility, indeed, the inevitability of the revolutionary course. The dominance of metaphors such as rushing waves, torrents, and mighty currents—Robespierre's *tempête révolutionnaire*—are clear indication of the sense in which the revolution, although begun by human agents with the clear intention of establishing absolute freedom, could not ultimately be seen as their work. The shock of the realization, both on the part of the participants as well as of its spectators, that men were unable to control their own actions through willful aims and purposes—that what they had instigated was to pursue a course whose outcome was entirely unforeseeable and so did not belong to them—"transformed itself almost immediately into a feeling of awe and wonder at the power of history itself" (*Rev* 51).

When viewed against the powerful backdrop of a revolutionary process that seemed to be teetering precariously on the verge of a boundless sublime,[28] Arendt contends that Hegel's philosophy of history was a revolution in its own right. Not only did he respond to this sublime moment in history, she suggests, by revolutionizing philosophy (that is, by articulating philosophy's "timeless absolute" in terms of world history), but in so doing he had also sought to grasp the revolution conceptually: to understand it not as an isolated historical fact but as a kind of "revelation," one that possessed the power to shed light on the entire historical process, of which it was the culminating moment, as the universal truth of spirit.

Arendt laments the fact that the French Revolution would almost exclusively be taken up as a challenge to rethink history from the perspective of the by-stander, the result of which, she argues, would be the practically total eclipse of a consideration of its implications for political action (*Rev* 52ff.).[29] The authority of philosophical hindsight, she argues, meant that everything "that had been political—acts, and words, and events—became historical." Politics, according to this account, is only meaningful as a "has-been." When political action no longer finds its ground in the examples set by history, there is indeed an important sense in which politics and history part company: Once history has become the successive narration of unrepeatable events, political action is more or less left to its devices (one consequence of which is, of course, that history will reappear in the political redeployment of "historical necessity" characteristic of fascism, conservatism, and certain forms of vulgar Marxism).[30]

Despite Hegel's own articulation of the development of history in patently solar terms—from its "dawn" in the East to its "setting" in the *Abendland* of the West—I am nonetheless hesitant about the conclusion Arendt draws—namely, that Hegel would ascribe the machinations of brute necessity to the movement of history.[31] However, I would like to take up the question of what she calls the "backward-directed glance" of philosophical history in relation to this doubling of revolutionary time: More precisely, what might ultimately be at stake when the revolutionary moment is formalized as the temporal modus operandi of a historical process? To begin to formulate an answer to this question, we must situate Hegel's unqualified show of contempt for the "historical example" in relation to his own philosophical history. For although his description clearly seeks to contain and limit the effects of a historical "repetition-compulsion," thereby calling the present to the power of its own irreducible singularity, on another, related level it also acts as a powerful resource for the emergence of a linear temporality. To make this last point clear, let us return to the basis of Hegel's criticism: "In this respect [that is, the vague memory of history against the exigencies of the present], nothing is more trite than the repeated appeal to Greek and Roman examples, which was so commonplace at the time of the French Revolution. Nothing could be more different than the nature of those peoples and the nature of our times [*die Natur unserer Zeiten*]" (*IPH* 8/17, translation modified). The final sentence of the passage articulates the difference between *then* and *now* on the basis of a shift from "the nature of those peoples" to "the nature of *our times*." Of course, what is at stake here is the difference between radically different historical epochs—that of the revolutionary present over and against those of Greek and Roman political cultures.

Less obvious, though, is what might be at stake in spelling out that difference by introducing the word "times" to characterize modernity. One way of conceiving this multiplication of time in terms of historical understanding—and probably the one foremost in Hegel's mind[32]—is that the foreclosure of the past's repetition allows for the various stages of spirit to become differentiated into *Zeitgeist*s; that is, they become divided and organized into discrete and unrepeatable historical epochs and eras. Although not a term that Hegel uses in this context, the notion of *Zeitgeist* is implicit to the passage, governing its organization of spirits on a basis of their incomparable difference.[33] Whereas for the Greco-Roman conception of history, historical examples would repeat themselves ad infinitum for an unchanging human nature,[34] Hegel's understanding of history implies that for postrevolutionary Europe, there appears to be nothing but *times*, in the plural.

THE MO(U)RNING OF RUINS

By way of elaborating this claim, let us draw out three of its implications for Hegel's thinking of historical time. To begin with the most obvious one: Hegel's notion of historical development cannot tolerate repetition insofar as it would suggest that a determinate historical shape possessed political potential beyond its own time. In other words, the exemplary repetition of an event would demonstrate its excess with respect to its own historical conditions and to its own moment. When, for example, Hegel writes that "World-Spirit . . . embodied in each shape as much of its entire content as that shape was capable of holding,"[35] this is to suggest that the determinate shape of spirit is utterly in sync with its own time—that *Zeit* and *Geist* are, historically speaking, never out of joint—and, what is more, that there is never more to spirit's determinate shape than its own time can accommodate or handle. Were it the case that events simply repeated themselves in the political sphere, the temporality of Hegel's own philosophical exposition of history would be placed in jeopardy, would itself be out of joint. What he describes in the *Philosophy of History* as "the long flow of time [*in dem Verlauf der langen Zeit*]" (*IPH* 22/33); as the "unfolding of spirit in *time*" and the "restless succession [*rastloser Aufeinanderfolge*]" of various historical formations (*IPH* 75/97) or, alternatively as the stages that "have unfolded themselves successively [*nacheinander ausgebildet*]" (*IPH* 82/105) all give a sense that what is at stake in Hegel's dismissal of historical repetition is the linear and irreversible time of world history itself: All the historical stages of spirit, he writes, are "themselves only moments [*nur Momente*] of the one universal spirit; through them, it elevates and completes itself in history into a self-comprehending *totality*" (*IPH* 82/104, translation modified). The complete linear narration of World History—on the one side, the shapes of spirit traversing "the long passage of time";[36] on the other side, its accumulation of them as one overarching spiritualized narrative—means that modern historical consciousness, including that developed by Hegel, is constituted by and as an exposure to a multiplicity of times at once.

Secondly, that history is not conceived by Hegel as a storehouse of examples to be redeployed for political purposes also means that the determinate shapes of the past do not themselves exert everlasting political power; they might be very well be outstanding, but that does not mean that they govern past their own time or that they should be emulated. To the contrary, outstanding political moments, those of rupture, transformation, and revolution, are exemplary for the insights into the temporality of politics they permit—namely, they provide us with the means of understanding how politics is not *borrowed* from the example of a historical "has-been" but rather is *born* in the present. Heroic individuals, while having "no consciousness of the Idea at all," Hegel writes, had "insight into what was needed and what was timely [*was an der Zeit ist*]: Their insight was the very truth of their time and their world—the *next species* [*die nächste Gattung*] so to speak, which was already there [*bereits vorhanden war*] in the inner source" (*IPH* 33/46, emphasis added). The claim that the future "was already there in the inner source" is, of course, one that can only be made a posteriori. On that basis alone, it is easy to imagine how the language of "Idea" and "inner source"—*das Innere*—could be marshaled as evidence of Hegel's metaphysical allegiance to an overarching philosophical necessity over the contingencies of history. Indeed, Hegel might even appear to be ultimately explaining away contingency, through recourse to a mystical and inhuman drive or propulsion toward wholeness.

Although there is indeed an air of mystery to all this, we would be mistaken to interpret the relation between "Idea" and history in terms of such a dualism.[37] Rather, the implicit challenge of the passage lies in how to think necessity—that is, the meaning of necessity as well as the necessity of meaning—in a way that binds it to political risk and contingency. If for Hegel, the present is utterly self-grounding, that does not mean that its necessity can be known in advance. In fact, he is clear on the point that the present cannot see its own ground and for that reason, considers itself to be free and independent from it. This could only mean that the present is never entirely present to itself and that moreover, it can only experience itself in its self-differentiation.

At this point, what can we say about the future? Let us recall how Hegel maligns attempts to neutralize or blunt the present through an idealistic projection of the future or through the repetition of a past example. Striking in this regard is how the passage cited above locates the future—the "next species": a vivid and forceful, if problematic, collective futurity—not in a philosophical "ought" or a historical "has been" but in the potentiality of the present, in its very self-division. If the future is able to appear at all in the present, it could only do so in the form or the appearance of the latter's restlessness, its own openness to new arrangements and new political possibilities.

In other words, the future for Hegel is not *sometime*—that is, some other *time* coming to the present from a determinable place (either from the region of thought or from the domain of objective history); rather, it happens. The "happening" of the future cannot possibly be understood within historical time conceived as a continuous flow of homogeneous presents, identical to themselves. For, in the continuous flow of time or in a pure and self-same present, it is, I think, relatively obvious that nothing can happen. At another level: If we look ahead to Hegel's argument regarding historical development, while the contingent happening of the future is no doubt *necessary* for the development of spirit, the necessity of its happening only becomes legible retroactively or after the fact, as a result of its having occurred. To the extent that, within the framework of the *historia magistra vitae*, historical examples have already demonstrated this necessity— that is, by having already happened—Hegel seems to be objecting to their redeployment principally on the grounds that they have already been shorn of the risks of contingency and openness (this is a point to which we shall return later in the chapter).

Finally, Hegel's strict censure of historical repetition also means that the modern modes of relating to history are predicated upon the irretrievability of the past as such. In this respect, they are almost necessarily governed by loss and mourning. In one famous instance, he considers the "slaughter-bench of history" in terms of the grieving response it provokes:

> When we look at this drama of human passions, and observe the consequences of their violence and of the unreason that is linked not only to them but also (and especially) to good intentions and rightful aims; when we see arising from them all the evil, the wickedness, the decline of the most flourishing nations mankind has produced, we can only be filled with grief for all that has come to nothing . . . we could paint the most fearful picture . . . and with that picture we could arouse feelings of the deepest and most helpless mourning, not to be outweighed by any consoling outcome. We can strengthen ourselves against this, or escape it, only by thinking that, well, so it was at one time; it is fate; there is nothing to be done about it now. And finally—in order to cast off the tedium that this reflection of grief could produce in us . . . —we return to the selfishness of standing on a quiet shore where we can be secure in enjoying the distant sight of confusion and wreckage. (*IPH* 24/35)[38]

Here, grief is a moral response to the drama of history, one whose outrage sees only brute meaninglessness. On one level, it is the helpless feeling of a spectator to human misery: Its only recourse is to the dull and fatalistic sensibility of "so it was at one time" (*es ist nun so einmal gewesen*). But on another level, Hegel suggests that its powerlessness can also be harnessed and turned into a negative resource of self-preserving aggrandizement. In this, it is not entirely innocent of the horrific pile-up of history to which it bears witness. This witness to history cannot be bothered to pursue explanations any further, Hegel writes, for "it is far more characteristic of such reflections to enjoy the misery of the empty and fruitless sublimities of that empty outcome [ie. the picture of history's brute meaninglessness]" (*IPH* 24). Thus, the kind of grief provoked by the scene of history's slaughter-bench is, in its own way, horrific: Outrage over the miseries of history is coupled with a not-insignificant amount of *Schadenfreude* produced in a subject whose squeamish delight is concealed—but just barely—by its own too easily self-satisfied and disengaged resignation.

Later on in the text, having taken leave of history's "confusion and wreckage," Hegel will return to the question of mourning in the context of historical loss. Specifically, he will situate it in closer proximity to his own philosophical project by conceiving it to be the proper response to an understanding of history as ubiquitous change. He writes,

> This restless succession of individuals and peoples that are here for a time and then disappear suggests one prevalent thought, one category above all, that of universally prevalent change. And what leads us to apprehend this change in its negative aspect is the sight of the ruins of some vanished splendor. What traveler, amidst the ruins of Carthage, Palmyra, Persepolis, or Rome, has not been led to contemplate the transiency of empires and of men, and to mourn at a once vigorous and rich life that is now gone? This is not a mourning that dwells upon personal losses and the transiency of one's own aims; instead, it is a disinterested grief at the decline of a radiant and cultured life. (*IPH* 76/97)

The work of mourning that is done in response to lost grandeur does not return to or reflect back on itself—it is a disinterested (*uninteressierte*) form of contemplation (*Betrachtung*). Remaining squarely focused on its object, it also incurs no disavowed debt to the past in the weird form of a self-interested backlash. As Hegel himself implies, it is the beautiful grief of a tourist.

How is it that Hegel uses mourning to characterize a traveler's responsiveness to ancient ruins, the very same idiom used to articulate the confused response of moral outrage to historical wreckage (*Trümmermasse*)? It is tempting to accuse Hegel, even circa 1830, of conflating two experiential registers that should have remained distinct and, moreover, of neutralizing the difficulty of one experience of history through the seeming ease of the other—the scene of Carthage is, after all, a scene of pretty straightforward enjoyment. From our own vantage point, nothing could seem more implausible or historically outdated: The *Trümmermasse*, as well as the moral outrage it might provoke, has certainly come to prevail in critical historical consciousness over any mournful celebration of vibrancy.[39]

Even if his privileging of historical ruins over *ruined history* does "date" Hegel somewhat, we cannot simply leave it at that. For Hegel will have made the stakes clear: Both instances articulate mourning as the modern response to history's loss but so too do they both remain at the level of a fixed subjective understanding, relating to loss as to an object radically distinct from them. While in the former instance, the "feeling" self confirms and even reifies its independence from history by grieving over the latter's sheer negativity, the mourning traveler still conceives of history as something foreign to him; as laudable as his response of mourning may be, the salient point of his exteriority—at once empirical and speculative—is that he is not at home. *Both* instances of mourning are thus unbefitting of science, but not so much because their perspective is one of mourning. Rather, the problem is that because they involve the one-sidedness of a subjective gaze, world-history is presumed unable to return the gaze and so "is seen" only in its passivity. As such they violate the condition of *Wissenschaft*, which for Hegel is that of a face-to-face encounter between two rational beings: "To him who looks at the world rationally, the world looks back rationally. The relation is mutual" (*IPH* 14/23, translation modified).

Hegel's own gesture will thus be to relegate these instances of subjective dispossession and loss along with their spiritual homelessness to a moment of the text's development. In particular, demonstrating their one-sidedness is what will enable him to provide an account of how it is that the loss of history is the condition for spirit's recuperation of it as its own spiritual gain.

In fact, the instance of mourning the glory of past cultures does come awfully close to setting an example, though, in that it provides Hegel with a segue into a philosophical exposition of historical change (*Veränderung*). The passage from a wholly self-interested mourning to "a disinterested mourning" prepares the text's transition to its properly philosophical articulation that, as we saw in Chapter 3, can place thought in relation to a kind of mourning. Here, a *philosophical* mourning would not so much disinterestedly view history as irrecoverably lost, as it would match spirit's own compulsive and irresistible drive (*IPH* 56) to assume the loss of history's finite determinations as, in truth, its own infinitizing act of self-recuperation in thought.

In particular, the mournful understanding of historical ruins seems to "work" in a way that the sublime reaction to history does not because of how the grief of the former is expressed in relation to time, specifically to lost time or transience (*Vergänglichkeit*) and finitude. It raises the question of finitude, namely, by grappling with a tension implicit to ruins between the vitality of life on the one side, and vanishing, disappearance, and decline on the other. What are ruins, after all, if not a ghostly "third term" between the living and the dead, a *vibrant decay* or intermingling of life and death, one that is utterly irreducible either to the one or the other? While the traveler finds this inextricability simply *moving*, Hegel will actually set it into motion, opening it up to thought by pressing the contemporaneous appearance of life and death out into a temporal logic. That is, by temporalizing as succession what is mournfully experienced as the commingling of life and death, Hegel will open up the subjective loss of history to the *thought* of spirit's most productive principle. The passage immediately following Hegel's brief excursion to Carthage invokes the vague outline of a logic of succession: "But the next consideration that is linked to that of change (*Veränderung*) is that this decline is at the same time the emergence of new life—for although life leads to death, death also leads to life [*aus dem Leben Tod, aber aus dem Tod Leben hervorgeht*]" (*IPH* 76/98). Being too vague (or perhaps too vaguely poetic) a description for the philosopher, Hegel will then go on to specify that "the abstract thought of change transforms itself into the thought of Spirit [*in den Gedanken . . . des Geistes*], manifesting, developing, and perfecting its powers in all aspects of its full realization" (*IPH* 77/98).[40]

The affected sense of historical *finitude* evoked by ancient ruins—for the traveler it is a lost culture, closed off to thought and open only to feeling—has prepared the way for a rather more disaffected philosophical consideration of history's speculative nature. The phrase "the thought of Spirit" (*den Gedanken des Geistes*) in this passage makes it clear that the stakes of this thought itself will be vigorously two-fold: They will involve both the thought that properly belongs to spirit (that is, its own perforce "timeless" activity) as well as a thinking that is proper to spirit's history—that is, one befitting its true essence.

We will see in a moment how, at the very end of the section (*IPH* 82ff.), the modality of spirit's exteriorization or expression will be constituted as the spacing of world-historical spirits in thought. Strangely enough though, at the point of the text where we just left off, no mention is made of historical succession; right where one might expect such an exposition, instead Hegel considers the life and death of peoples in terms of the natural or biological stages of individual life span. The natural course of the ages of life, from birth and youth through to old age and dying, has been made to function throughout the text as a *hypotyposis*, the sensory translation of a logical process.[41] Because humans go through changes in age, it is they who most fully embody degrees of potentiality. Furthermore, the degrees of potentiality that characterize human life span are particularly amenable to a translation into temporality. At this stage of the argument, "from manhood to old age" is the stage of life that interests Hegel most, even leading him to the catachrestic suggestion that entire peoples have died of boredom (*IPH* 78).

There is a special two-fold intensity registered in the hypotyposis here: In one sense, it obviously runs the risk of over-endowing spirit with the character of finitude. In light of this possibility that the thought of spiritual development be overwhelmed by the organic naturalism of the sensory translation, Hegel will almost immediately cut it short by appealing to a "higher form [*höhere Gestalt*]" (*IPH* 81). But precisely this "higher form"—which is the realm of thought—is no less what returns spirit to the human sphere, since it is this activity that most properly defines human freedom.[42] The life that proceeds from the death of Spirit's determinate form, he argues, is *not* a "uniform repetition of the same mode of existence" as it is for a natural species but is rather the birthplace (*Geburtstätte*) of a *higher* form of life on the order of a speculative *Aufhebung*: "The determinate form of spirit does not merely pass away naturally in time, but is sublated [*aufgehoben*] in the self-activating, self-reflecting activity of thought. Since this sublation [*Aufheben*] is an activity of thought, it is also a preserving and a transfiguring [*es ist zugleich Erhalten und Verklären*]" (*IPH* 81/103, translation modified).[43] Although the upbeat tenor of this passage makes it seem as if spirit experiences no pain or loss as it makes the transition from a finite determination to the negation of that determination in thought, Hegel is himself constantly at pains throughout the text to convey a sense of brutal confrontation and injury. Not only are periods of happiness and harmony the "empty pages of history" (*IPH* 29); spirit's journey is conceived as a process of development in which it encounters itself as its "own truly hostile hindrance"; it is a "hard and endless struggle against itself" (*IPH* 59).

What means does spirit have at its disposal to wage this battle, one whose sole aim is to reduce the resistance of (its own) history to itself?

It has, in fact, just been named: thought's own activity of *Aufheben*, what the *Logic* calls "one of the most important notions for philosophy."[44] On the one hand, the *Logic* defines *Aufheben* as a simple negation; it means "to cause to cease, to put an end to." On the other hand, it also means "to preserve, to maintain."[45]

With regard to the passage from the *Introduction to the Philosophy of History*, while *verklären* does mean "to transfigure," its meaning is not restricted to the almost exclusively religious connotations of the English "transfiguration." Its more literal meaning is *both* "to make clear" *and* "to make unclear" (a doubling or inversion that is enabled by the suffix *ver-*, which can either invert the meaning of the root verb or denote its completion or perfection). In everyday German parlance, *verklären* is most often understood in terms of memory; it is a thought process by which details are faded-out or omitted, usually with the result that the past is given a more favorable impression.

It is easy to see how both of these meanings—both a "clarifying" and a "blurring out"—are at play in Hegel's usage of the term. The point, though, is not so much to show how Hegelian memory inevitably slides toward nostalgia as it is to discern the centrality of this process for any kind of memory: Although *verklären* is not among the host of words that Hegel praises for their speculative import, is it not in some sense obvious that every act of clarity or focus involves a blurring out or omission of other details? The relevance of this operation for the thought-activity of memory is, I think, relatively clear, for only when we are not exclusively in the domain of immediate particularity, itself a rare enough occurrence, are we able even to feel a sense of loss or to assess what has been lost. Without such a process of abstraction or omission, in other words, not only would memory itself be impossible, but—in a very real sense—so too would experience.[46]

From this it follows that the conjunction of the above passage's "preserving *and* transfiguring" does not so much signal the contrast of two distinct operations (or even the simultaneity of their occurrence) as it is an apposition or identity of the two terms, since the two meanings of *verklären* are already at play in preservation. This reading is borne out by the contention Hegel makes, also in the *Logic*, that "'to preserve' already includes a negative element, namely that something is removed from its immediacy and so from an existence open to external influences, in order to preserve it."[47]

The side of maintenance or preservation in the definition of the *Aufhebung* is thus not the fixed and positive counterpart to its negative side of cancellation or suppression; rather, preservation itself is always already involved in an economy of loss or omission. While the claim that the act of preservation must itself involve losing something or letting something go (in order, no doubt, to avoid incurring an even greater loss) may not seem particularly striking, the fact that Hegel emphasizes the two-fold meaning of *Aufhebung*'s one side of preservation—it is already both loss and gain—does raise the possibility that spirit's *Aufhebung* of history is not a rigid process remaining detached from everything it sets into motion, but that perhaps it is open to its own operation.

In the next two sections, we will explore more fully the implications of the possibility that spirit's *Aufhebung* of history is not simply a frozen testament to its own process of development. First though, we must take note of how spirit deploys the mechanism of *aufheben* to effect the transition from the immediate determination of its historical shape to a shape that puts up less resistance. At the very beginning of the *Introduction to the Philosophy of History*, Hegel had stated that "Thought is the mightiest epitomizer [*der mächtigste Epitomator*]" (*IPH* 7/16). The historian or philosopher who engages in the effort of writing "a history of the kind that surveys long periods, or the entire history of the world must in fact *give up (aufgeben)* the individual presentation of particular reality and draw on abstractions, epitomizing, shortening [*sich mit Abstraktionen behelfen, epitomieren, abkürzen*]" (*IPH* 7/16, translation modified).

Against the manifold variety of determinate particularities, histories that span long lengths of time must subject that material to a process of abbreviation. "Thought," as Hegel later writes in the text, "is the innermost infinite form itself wherein everything that exists is, in principle, dissolved—and chiefly the finite being, the determinate form" (*IPH* 80). The task of spirit, then, "to break through [*durchbrechen*] its own shell of sensuality" (*IPH* 61) implies that spirit's interiorization of its history depends on its *giving up* this sensual plenitude or indeed on breaking with it, leaving it behind.

We might sum up this process through recourse to a notion of *reduction*: A historical epoch gains momentum only by giving up or breaking with the potentially infinite mass of particular details, a process of relinquishment by means of which it takes on a simpler, abbreviated form. Reduction involves a kind of blunting operation or abstraction, one that we might understand in terms of how it drains a vital entity of life, paring down its multiplicity of determinations to a so-called "essence." In this sense, reduction might correspond to an abstraction that *over*-simplifies, as is the case for instance when we speak of an argument or formulation as being "reductive": Its lack of force is attributed to its having ignored or deadened important detail, its having left out too much.[48]

However, despite appearances, a reduction can just as easily be understood as a distillation of life, its concentration or even intensification. Accordingly, even as it blunts the phenomenon and robs it of detail, color, and sensuous vitality, the operation of reduction also has the potential to distill an epoch or era, to concentrate it, perhaps even to sharpen or intensify it.[49] In fact, Hegel suggests that this process of simplification is the only way in which a determinate historical epoch can be blunted and overcome—in terms of its immediate particularity—and at the same time retained in the form of a universal yet nonetheless highly articulated and distinct shape, yielding an import not exhausted by or in the moment of its occurrence.[50]

For Hegel, the consequences of this process of condensing or abbreviating historical events over "long periods" into simpler determinations are two-fold: On the one hand, those determinate historical shapes are granted longer life by being reduced or sharpened to a single attribute: "Every moment . . . is incomplete Spirit, a concrete shape in whose whole existence one determinateness predominates, the others being present only in blurred outline."[51] On the other hand, by virtue of their reduction to single traits or characteristics, history's moments might be granted not only an unprecedented degree of longevity but also of accessibility, no longer being "something peculiar in the heads of a few people."

Specifically, abbreviated historical events achieve the degree of articulation required for them to "stand arrayed in their firm relationships" and to become "exoteric, comprehensible, and capable of being learned by all."[52] While Walter Kaufmann contends that in this passage, Hegel is arguing that "the time has come for all men to demand equal access to philosophy,"[53] by implying that history might be granted a practically unlimited accessibility through this process of conceptualization, is Hegel not also admitting that it becomes accessible only insofar as the pared-down version of its moments has stripped them of all contingency, even to the point of killing them off? In light of what seems to be a life-destroying process of formalization, can we go so far as to suggest that the mode of access to history remains *open*?

Despite the initial impression that spirit's consciousness of its own development is beholden to a process that deadens or neutralizes it, Hegel nonetheless sees in spirit's rescission an animating force, one heralding a new life for its historical shapes. By sublating (*aufheben*) "the reality, the subsistence of whatever *it is*," spirit "gains [*gewinnt*] the essence, the thought, the universal concept of that which *it merely was*." In so doing, Hegel asserts, spirit "gives a new determination [*neue Bestimmung*] to its principle" (81/104), an "affirmative, richer, and more concrete determination" (67).

Spirit's negation of its own manifold particularity is a process allowing it to reduce the resistance of its own moments to itself. Having reduced its variety of immediate particularities to a single stroke or unique characteristic, each stage of world history has been prepared to become a "moment" of the speculative narrative. In turn though, Hegel suggests that that very operation also creates a space within which those by-gone moments retain or recuperate their singularity as their own *force of survival*. Quoting, at some length, from the final passage of the section:

> Because we are concerned only with the idea of Spirit—and we regard the whole of world history as nothing more than the manifestation of Spirit—when we go over the past, however extensive it may be, we are really concerned only with the *present*. This is because philosophy, which occupies itself with the True, is concerned with what is eternally present. Everything in the past is un-lost to philosophy [*alles ist ihr in der Vergangenheit unverloren*]: the Idea is ever present, Spirit is immortal, ie. Spirit is not passed and it is not not yet [*nicht vorbei und nicht noch nicht*], but is essentially *now*. This is as much as to say that the present form of Spirit contains all the earlier stages within itself. Certainly, these stages have unfolded themselves successively and independently; yet what Spirit is, it has always implicitly been (*an sich*). The difference lies only in the degree of development of this implicit nature [*dieses An Sich*].[54] The life of the ever-present Spirit is a cycle of stages: on the one hand, the stages co-exist side by side [*nebeneinander*]; on the other hand, they appear [*erscheinen*] as past. But the moments [*die Momente*] which Spirit seems to have left behind it, it also possesses in its present depth [*in seinem gegenwärtigem Tiefe*]. (IPH 82, translation modified)

The implications of this development are well known: The compressed, distilled or blunted chronology of world-history will, in the end, have been an exact match for the logic of spiritual self-actualization. Hegel's word for this has repeatedly been *Veränderung*, change, literally a "making other." Having recognized all contingent change as the necessary speculative development of the *An Sich*, Spirit has no more reason to expect change, at least not from the side of "free contingent happening."

Still though, there is a strange and equivocal pitch registered in this passage: On the one hand, it clearly possesses the force of a momentous dénouement—the linear time of historical occurrence does, after all, come to an end here. On the other hand, though, there is an odd sense of a lingering or opening-out to the passage, despite (or because of) its being situated right at the level of a systematic closure, one with which Hegel's thought has come to be inextricably associated.

The sense of opening-out might very well be a product of the text's status: As the lectures' introduction, what we are calling an *opening-out* might consequently be understood to be a prelude or preamble to a *filling-in* of the historical narrative.[55] After all, only when spirit's historical journey has come to an end is it finally able to narrate that journey in its entirety; spirit *now* contains "the moments" within itself; it possesses them in its "present depth." The "restless succession" of a diachronic historical process—*rastlose Nacheinander*—becomes a synchronic "side by side" of its moments, a *nebeneinander*.

In one sense, this spatial description of "side by side" captures how events are narrated as the writing of philosophical history. But, with the passage's suggestion that philosophy relates to history as spirit does (that, like spirit, it too is concerned with what is eternal in history), the ambivalence of the word Hegel uses to characterize the philosophical relation to history—the latter is *unlost* to philosophy—implies too that spirit relates to its own history as *unverloren*. While it might be tempting to interpret this phrase as one of fixed position or location—and in fact, the Rauch and the Sibree translations both give "Nothing is lost to philosophy" for this phrase, effectively neutralizing its oddness—Hegel's precise phrasing, that "everything is un-lost to philosophy," is a much more ambiguous claim, suggesting perhaps that while spirit and philosophy do indeed have this history within it, its philosophical or spiritual organization is anything but fixed or secure. "Un-lost" seems to characterize at once a confident knowing—that all of history's significant moments are there, reduced to their singular traits or characteristics—at the same time as it hesitates over its exact organization or modality. Whatever weight or status we might want to accord this formulation, Hegel's point here seems to be that the site of uncertainty is not on the nether-side of knowledge—either as a philosophical unknown or a historical fact—but is within the structure of knowing itself. According to this reading, we might read the path of the historical narrative not so much as the triumphant and fixed "end" of history, but rather as its furtive beginning.

CODA I: FLAYING SPIRIT

Turning to the *Phenomenology of Spirit*, we also find the uncertain provenance or modality of spirit's discursive organization, but this time with a clear sense as to its necessity. For not only is it the case (as we have just seen) that spirit must forfeit the rich variety of the sensuous in order to compress its finite temporal moments into a side-by-side arrangement of historical stages or stations, the *Phenomenology* suggests that spirit must also submit *itself* to that process. In particular, it must surrender itself to the various attempts made to know it, ones that, for their part, have refused to surrender much of anything at all: "Instead of tarrying with [the real issue], and losing itself in it, this kind of knowing is forever grasping at something new" (*Phen* 3).

Hegel's primary concern here is with the fixity of the subjective understanding in relation to the "objects" it investigates. Here I am referring to the sections of the *Phenomenology's* preface where Hegel maligns the "pigeon-holing process" (*Phen* 32) of "lifeless Understanding [*toter Verstand*] and external cognition" (*Phen* 31). Hegel uses a singularly striking description to characterize this activity of the understanding: It labels and categorizes spirit, he writes, "like a skeleton with scraps of paper stuck all over it [*einem Skelette mit angeklebten Zettelchen*]" (*Phen* 31). Such attempts might make spirit "easy enough to interpret" but Hegel suggests that the knowledge they produce is as good as dead. Ashamed, shocked even, by the schematic and lifeless products of its own reflection, the understanding then pushes the "essence of the thing" back onto the pure whiteness of a infinitely blank page: It "submerges them all in the void of the Absolute, from which pure identity, formless whiteness [*formlose Weiße*] is produced" (*Phen* 31). As such, the lifeless determinations of the understanding—the scraps of paper—are entirely consistent with a conception of spirit as absolute and self-same identity. The one—spirit as infinitely and formlessly blank—is the reaction of the understanding to its own life-destroying and formalistic method of bookkeeping.

The radical diremption of spirit from the understanding is the product of a thinking activity that begins with the assumption of a radical incommensurability between the process of knowing and what is known. As such, its attempt to overcome the one-sidedness of its aim—to know spirit objectively—is what ultimately keeps it locked in that confrontational subject-object relation. Such a cognition assumes spirit to be "a fixed point to which, as their support, the predicates are affixed by a movement belonging to the knower of this Subject, and which is not regarded as belonging to the fixed point itself" (*Phen* 13). But, as Hegel adds immediately, even this necrophilic encounter is a fate spirit must endure. The next paragraph states the following: "The excellent, however, not only cannot escape the fate of being thus deprived of life and Spirit, of being flayed and then seeing its skin wrapped around a lifeless knowledge and its conceit. Rather we recognize even in this fate the power that the excellent exercises over the hearts, if not over the minds, of men; also the constructive unfolding into universality and determinateness of form in which its perfection consists, and which alone makes it possible for this universality to be used in a superficial way" (*Phen* 31). If the understanding formalizes the determination of spirit to the very point of killing it—and then of having to resuscitate it elsewhere . . . as a blank—it is nonetheless also the case that its deadening procedure *sustains* spirit by reducing it to the determinate form of little scraps of paper. The problem with this kind of knowledge is, surprisingly perhaps, not the fact of the *Zettelchen*—though at first glance they hardly seem a very fitting destiny for spirit—but the fixity of the understanding with regard to them, "the standpoint of consciousness which knows objects in their antithesis to itself" (*Phen* 15). In other words, Hegel praises the understanding for having pared down spirit's concrete immediacy to a series of simple and abstract determinations, the same process we saw articulated in the *Introduction to the Philosophy of History* as the means by which an historical moment, epoch or era makes its way into, and takes its place in the speculative narrative. The suggestion here is that the formalizing reduction of the determinate moment produces a new determinacy in the form of an *inscription*.

This process doubtless meets with Hegel's approval insofar as modern pedagogy offers a kind of shortcut to universality. Retracing spirit's "long passage of time" is less arduous for those moderns who seek to appropriate its history since "its forms have been reduced to abbreviated, simple determinations of thought" (*Phen* 17). What is articulated here as thought-determinations constitutes a speculative version of the lifeless aggregate—the scraps of paper—produced by external cognition. In historiographical terms, their counterpart would be given by a detached understanding that views history as an amalgam of objective facts or, alternatively, as a dramatic and incomprehensible scene. In fact, these characterizations of the understanding in the *Phenomenology* will have already formalized and condensed all the perspectives "on" history that Hegel will come to trace throughout the *Introduction to the Philosophy of History*: She who mourns history as the loss of great culture; he who takes sublime (dis)pleasure in his own stance on the meaninglessness of history; and even the historian who, believing that it "is dealing with history as a raw material," and that it "has merely to take in information—i.e. of what is and has been, of events and actions" (*IPH* 10), has raised his or her own purported thoughtlessness to the principle of a modus operandi.

To overcome this confrontational stance, Hegel develops a notion of modern *Bildung* that places it in close proximity to memory, or inwardization: "Formative education, regarded from the side of the individual, consists in his acquiring what thus lies at hand, devouring his inorganic nature, and taking possession of it for himself" (*Phen* 16). In this regard, theorists have frequently noted how education as Hegel understood it is related to the conceptual reduction that allows spirit to appropriate its speculative content and how both are articulated in relation to processes of inwardization or devouring. "*Erinnerung* is a process of *Innerung*, of inwardizing," writes Donald Verene, and furthermore "this inwardizing is the basis of *Bildung*." For Timothy Bahti, the Hegelian subject—that is, both the scholar of spirit's scientific history *and* spirit itself—is, of necessity, an eater. In his reading of the tropes of spiritual digestion in the final paragraphs of the *Phenomenology of Spirit*, he writes, "under the sign of digestion, Hegel will apparently suffer no indigestion: Absolute knowing will digest absolutely."[56]

Less frequently though, have considerations of this sort gone beyond the sense of a dialectical necessity, whose routine automaton-like processing might generate the sense that the historical narrative of spirit would only be the correlate of a proprietary subjectivism all the more edified in being assured not only that it has history on its side, but that it has it on its "inside." However, in light of Hegel's demand that philosophy *not* be edifying, is it possible to read the implications of this reciprocity otherwise?

CODA II: SPECULATING ON THE EXAMPLE

You sometimes have to take books out of libraries, and sentences out of books: that's a way of giving them another chance or letting them run another risk.

—Jean-Luc Nancy

The essential thing is not only an insight into the dependence of the singular [*des Einzelnen*] on the whole, but just as much that every moment itself, independent of the whole, is the whole.

—G. F. W. Hegel

While the modern understanding has already reduced knowledge to a form suitable for its intellectual presentation and so has made the task of the modern pupil easier as it traces and internalizes "the history of the cultural development of the world"—perhaps even learning that history by rote (*Phen* 16; 24)[57]—the act of repeating the same story over and over again, according to Hegel's own assessment, is always at risk of haplessly falling into a "shapeless repetition of one and the same formula . . . thereby obtaining merely a boring show of diversity." As such, Hegel suggests that it remains the task of modernity to achieve a way of thinking that reanimates these inscriptions, and frees "determinate thoughts from their fixity so as to give actuality to the universal, and impart to it spiritual life" (*Phen* 20).

According to this injunction of release and liberation, universally determined moments or thoughts are not dead or fixed at all, but are immanently open to reactualization. In particular, they come to life when they become unfixed from their routine repetition, an unfixing that occurs when pure thinking recognizes *itself* as a *moment*. "Thoughts become fluid," he writes, "when pure thinking, this inner *immediacy*, recognizes itself as a moment, or when the pure certainty of self abstracts from itself—not by leaving itself out, or setting itself aside, but by giving up the *fixity* of its self-positing, by giving up not only the fixity of the pure concrete, which the 'I' itself is, in contrast with its differentiated content, but also the fixity of the differentiated moments which, posited in the element of pure thinking, share the unconditioned nature of the 'I'" (*Phen* 20). Kaufmann, in his reading of this passage, points out that the unnamed target here is Kant, who thought to be offering "a timeless analysis of human nature" independent of what happens, and considered his own concepts to be "fixed and rigid and final."[58] In this regard, Kaufmann suggests that the real force of the passage lies in how it shows Kant giving "us an analysis of only one . . . *Gestalt des Bewußtseins*, one manifestation of the spirit, one episode in the *Phenomenology of the Spirit*"[59] The gap between the fixed gaze of the "I" or the "I think" and an object— a gap that also sustains the bifurcation of the determinate inscriptions and the "object" to be known—falls away or is suspended, suggesting that the rigidity of its confrontational stance was not, in fact, the "last word" and that it might have run its course. In other words, while this particular epochal perspective was no doubt both logically and historically necessary, the time had perhaps come for it to show its own contingency. Contrary to much Hegel criticism, this statement also implies that speculative thought does not eliminate the possibility of perspective; in advocating a break from the rigidity of a subject-object relation, it seems rather to open up a multitude of perspectives.

How can we consider this statement in terms of the implications that it might have for history and in particular, for the question as to the modality of Spirit's manifestation at "the end of history"? Firstly, the suspension of pure thinking calls into question the notion that a stark opposition exists between the past and the present. No position or mode of understanding is "outside" history; Hegel demonstrates that even a position that claims for itself the putatively "outside" perspective of spectator is itself only a moment of that history. In that respect, his call for the unfixing of that moment also implies the potential for a more malleable relation between the past and the present and for a more fundamental experience of their mutual occurrence.

This call to unfix the rigid gaze of the "I" clearly indicates an important dimension of that experience: Directly related to the suspension of fixity, it involves the claim that not only is the self released from fixity but that so too is its differentiated content released from rigidity, by its "giving up . . . the fixity of the differentiated moments." If a release from fixity suggests a liberation of pent-up and contained energy, this can only mean that those moments retain a potential in excess of the fixity ascribed to them. In this respect, the transition from temporal moments to their reentry as speculative "moments" (that is, as so many differentiated doctrines, traits, figures, stages, and monuments of the past) appears as a process of differentiation and spacing by virtue of which those moments had retained the potential for sustained life in the mode of an immanent *detachability* from their fixed position. But what is detachability, finally, if not the condition under which a "moment" might take on an exemplary force—a force, that is, of exemplarity?

To situate this proposition and to begin drawing out its implications, let us briefly retrace our steps. Firstly, we saw how Hegel's dismissal of the possibility that political action can ever find a pregiven foundation in history was part of a larger development that sought to give an account of the risk and openness of the present. Secondly, we traced how it is that bracketing the political redeployment of history as so many "tried and true" examples allows history's abbreviated moments to be arranged within a spatial totality. In other words, this momentization of the historical epochs is the condition for their being taken up in differentiated relation to each other. One way of understanding this "difference in unity"—and by far the most common—is that those moments become meaningful and necessary (timeless, in other words) only as moments within the entire sequence of history, World History.

However, this perspective is complicated when focus is brought to bear on the labor of momentizing itself. What that procedure suggests is that the singular uniqueness of the historical moments—each of them is finite, has had its moment—is precisely what allows them to be differentiated as inscriptions or as written moments: distinct, singular, and so potentially detachable from the fixity of the position which they are given in any one mode of historical or philosophical understanding. Of course, Hegel focuses on the external cognition of the understanding to draw out the implications of this fixity but in our own considerations of fixity, we would have to include how we understand the task of reading Hegel's own speculative history, especially when that history is read—as it so often is—as a narrative succession of moments frozen in terms of an fixed and unchanging mode of relation.

Furthermore, the possibility that no moment is simply fixed "for all time" suggests—strangely enough, perhaps—that we might articulate its timelessness as the force of an immanent contingency. Narrative history, we might recall, is only possible by virtue of (at least) a twofold differentiation: the difference of successive moments from one another, allowing one mode of their appearance to be "points" on a line, and the immanent difference of the moment within itself—the condition for something to happen in history. To be sure, the rupture of happening as such is not recuperated in a linear narrative (much less in "historic time") as a *moment*. As Jean-Luc Nancy has suggested, it could never be represented as a moment, narrative or otherwise, for the happening of rupture (and the rupture of happening) is what gives birth to the moment itself.[60] Still though, will the trace of this rupture not somehow have been retained—even if in blunted, intensified, or reduced form—in the spacings of the narrative itself, namely as the detachability of its moments, each of which remains thus exposed to the possibility of (another) contingent exposure?

At one level, all we are doing here is formalizing in terms of its implications for history what could have escaped no reader of Hegel: that a great deal of the force of his texts lies in how their own moments are eminently and thoroughly detachable from their position in a historical narrative, demonstrating their potential for new organizations and new exposures. The most outstanding of these moments is undoubtedly the "Master-Slave" dialectic, but no less could we cite "the beautiful soul," "the cabbage heads," "the pyramid," "the many-eyed statue," "Antigone," "phrenologist," "*Aufheben*," "the knight errant," "I," "the pissing organ," "the Reign of Terror," "dough and bones"—the list could, of course, go on. Will these singular moments not have been the means by which we have all begun to read Hegel, possibly even (for better or worse) committing him to memory?

A helpful perspective for assessing the peculiar impact of Hegel's moments involves the intricate way in which they sustain relations to both temporal and logical categories. In this respect, they appear as both *instants* and *instances*. They are the determinate moments that have happened—appearing in the form of contingent happenings—and, at the same time, they are exemplary singularities, whose demonstration of force and necessity makes them irreducible to a fixed instant of a chronological succession. Whatever might be at stake in a notion of their speculative exemplarity would have to involve consideration of this doubling; that is, the speculative example would have to be situated right at this intersection of the accident and its logical necessity, without merging them but also without granting ultimate privilege to either.

The disdain Hegel shows for historical examples is grounded in how their deployment flattens out the complexity of both the past and the present, with the result that the latter is spared the risk of its own experience. In this respect, might it not be worthwhile to risk conceiving of a speculative example, one that might unsettle the present in which its necessity erupts again, perhaps even exposing that present to its own contingency?

CODA III: PROBING NECESSITY

Having just broached the question of necessity and contingency while attempting to open up an unpredictable future for the past, it is crucial to ask whether or not the whole itinerary of Hegel's philosophical history had been rigged from the beginning. To be sure, Hegel has often been read in terms of how he explicates the auto-development of an anonymous Subject or Reason. The following description, for instance, signals the sheer inevitability of this development with its own strangely repetitive use of the word "necessity." "The fact" is, writes Charles Taylor, "that this set of stages [of World History] is itself necessary, according to the Concept. It is necessary to its self-realization that Spirit move from the greatest outwardness to full self-consciousness. But in the same way the stages on the road are set by necessity; each must work itself out . . . since the beginning point and the goal are set out by the Idea, hence by necessity, so are all the intermediate stages necessary"[61]

If all history is as necessary as Taylor's comment insists, this only begs the question of what role contingency has had to play in that history, as well as the question of why Spirit must go through this history if it was all simply preordained or destined to happen. How, if Spirit really does go about applying its own necessity to everything it encounters, would its development escape Hegel's own charge of being "a boring show of diversity . . . nothing more than this sort of repetition of the same formula"?[62] Countering this propensity, when Hegel states on the very first pages of the *Phenomenology* that "the real issue is not exhausted by stating it as an aim, but by carrying it out, nor is the result the actual whole, but rather the result together with the process by which it came about" (*Phen* 2), the injunction here is to think necessity—the aim or result—together with contingency. In this respect, when Hegel characterizes the rupture of spirit into the human world as "an accident as such, detached from what circumscribes it" and contrasts it to "the circle that remains self-enclosed," which "has nothing astonishing about it," the point is to highlight, emphatically, the astonishing nature of contingency, or what he famously calls "the tremendous power of the negative" (*Phen* 18–19).

Still though, there is a sense in which our attempt to discern a degree of openness or contingency in history's logic of necessity—through recourse to its performativity as well as to the specific mode of its exemplarity—is quite easily called into question, and perhaps even as a function of the destiny of these passages themselves. Are we not patently contradicting everything Hegel says about the *final* destiny of necessity and contingency—namely, when in the *Introduction to the Philosophy of History*, he subjects the privilege granted to the contingent in the *Phenomenology* to a radical inversion, the result of which being that all contingency is ultimately resolved into the pure necessity of spirit?

This conclusion seems self-evident when we string together phrases from the *Introduction to the Philosophy of History* such as "the infinite necessity of [freedom] bringing itself to consciousness and thereby to reality" (*Phen* 22); "the final goal toward which all the world's history has been working. . . . This is the one and only goal that accomplishes itself and fulfills itself" (*Phen* 22–23); "the immanent development [i.e., the contingent events of history] [is] necessary" (*Phen* 28), or even the *Logic*'s "contingency is absolute necessity."[63] Taking these instances of inversion as our cue, we would have to conclude that in the end necessity predominates, that every chance occurrence had already been given a predetermined meaning. Would it not be precisely this aspect of Hegelian thought that seals its fate as irrelevant for our day (or for any day at all, given that to be in time is to be exposed to contingency)? The prospects look dim indeed, both for the future of politics—as one interpreter has put it, for Hegel "contingent history does not cease, but its significance is fully revealed"[64]—as well as for the future of the past—"One feels that the system would allow of accommodation to very wide changes in the course of history if we were suddenly to discover that our knowledge of the past had been mistaken."[65]

The numerous variations on "the contingent is necessary" found in the Hegelian corpus are, according to just as many variations in interpretation, commonly taken to mean that the contingent is (in truth) just a clumsy or awkward version of necessity, or that Spirit masterfully reveals its own necessity by going through the motions of contingency, and ultimately by subsuming it, effacing it, canceling it, neutralizing it.

However, John Burbidge's "The Necessity of Contingency" and Catherine Malabou's *The Future of Hegel* offer a more complicated picture of the relation between necessity and contingency in their readings of the *Logic*. It is beyond the scope of the present work to retrace their steps fully; we will limit ourselves to a few of their insights. In the section of the *Logic* entitled "The Absolute Relation," we find that necessary being is self-causing and for that reason, cannot be other than it is. Hegel writes: "Necessity is being, *because* it is—the unity of being with itself, that has itself for *ground*; but conversely, because it has a ground, it is not being but is altogether *illusion, relation* or *mediation*."[66]

Pure necessity is necessarily *blind*[67] for the reason that it cannot see the contradiction of its own ground. Because it is self-grounding, Malabou argues, "there is a contradiction inherent" to it, as there is "in every ground in so far as that ground is 'relative' (i.e., in relation, in *Beziehung*) to what it grounds" (*FH* 163). In drawing attention to the way in which necessary being, in order to be self-causing, must relativize itself or place itself in relation to itself, Malabou is also pointing out how it is also dependent upon itself: In order to ground itself, it must posit itself as its own ground. But to do that, necessary being must also split with itself, breaking with its own ground in order to relate to itself as the grounding of the ground.

When Hegel speaks of an "absolute contradiction [*den absoluten Widerspruch*]" (*Phen* 28) in this context, it is to the contradiction of self-grounding that he is referring. Burbidge puts the point in the following way: "As that which constitutes its own ground—as self-constituting—[that relation] is absolutely necessary. Thus absolute necessity gives rise to contingency as the ground of its own necessity. . . . Without these contingent, determinate moments, absolute necessity could not be established as necessary."[68]

In other words, one aspect of necessity must break with or repel the other, causing one to be active and the other passive. Hegel speaks of a "passivity posited by its own activity" and demonstrates that in a prior moment, necessity "repels itself from itself."[69] By virtue of the self-grounding activity of necessary being, necessity is never its own ground, but must experience itself as passive in relation to its own activity. Although necessity has its own source within itself, it feels itself to be independent from it. In other words, it experiences its own ground as something other than itself: either as something that has happened to it, befallen it as if from the outside, or as the ground to which it must necessarily fall.[70] There can be no question here of which element is active and which passive—which contingent and which necessary—for both are essential to the act of self-grounding. The point of their co-implication is that contingency arises *out of necessity* (in both senses of the phrase) and takes on the force of necessity. At the same time, necessity, setting itself up as an experience of self-division over which it exerts no mastery, thereby takes on the force of contingency. As Burbidge puts it: "This play of countervailing forces . . . generates, even as it transcends, the repelling moment of contrast and counterthrust. This necessity is necessity absolute. For it alone establishes the absolute necessity of contingency."[71]

According to these readings, the contingent is neither subordinate to nor derivative of spirit's necessity. The two coincide absolutely: Contingency arises out of the very logic of necessary self-grounding. This means that necessity's unfolding in the realm of "free contingent happening" stems from a process whereby spirit acts on itself in order to be self-grounding. The result of that process—the final contraction into itself of the contingent happenings making up the act of grounding itself—can only be the expression of that original contradiction arising at the heart of necessity, that of its self-division.

How might this logic of necessity's originary self-relation—that is, the necessity of contingency—help us to draw out the wager of what we have called speculative exemplarity? First of all, it has the merit of highlighting the one-sidedness of the claim that all necessity has simply been worked out and that nothing of any import will ever happen again. But it does beg the question. How can the import of an occurrence ever be weighed or measured against the "end of history"? That is, does "what happens" do so in accordance with an a priori foundation—ie. Is it fated to happen?—or conversely, is it the case that "what happens" will itself found or ground meaning? What the claims made in the *Logic* suggest is that in the face of something happening, it is impossible to organize necessity and contingency, much less the relation between "meaning" and "event," along a temporal continuum or in a sequential order. Whatever happens does not arise from a preexisting foundation, but "what happens" is also not foundational. In fact, Hegel would no doubt be tempted to dismiss as *mere* speculation any attempt to give one priority over the other, for their co-implication is primary. Might this not be precisely what Absolute Knowing, at the end of its long and torturous history, knows?

In one sense, this should—in principle at least—cancel the tendency to speculate on history in terms of whether or not it could have been otherwise, even if necessity's originary entanglement with (its own) contingency might seem to provide the impetus for such a thought. Indeed, the present might always find the question of another origin or another outcome to be an irresistible, if vertiginous, one. The crucial point, though, would be that the question itself, along with all the anxiety and unrest produced by it, is not one that comes from history per se. Rather, it is an agitation that "happens" in the present: from the resources of its own multiple historical perspectives, from its own sense of unrealized possibilities, from its own openings.[72]

In another sense, it is easy to see how the experience of vertigo produced by the question of another history is neither appropriable by consciousness nor, strictly speaking, is it available to the work of mourning conceived as integration or assimilation. All the same, one must be wary of hastening to the conclusion that what we are invoking here is the easily dismissible "non-reality" or nonactuality of a phantom nostalgia (that is, a nostalgia not for the "way things were," but for the way they were not). What will occupy us in the following and final chapter is how this unassimilable "experience" might offer the opportunity to conceive an other mourning, the mourning of a possibility that is neither historicizable nor actualizable as an "event." What will be at stake is a *missed* chance that, precisely because missed or unaccomplished, might very well remain in the present as the nonappropriable trace of the other.

For now though, perhaps it is enough to suggest that the question of other possibilities, historical or otherwise, could only ever arise where there is a sense or an experience, itself paradoxical, of lost necessity. If one can risk a generalization, this loss is perhaps what most fully characterizes our own epoch vis-à-vis its relation to history. In any case, it undoubtedly accounts for why Hegel's history strikes so many of its readers as being a "thing of the past."[73] Though in another sense, Hegel will also have made it clear what the stakes might be in conceiving the present as a radically contingent occurrence, or as a "mad and foolish happening" (*IPH* 39): the tacit, even if despairing, acceptance of its brutal necessity.

In this respect, might not a crucial dimension of the exemplarity of the speculative moments lie in their potential to act as a jarring reminder of the eruptive dimension implicit to necessity—the trace of a *reminder*, that is, and *not* a memory? If that is the case, then reading historical moments pace Hegel might restore a degree of risk to the act of citing an example from history, if only by attending to the ways in which the necessity of its meaning (as well as the meaning of its necessity) has always been inseparable from the eruption of its happening. Not only might this attentiveness generate a more forceful or even jarring reading of any single moment from the past; its force might be enough for the present to turn spontaneously—that is, both unexpectedly and on its own—to the contingencies of its own deployment of history's examples, perhaps even to begin writing another kind of "history." It seems that for Hegel, there is always time left for that.

CHAPTER FIVE

In Lieu of a Last Word

Maurice Blanchot and the Future of Memory (Today)

Wild animals run from the dangers they actually see, and once they have escaped them worry no more. We however are tormented alike by what is past and what is to come.

—Seneca

. . . la responsabilité la plus folle (celle de la mémoire) . . .

—Christophe Bident

Impatience is the failing of one who wants to withdraw from the absence of time; patience is the ruse which seeks to master this absence by making of it another time, measured otherwise.

—Maurice Blanchot

To end with a discussion of the work of Maurice Blanchot is rife with difficulties, two of which I will mention by way of beginning. The first involves the sheer difficulty of reading his work. While to be sure, this seems to be something of a "side issue," it is one with important consequences: An encounter with Blanchot's texts—whether those of his fiction, his criticism or the aphoristic, fragmentary texts of the later years—induces a deep feeling of exposure and vertigo, the negativity or indeterminacy of which is hardly conceivable as a mediating moment toward a higher reconciliation, be it one of judgment, of an experience of sympathy or of understanding.[1] Even the genre of the "encyclopedia entry," that avatar of sober academic assessment, seems to lose its footing when it draws attention to this experience, in one case asserting that Blanchot's oeuvre "has struck many serious commentators as being uncannily, disempoweringly infectious" and that, while his significance is undoubtedly formidable, its impact has proven extremely difficult to assess.[2] Given the difficulty of such an experience, the fascination of reading Blanchot is bound to be accompanied by an undeniable feeling of resistance, by a refusal to be led to a confrontation with something opaque on which one's consciousness can find no hold.

How, then, to answer to the groundlessness of this reading? How to respond in such a way that does not simply recover from or shut down the unsettling experience (or unexperience) to which this writing exposes us, where it seems to be the very ground of experience itself that is called into question? Though, as we shall see, this calling-into-question itself implies that we are already near to a singularly Blanchotian motif, nothing about its proximity should provide us with an overly hasty feeling of comfort or security, let alone with the ease of feeling as if a certain "solidarity" has been achieved.

Related to the sense, only barely touched upon here, in which Blanchot's texts leave us alone and in no position ("to approve or disapprove, believe in or doubt" says one of his readers and translators[3]) is an even more intractable objection to giving a reading of Blanchot's texts (in) the place of an ending: Over the course of roughly fifty years, he consistently submitted the notion of the "end" to rigorous critique, exposing its ground to be the ethos of a "successful" work of mourning that seeks to limit and contain the possibility of an other exposure. In keeping with Blanchot's most trenchant demand, then, it will have to be a question of another mourning, or of a *mourning after*.

Nonetheless, impatience is my failing. The impatient reader in me still wants to get to the end, wants to put "a term to the interminable,"[4] still wants to ask: "What is *mourning* though, if its ethos of putting a term on the past is not somehow intimately linked to *morning*, to the very possibility of a new moment, a new beginning, to the dawn of something new?" What is it, indeed, that links mourning to morning? The question may not be quite as simple—or not quite as complex—as the homonymic play between the two words suggests. Before we can approach what is at stake in Blanchot's problematization of mourning, then, this question of what aligns *mourning* so closely to *morning* or with the dawn of new beginnings must itself be raised.

From Hegel to Nietzsche and Freud, each makes a claim that stakes the vitality of the present on its ability to assimilate what is lost. Assuming the familiar simplifications, whether the claim is conceived along the cultural lines of an organic assimilation put to

the service of the subject's own self-constitution, of an obsession
with the ego's successful *Trauerarbeit* following a loss or of scolding
one's own century for its pathological sense of history, in all cases,
the chief exigency is that the potentially crushing weight of the dead
must be transformed into something more liberating.[5] "*There is a
degree of sleeplessness, of rumination, of historical sensibility,*"
writes Nietzsche, "*that injures and ultimately destroys all living
things, whether a human being, a people, or a culture.*" For a vital
and life-affirming balance to be stuck, the past must "not become
the grave digger of the present"; that is, a people, an individual, or a
culture must succumb to the power to "assimilate what is past and
alien, to heal wounds, to replace what has been lost."[6] Likewise,
for Freud: "The fact is . . . that when the work of mourning is completed the ego becomes free and uninhibited again [*Tatsächlich wird
aber das Ich nach der Vollendung der Trauerarbeit wieder frei und
ungehemmt*]."[7]

Despite the more complicated reading I hope to have generated in
Chapter 4 regarding the future of a dialectically recuperated past,
nonetheless it is Hegel who will have set the stage for this *Trauerspiel*.
Indeed, the preoccupations with grief and mourning that we have
discerned in Hegel's treatment of how objects pass from sensuality to
intelligibility—marking their passage into knowledge as philosophical history—confirm the sense that mourning is the mechanism that
will ensure spirit the return to itself of all its moments.

For mourning to be "successful," all three accounts suggest that
what has been lost must not only be relinquished but must also be
made to reappear. If mourning emerges as the work that successfully
disarticulates the past and the present, it still remains difficult to
know how to situate this disarticulation in relation to the paradoxical
necessity that the loss be made to appear. On the one hand, this disarticulation between past and present is clearly on the order of a rupture
or break; on the other hand though, it can only be the outcome of an
articulation, determination or assessment of what is lost. To bring the
loss to an end, one must claim to know it and to know its reach; one
must mourn as if one knew what it was and could represent it as a figure for, or an object of, knowledge.

The disarticulation of the past from the present thus implicitly presupposes a figure or presentation of *what it is* that has passed. Whether
it be in the form of a concept, a monument, a narrative account or a
"lesson learned," the demand for a safe or nonpathological return of

the past through its *figure* is everywhere present where, by assimilating the past, attempts are made to get out from under it and to neutralize its potentially deadening blow to the singular vitality of the present. Conversely, the inability to figure the loss (or, indeed, the refusal to do so) obstructs the possibility of mourning and is associated, for Freud, with a breakdown of the very principle of subjectivity ("an impoverishment of his ego on a grand scale [*eine großartige Ichverarmung*]" [MM 254/431]), writes Freud); with a passive stance that masks a deeper attitude of open hostility toward overcoming the loss and, finally, with an almost total loss of interest in the quotidian world (of politics, of community).

In the thought-provoking protest against melancholia that takes place on the pages of *Mourning Becomes the Law*,[8] Gillian Rose echoes these thinkers by summing up what she sees as the none-too-inspiring political consequences at the heart of a "process of endless mourning" or "everlasting melancholia" (*ML* 11): a "refusal to let go" (*ML* 11) that results in a self-imposed "impotence and failure" (*ML* 10); a flight from and renunciation of the difficult political risks involved in self-positing and learning from one's own limitations; "impotence and suffering" (*ML* 51); an evasion of responsibility, as well as a self-absorbed indifference to questions of justice.

In the book's penultimate chapter[9]—which is also a moving account of private grief—explicit aim on all these fronts is taken at the oeuvre of Maurice Blanchot who, in Rose's estimation, represents a particularly extreme example of this melancholic paralysis (*ML* 14). Rose objects in particular to his notion of *désoeuvrement* (worklessness or unworking) and draws attention to how it stalls the work of mourning, interrupting its movement of restitution and jamming the gears of a dialectical relation to the past: "For Blanchot, the letting go of mourning is not for morning or dawning, for commencing, but for the endless reality of ending, which our workful beginnings can only, and must always, violate" (*ML* 104). In Rose's account, Blanchot's refusal to "let go" of mourning is tantamount to a refusal of responsibility and to a blanket rejection of the premise that we can learn anything from the past.

It is explicitly in light of these characterizations of Blanchot as a melancholic par excellence that Rose performs a vigorous critique of Blanchot's reading of Hegel in his 1949 essay "Literature and the Right to Death."[10] According to Rose, the essay evinces a melancholic stance at practically every level, but she places special emphasis on the way in which it throws the Hegelian dialectic into violent reversal: Whereas the sequence of the Hegelian presentation proceeds from naming and moves on to action and then to ethical substance, Blanchot, she writes "moves from action and the thing itself (*la chose même*) to the name (*la chose*) and its ungraspable remnant, and thence to the absolute meaning of meaning" (*ML* 117). The claim that mourning in Blanchot is tied to what remains ungraspable within language is what provides Rose with the grounds for the contention that his unworked mourning involves turning one's back on the future, in order precisely to turn back toward the unredeemable loss in a gesture of "*poiesis* or 'making,'" one that "does not involve working through, nor acceptance of, the inevitable negation by which meaning is secured" (*ML* 104).

Ultimately, the task here will not be to square Rose's complaint—as urgently expressed as it is polemically so—with Blanchot's writing but to assess what might be at stake in Blanchot's tarrying over the issue of language for an understanding of how it can be situated in relation to mourning. In what follows, I will examine "Literature and the Right to Death" for its philosophy of language and will concur with Rose's assessment that the language of Blanchotian mourning cannot be read as the expression of a work of recovery, self-empowerment or cultural accrual.[11] Unlike Rose's however, my reading of that language will suggest that the divisions and ruptures of language that Blanchot draws out—excruciatingly, exquisitely—have temporal implications that, while certainly at odds with that of a teleological history, open up the possibility of a nonredemptive account of memory. Turning to a late text, *Après coup* (1983), I will then attempt to gauge the "practical" implications of this temporality for a sense of how it might be conceived in relation to history.

POSING A QUESTION

Every time we speak, we make words into monsters with two faces, one being reality, physical presence, and the other meaning, ideal absence. But ordinary language limits equivocation. It solidly encloses the absence in a presence, it puts *a term* to understanding [*elle met un* terme *à l'entente*].
—Maurice Blanchot

It will certainly come as no surprise to readers of a certain Hegel: By asking after the essence of literature—that is, in posing the question "What is Literature?"[12]—philosophy will have already begun chanting its funeral dirge. For when posed in reflexive and cognitive form, the question itself will have already presupposed the overcoming of the "what" under consideration; it will already have the answer at its fingertips, will have already consigned literature to the status of a determinate object, the essence of which having already departed from literature per se so as to emerge in the registers of philosophy or conceptual analysis.

Refusing to allow philosophy to get at its booty with such seeming ease, Blanchot's "Literature and the Right to Death" contends from the outset that literature has some questions of its own. To be more precise, its questionability is *not* the exclusive domain of philosophy but has an irreducibly literary dimension. The question of literature, Blanchot asserts, is coextensive with literature itself and as such, is neither incidental to literature nor is it a threat that comes to it from the outside. In other words, self-questioning is present at literature's very commencement: Supposing, he writes, that literature does "begin at the moment when literature becomes a question," the question is addressed "to language . . . , by language which has become literature" (LRD 300–301).

It is thus from very early on in Blanchot's essay that philosophy gains a rival in literature; there is something in "the literary Thing" (LRD 301) that refuses to be given as knowledge and refuses too to give itself up to the conceptual rigor of philosophy. In what might this refusal consist? To get at what is at stake here, Blanchot's excursus on the "word" will prove crucial insofar as it acts for him as a focal point from which to draw out the striking differences between what we might call a philosophical bearing of death and a literary one.

In the second half of the essay,[13] Blanchot recalls the claim made by a youthful Hegel (not without placing him near Hölderlin, his "friend and kindred spirit") that the act of naming is always and irreducibly an act of annihilation: "In a text dating from before *The Phenomenology*, Hegel . . . writes: 'Adam's first act, which made him master of the animals, was to give them names, that is, he annihilated them in their existence (as existing creatures)'" (cited in LRD 322–23). The act of naming can be understood here as a form of mastery; indeed, as one of the opening sentences of the essay's second half explicitly suggests (one prior to the citation of Hegel), naming can be linked to control and domination. Alluding to the phrase "*Je dis: 'une fleur'*" from Mallarmé's *Crise de Vers*, Blanchot writes: "When we speak, we gain control over things with satisfying ease. I say, 'This

woman,' and she is immediately available to me, I push her away, I
bring her close, she is everything I want her to be" (LRD 322).

If such is the kind of language most of us would be content to live
with—it is, as Blanchot says, "life's ease and security"—it will immediately give way to the hint of an even greater power, greater in that it
is both "disquieting and marvelous." Again echoing Mallarmé's celebrated phrase, Blanchot writes:

> I say, "This woman." . . . A word may give me what it means, but
> first it suppresses it [*mais d'abord il le supprime*]. For me to be able to
> say "This woman," I must somehow take her flesh-and-blood reality
> away from her, cause her to be absent, annihilate her. The word gives
> me the being, but it gives it to me deprived of being. The word is the
> absence of that being, its nothingness, what is *left of it* when it has
> lost being [*Le mot me donne l'être, mais il me le donne privé d'être.
> Il est l'absence de cet être, son néant, ce qui demeure de lui lorsqu'il
> a perdu l'être*]—the very fact that it does not exist. Considered in this
> light, speaking is a curious right. (LRD 322/312, emphasis added)

Several aspects of this dense formulation need to be drawn out. First
of all, as in its first usage, the act of substituting *une femme* for *une
fleur* is clearly not fortuitous: *Une femme* lends to the elaboration of
the relation between language and annihilation an intensity or disquiet that could never be matched by reference to a flower.

Related to the passage's sense of increased intensity is the intricate relation it establishes among speaking, being, and nothingness.
With regard to the phrase that begins with "the word gives me the
being but it gives it to me deprived of being," the first and most obvious interpretation to present itself suggests that the name or word
only signifies by virtue of its having robbed the entity to be named of
being pure-and-simple, its "flesh-and-blood reality." Or to put it in a
slightly different way, the name drains or divests what is named of its
vital being.

The next sentence, however, qualifies this interpretation. If the
three phrases of the second formulation—"absence of that being,"
"nothingness" and "what is left of it" (*l'absence de l'être; son néant;
ce qui demeure de lui*)—are apposite and are to be understood as
specifications of "the word," what Blanchot seems to be suggesting is
that nothingness itself has *survived* in the word. Furthermore, if "to
survive" indicates a prior existence, the implication is that nothingness was already there in the entity *prior* to naming. According to
this reading, language does something other (and less) than divest an

entity of the plenitude of its own being. Rather, it seems to complete an already-existing division of the entity *from itself.*[14] The following contention, made some paragraphs later, confirms this reading at the same time as it redoubles, once again, the intensity of the claim:

> Of course, my language does not kill anyone. And yet, when I say, "This woman," *real death has been announced* and is already present in my language, my language means that this person, who is here right now, can be detached from herself, removed from her existence and her presence, and suddenly plunged into a nothingness in which there is no existence or presence; my language essentially signifies the possibility of this destruction; it is a constant, bold allusion to such an event. My language does not kill anyone. *But if this woman were not really capable of dying, if she were not threatened by death at every moment of her life, bound and joined to death by an essential bond,* I would not be able to carry out that ideal negation, that deferred assassination which is what my language is. (LRD 323)

As the development of this passage suggests, Blanchot defers the moment of "ideal negation" in order to underscore the ground on which it takes place: Mortality is the sole condition upon which language can proceed to that idealizing destruction of a singular, flesh-and-blood reality. While in one sense, this formulation can be read as an expression of the structuralist argument regarding the conditions for signification in general (that signification depends upon the potential absence of the speaker and referent), Christopher Fynsk has argued that a far more unsettling death is at stake here, in that "a 'real death' has occurred. This woman negated when I say 'this woman' must have been '*really capable of* dying,' bound *essentially* to death. Language is thus constantly referring back to its origin in the essential bond between the existent being and the possibility of the death that offers this being to language."[15] What is most forceful in Blanchot's contention, Fynsk asserts, is that what exists prior to language is not life pure and simple, but life already bound to death.[16] In turn, the claim that "my language essentially signifies the possibility of that destruction" implies that the destruction itself is *prior* to language and that the very possibility of language consists in the offering of existent beings of themselves to language through and as their own dying.[17]

Since language begins in negation and its meaning "derives not from existence but from a retreat before existence" (LRD 324), different understandings of it become possible. Everyday language asserts that the living thing is contained in the word. This assertion is certainly not wrong, Blanchot claims, since even if it be admitted that the word "excludes the existence of what it designates," common language is still able to refer "to it through the thing's nonexistence, which has become an essence" (LRD 325). In fact, here common language finds itself on even more solid ground. For, by emphasizing its expression of the *nonexistence* of things, Blanchot explicitly, if ironically, suggests that it has also secured for them something resembling everlasting life: "Things can change if they have to, sometimes they stop being what they are—they remain hostile, unavailable, inaccessible; but the being of these things, their idea, does not change: The idea is definitive, it is sure, we even call it eternal" (LRD 325).

Literary language, however, remains torn. It is "made of uneasiness"; its position is "not very stable or secure." On the one hand, language involves it in a deceit and a contradiction: While desiring to attain the absence of the thing absolutely, it nonetheless perceives that the "non-existence of the cat" is a "non-existence made *word*"; that is, it perceives its language as a completely material and objective reality. Here the word is an annoying embarrassment, a stupid block or hindrance that maliciously attests to the failure of language to attain the infinite movement it seeks and that can only be mitigated by "an endless sliding of 'turns of phrase' which do not lead anywhere. Thus is born the image that does not directly designate the thing but, rather, what the thing is not; it speaks of a dog instead of a cat" (LRD 326).

On the other hand, literary language cannot help asking after what was lost. Tormented, it cannot recover from that "murder Hegel speaks of":

> It recalls the first name which would be the murder Hegel speaks of. The "existant" was called out of its existence by the word, and it became being. This *Lazare, veni foras* [Lazarus, come forth] summoned the dark, cadaverous reality from its primordial depths and in exchange gave it only the life of the mind. Language knows that its kingdom is day and not the intimacy of the unrevealed; it knows that in order for the day to begin . . . something must be left out. Negation cannot be created out of anything but the reality of what it is negating; language derives its value and its pride from the fact that it is the achievement of this negation; but in the beginning, what was lost? The torment of language is what it lacks because of the necessity that it be the lack of precisely this. It cannot even name it. (LRD 326–27)

How can one seize hold of what is prior to the word, how is one to get at that primordial truth of things before language, when all that language has at its disposal is precisely the idealizing negation that causes that truth to retreat or that pushes that truth away? "How can I recover it, how can I turn around and look at what exists *before*, if all my power consists of making it into what exists *after*? The language of literature is a search for this moment which precedes literature [*Comment le trouver, comment me retourner vers ce qui est avant, si tout mon pouvoir consiste á en faire ce qui est* après? *Le langage de la littérature est la recherche de ce moment qui la précède*]" (LRD 327/316).

One might be tempted to read these formulations as an attempt to retrieve the timelessness of a prelapsarian purity. Indeed, Blanchot's various references to "this woman," "the flower," "the cat as it exists," "what man rejects by saying it," etc. do little to dispel such a reading, invoking as they do an Edenic paradise of utopian fulfillment.[18] Is Blanchot's characterization of language here not, in fact, that of an impossible and tormented commitment to the *before* which the *afterwardsness*[19] of words—the *after-words?*—can only ever honor by violating? Before attempting to answer this question, let us continue to follow the movements of the text. For contrary to what one might expect, it is not to the *before* of a living Lazarus on the nether-side of language that Blanchot will draw attention but to what remains unassimilated by any model of designation or representation. Almost immediately following the long passage cited above, Blanchot writes that the loss that torments literature, all the more intense for being insurmountable, is the all-too-literal "cadaverous 'reality'" of the corpse: "Lazarus in the tomb and not Lazarus brought back into the daylight, the one who already smells bad, who is Evil, Lazarus lost and not Lazarus saved and brought back to life" (LRD 327). Next to its difficult sensibility, what is, I think, most exceptional about this passage is how the corpse is put "to work" as an emblem or figure of the *before*. By most standards, this choice would seem unconventional in the extreme. For if a corpse can be said to "work" as a figure at all, would it not be most likely to do so as a figure of the *after*, of the unworked and unworkable remainder of mortal existence? Or is there a sense in which the *before* already bears within it its own after-life? We will come back to this.

Whereas language had earlier acted as a hindrance and a barrier to ideal negation, at this stage of the argument it becomes the writer's only hope. "What hope do I have of attaining the thing I push away? My hope lies in the materiality of language, in the fact that words are things too." Referring back to the understanding of language as "ideal negation," one for which the dead letter posed an irritating hindrance, Blanchot continues, "just now the reality of words was an obstacle. Now it is my only chance" (LRD 327). The chance for language to grasp what it has left behind turns out, in fact, to be very much within reach; it lies in the very materiality or *thing-ness* of language itself. As such, the flight of literature into the physicality of language will foreground the latter's "rhythm, weight, mass, shape," even the smear of the ink and the sheets of paper on which one writes. Its desire? To "become senseless" (LRD 327).

As Blanchot well knows however, this very attempt will turn out to be "a tragic endeavor": Ultimately, literature cannot not reveal. The insanity of the effort to do so turns on an elaborate paradox, that of attempting to become "the revelation of what revelation destroys" (LRD 328) or to become antisense, which cannot help surreptitiously importing a meaning into this meaningless matter.[20] "If it were to become as mute as a stone, as passive as the corpse enclosed behind that stone," Blanchot writes, "its decision to lose the capacity for speech would still be legible on the stone [*la décision de perdre la parole continuerait à se lire sur la pierre*] and would be enough to awaken that false corpse" (LRD 329/318). Even in the purest poetic spirit of refusal—of ideality, signification, and negation—literature, it seems, cannot help inscribing an epitaph on the tomb; it cannot avoid spiriting the corpse.[21] After having established that every attempt to ground language either in its idealizing and eternalizing negation (pure sense) or in its brute materiality (pure senselessness) is doomed to find itself caught in a contradiction, Blanchot then turns to the question of their intermingling.

In an attempt to catch more precisely the irreducibly double-aspect of language, Blanchot returns to it in his summary of the two "sides" (*deux versants*) of language. The first side, that of "meaningful prose," aims at expressing "things in a language that designates things according to what they mean" (LRD 332). This is the prosaic and healthful language of ideal negation, whose distrust of words, paradoxically enough, makes it perfectly adequate as everyday communication and speech. The second side is characterized by a "concern for the reality of things," by "the being which protests against revelation" (LRD 330/319). On this side, "words are transformed . . . in them, physical weight is present as the stifling density of an accumulation of syllables that has lost all meaning" (LRD 331).

For our purposes, the particular constitution of each side is of less importance than is the question of their interrelatedness: Each is "contaminated" by the other—the language of ideal negation cannot escape its own irreducible materiality while the language of pure materiality cannot avoid signifying its own decision, even if it is one of a refusal or abandonment of meaning. But for Blanchot this does not imply that one side of language simply collapses into the other, or that their differences are ultimately reconcilable at a higher order of consciousness. Their enduring relation as *partage*—that is, an experience of both sharing and division—is crucial. Blanchot writes: "Literature is divided [*est partagée*] between these two sides. The problem is that even though they are apparently incompatible, they do not lead toward distinctly different works or goals, and that an art which purports to follow one side is already on the other" (LRD 331). What might be the implications of this *partage* between the two sides of language—an indivisible division, signifying both an incompatibility and an inseparability, an intimate proximity and an infinite distance, etc.—for our understanding of language or for an understanding of how consciousness might encounter it, say through practices of writing or reading?

Such a question raised at this particular juncture is far removed from the question of writing or readership that was posed in the first half of the essay. There, it was a question of a reading public or an audience whom a writer might attempt to keep in mind as she composes her works, but whose presence in the end would effectively prevent both the writer from writing and the reader from reading (LRD 306–7). What is at stake here involves the ordeal consciousness might possibly undergo when exposed to language's two sides and the issue as to whether or not it can maintain any hold on its own experience.

In the first place, the most obvious aspect of language is that in order for it to be legible, words must "mean." That is, they must point beyond themselves to that which in them enables representation, illumination, and comprehension. However, prior to any comprehension, understanding or illumination, it is the nonrepresentational and senseless materiality of language that first constitutes the ground or substratum of such a reading.

In the second place, a more complex and difficult issue involves the sense in which that same materiality, while making the act of reading possible, is also what possesses the potential to undermine or destabilize the security of the insights it may afford. For is it not the case that

language's materiality is precisely that aspect of linguistic power that
resists accommodation to consciousness and as such, might threaten
its sure footing? Whatever else one might hazard to say about it, the
attempt to ground oneself with any kind of certainty in language is
bound to produce an experience that is, at the very least, confusing:
"Everyone understands that literature cannot be divided up, and that
if you choose exactly where your place in it is, if you convince yourself
that you really are where you wanted to be, *you risk becoming very
confused* [*c'est s'exposer à la plus grande confusion*], because literature
has already insidiously caused you to pass from one side to the other
and *changed you into something you were not before.* This is its treach-
ery; this is also its cunning version of the truth" (LRD 333, emphasis
added). If it is indeed true that neither the writer nor the reader can
possibly hope to find themselves on stable ground in language—if they
do, Blanchot claims, they will immediately find themselves changed
into something else—then tarrying with language means endlessly con-
fronting an illegibility that an act of reading or writing can neither
obliterate nor incorporate as an aspect of its own sense.[22] The most
we can say about such an experience, in fact, is that it bears the risk of
being exposed to "something else," to what Blanchot calls a "force that
is capricious and impersonal, and says nothing, reveals nothing . . ."
(330); an "impersonal power" with which "no one can do anything"
(LRD 331); "an impersonal spontaneity" (333). The matter of language
remains, then, as an uncanny trace of illegibility or a disquieting non-
revelation within every "enlightened" experience of reading.

At this stage, it might be helpful to go back over some of the terrain
we have covered thus far. First, we noted how literature is tormented
(in a way that philosophy and ordinary language claim not to be[23])
by the status of its own language in relation to what comes *before*—
which, as we saw, is neither immediate sense-certainty nor "the life
of the mind" but mortal life—that is, life that is already capable of
dying. In light of that contention, we then noted how Blanchot submits the conventional relation between the terms of *before* and *after*
to a complex and subtle transformation. For if their relation is normally conceived along the lines of a rupture or break, Blanchot's
contention is that the *before* is somehow continuous with the *after*,
the corpse being that dead aspect of mortal existence from which
language, thanks to its own materiality, ultimately manages *not* to
break; rather, the abject corpse passes into the afterlife of language in
and as the latter's very thingliness.

What at the level of the prepositions of *before* and *after* we might
be tempted to read as a temporal division reemerges, then, *within* language as its own division, the division of its very essence. That is to
say, the division of existent being is itself not overcome by language
but is carried into it. In precisely that sense, the relation between the
before and the *after* cannot be said to be structured around a radical
break or rupture—between, say, words and things—which might act
to immunize language against what preceded it; in fact, the dead letter of language has retained something of what refuses to give itself
as signification or, more accurately, what gives itself only in refusal.

Strictly speaking, then, between the *before* and the *after* there is
both continuity and discontinuity. On the one hand, there is a survival of what has been left behind but on the other hand, that survival
can only be conceived in terms of an enduring discontinuity within
language itself. For if the task Blanchot has set for language is to recuperate the corpse-like *before*, the *unheimlich* and abject stature of
which would be enough to stop anyone dead in their tracks, into the
after (what we called, only half in jest, "after-words"), the "accom-
plishment" of that task only seems possible by virtue of the division
inherent to language itself—namely, in its two sides that are simultaneously irreducible to and inseparable from one another. When consciousness attempts to find sure footing on these sides, it does so only
at the risk of losing its train of thought, of getting confused and losing
its place, its own mastery waylaid by a "something else" that, when
pursued, "vanishes into thin air" (LRD 335).

The movement here clearly cannot be described in terms of a pro-
pelling-forward, a progression, or a safe recuperation of what is past.
It would probably be more apt to describe it in Blanchot's terms as
the vacillation of a "strange slipping back and forth" (LRD 338) or,
stranger still, as the nagging distraction of a Kafkaesque "insect-like
buzzing" that never attains the status of an idea to be understood,
comprehended or explained, "because the inexplicable emerges in
it" (LRD 340). Indeed, Blanchot's complex presentation of language
makes any implications it might have for an understanding of its temporality deeply elusive. In fact, if we foreground the sense in Blanchot
that the effort of language is precisely to leave nothing behind—not
even the corpse—does this not violate the very condition upon which
a future seems possible, which is, as Blanchot himself acknowledges,
that "for the day to begin . . . something must be left out [*pour que le
jour commence . . . quelque chose doit être exclu*]" (LRD 326/316)?

Be that as it may, it nonetheless remains the case that the analysis of the *after-words* in relation to their *before* gestures toward a structure of retrospection, one whose transformations might very well be pointing to some other sense of futurity. Is it not the case, after all, that at a very minimum, retrospection can be said to be the attempt to give the past an other future?

The belated act of retrospection is often conceived in terms of how it belatedly confers on the past a sense of futurity. Lacan, for example, succinctly sums up the task of Freudian psychoanalysis as the opening-up of a space for retrospection so that the subject can restructure the event at a later date (Lacan's—*Freudian*—word for this belatedness is *nachträglich*) and can "reorder past contingencies by conferring on them the sense of necessities to come."[24] While Lacan underscores how this method is the means by which retrospection enables "an assumption of his history by the subject," it seems crucial to highlight how that act of assumption is inseparable from giving past events a sense of the future, one that Lacan describes in terms of "necessities to come." Now, if the potentiality of this future seems, in Lacan, to be circumscribed or captured by the sense of an after-the-fact anticipation or expectation of the present, the question remains as to how to situate Blanchot's structure of retrospection in relation to Lacan's.

Blanchot's formulation, in fact, seems to complicate the sense in which the futurity of the *before* is restricted to the one conferred on it by the belated anticipation of a retrospective act. In fact, the disquiet of his formulation arises from the sense in which, for Blanchot, the *before* is of a radically different order than a retrospectively ascribed "necessity to come." In particular, its force seems to be virtually indiscernible from the unworkable sense—the extreme blockage of which is maximized by its corpse-like illegibility—in which something of that "pastness" exceeds the grasp of a consciousness seeking to capture it without remainder and which consequently is not so much transformed by the *after* into something more accommodating or manageable—Lacan's necessity "to come"—as it is carried into the *after* as an enduring material remnant. In short, what may very well be at stake in this unreadable remnant of the *before* is its sustained potential to destabilize or disrupt a retrospective assumption of it. In this respect, perhaps we could propose that when Blanchot refers to the anonymity (or the "impersonal") of language, it is to a sense of this quasi-permanent and uncertain futurity that he is gesturing. Furthermore, at the risk of conflating two distinct registers of discourse, one might also suggest that what is given voice here informs what will be articulated, much later, on the opening page of *The Writing of the Disaster* as the time of the disaster:

> We are on the edge of disaster without being able to situate it in the future: it is rather always already past, and yet we are on the edge or under the threat, all formulations which would imply the future— that which is yet to come—if the disaster were not that which does not come, that which has put a stop to every arrival. To think the disaster (if this is possible, and it is not possible inasmuch as we suspect that the disaster is thought) is to have no longer any future in which to think it.[25]

In "Dreadful Reading: Blanchot on Hegel," Andrzej Warminski repeatedly asserts that in "Literature and the Right to Death," Blanchot rereads the Hegelian motifs of death and work "in an other place, to the side," that is, in terms of writing.[26] To which, I think, we could add that in doing so he also rereads and transforms the mourning-work of history. If Blanchot does turn the tables on history by rereading its dialectical mechanism in terms of reading and writing, is it conceivable that the tables be turned once again? That is, is it conceivable that Blanchot himself be asked to turn the tables and reread, in still an other place, his own writing in terms of history?

§

Every work is an occasional work: this simply means that each work has a beginning, that it begins at a certain moment in time and that that moment in time is part of the work, since without it the work would have been an insurmountable problem, nothing more than the impossibility of writing it.

—Maurice Blanchot

The text *Après coup* (1983) is among the few in Blanchot's oeuvre that scholars devoted to his work have seemed reluctant to engage in any sustained way. While the text is sometimes mentioned in the course of other analyses to support arguments that are not its proper focus, seldom is it taken to be a work with a force of its own.[27] The reasons for this lack of engagement are doubtless manifold—its brevity, its status as excursus or addendum (it is an after-word for the reedition of two little known interwar *récits*)—but one could speculate that what has proven to be more than a little off-putting for those readers of Blanchot who seek to trace the enigmatic textual force at work in Blanchot's writing *from inside of that writing* might be its curious *lack* of an inside.

Many aspects of *Après coup* indeed suggest that it belongs to the most conventional of genres, so much so that one of its readers has characterized it in the most neutral terms as "a brief retrospective essay" and another has argued that it goes "against the grain of critical approaches" to Blanchot's work and promotes "a consistent authorial identity above and beyond change in time."[28] To this we could add consideration of its writing style, which is uncharacteristically programmatic; its perspective, which has been suggested to foreclose theoretical readings in favor of a more direct or constative approach (exceptional as it is, Gary Mole suggests, Blanchot is here commenting "directly on his own work" [33]); and finally its tone, which oscillates between fatigue and a pedantry or parabasis. In short, if one can say as much, it is difficult to read *Après coup* as a text.

In this regard, the intention here will neither be to "rescue" *Après coup* from a supposedly undeserved theoretical oblivion nor to make an inflated claim for its importance within Blanchot's oeuvre. Rather, I simply hope to highlight the ways in which the text indeed adopts the conventional signs of a retrospective essay—the signature, the heightened awareness of time's passage and importantly, the retrospective aim par excellence of giving the past an other future—but that it does so in a way that transforms these conventions to a degree significant enough to warrant consideration. First, then, it will be necessary to say a word or two about the provenance of the texts collected in the volume and to highlight some of the latter's structural aspects. As I will suggest, its very make-up attests to the difficulties involved in establishing the time of Blanchot's writings. Uniting in one book writings of a radically discontinuous provenance, the collection itself speaks volumes about the forces of continuity and discontinuity that are put into play there.

Après coup was first published in 1983, having been written to accompany the reedition of two interwar *récits*, entitled "The Idyll" and "The Last Word."[29] These two stories were first published independently of one another in 1947, but they had been written over a decade prior to this: The 1947 version of "The Idyll" bears on its closing page the date "juillet 1936." As Michael Holland has suggested, this story must have already seemed like an anachronistic curiosity even on the occasion of its first publication in 1947. Not only was it over a decade old but it evinced a style, what Holland describes as "a relation between story and form of the most conventionally self-contained sort,"[30] that Blanchot was already in the process of surpassing.

What Holland leaves out of his account of the publication of these stories so long after their having been written is that, from the vantage point of *Après coup*, the interval between 1936 and 1947 had to have made the stories seem like a forlorn relic in an altogether different historical sense: I am, of course, referring to the devastation of the war. I mention this not to cast a stain on Holland's excellent account (it is of little relevance at this point of his analysis), but to place the dating of the stories squarely in the context of our focus on *Après coup*. It seems to me that the belated first publication of the stories generates the sense that, beyond any particular decision on Blanchot's part, "datedness" has to be seen as an essential aspect of their history, almost as if they were revenants coming from another world.

In any case, we have not yet reached the "last word" as regards the publishing history of these stories. Before their publication together with *Après coup*, the stories were then republished (with minor changes) together for the first time in 1951 under the title *Le Ressassement éternel*,[31] a volume that was again reprinted in facsimile in 1970. Finally thirteen years later, in 1983, *"Après coup" précédé par "Le Ressassement éternel"* appeared. As Holland contends, these two conventional stories, "however inert and self-contained in appearance," remain the single most reworked and continuously "rewritten" pieces of writing in Blanchot's entire oeuvre.[32] If the act of republication can indeed be conceived less straightforwardly than is usually the case; that is, if we can conceive it as a reflective act of rewriting or renarration, the issue immediately arises as to what status to accord the "postface" (as it is called in its English translation). Is it to be read as a "commentary on" that stands at a remove from the rewriting, or is it part of the putting-back-into-play of these texts?

A brief digression into the text's 1983 title suggests that Blanchot was doing something more complicated here too. While at one level the title *"Après coup" précédé par "Le Ressassement éternel"* confirms the compositional order of the text (that is, the postface comes after the 1951 *Le Ressassement éternel*), the sequence of the title actually reverses it, privileging the *after* over the *before*.[33] That is to say that the ordering of texts presents them in chronological order (1951; 1984) but that the title disrupts or destabilizes this ordering, turning *Le Ressassement éternel* into a sort of foreword for the "post-face" that follows. Furthermore, the title's emphasis on the 1983 *Après*

coup is such that the *après coup* reflection takes priority over the two
stories or at least renders the *récits* themselves secondary in importance to their uptake and replay in and as the preface to *Après coup*.
This repositioning opens up the possibility that *Après coup* is not
to be read simply as a detached and straightforwardly retrospective
commentary on a couple of fifty-year-old stories but as a central, if
not primary, aspect of their rewriting.[34] Though, that would be not
so much to say that *Après coup* is, like the narratives that "precede"
it, simply a fiction, as it is to say that the *ressassement éternel* of these
stories *from within* the space of *Après coup* provides Blanchot with
the opportunity to articulate a relation to history that is neither direct
nor, strictly speaking, chronological.[35] At the expense of a reflection
on the narratives themselves, then, it is to this aspect of *Après coup*
that the following pages will be devoted.

TIME LAPSE OR, BACK TO THE FUTURE

At the very core of *Après coup* is a concern with the relation between
writing and history. Rereading his early narratives, Blanchot considers them in relation to historical events—more precisely, to the event
of the Holocaust—that at least one of the narratives, "The Idyll," in
its evocation of a penitentiary workhouse with its "vast rows of show-
ers" and arduous yet pointless work-routines may be seen to parallel
in eerie ways, if not to predict outright. Though, the very first lines of
Après coup complicate its appointed task of retrospection.

In a gesture that will be familiar to readers of his other works (not
least, the first half of "Literature and the Right to Death"), Blanchot
first calls into question the project of reading retrospectively by problematizing the status of the writer as one who possesses authority over
his or her own work: "Prior to the work," he writes, "there is no artist—since it is the production that produces the producer. . . . But if
the written work produces and substantiates the writer, once created
it bears witness only to his dissolution, his disappearance, his defec-
tion and, to express it more brutally, his death. . . . Thus, before the
work, the writer does not exist; after the work, he is no longer there"
(*AC* 59–60). The author's time is quite literally impossible to measure, suspended as it is between the "not yet" and the "no longer" of
writing. Under these conditions, Blanchot is asking what authority
the writer can ultimately be granted to reflect on what he has written, when it is precisely his fate to be exiled from it. Both created and

destroyed by writing, the writer, it seems, is never there at the right time to reflect on what he has written, much less to reappropriate it or to explain it to others: "From the 'not yet' to the 'no longer'—this is the path of what we call the writer, not only his time, which is always suspended, but what brings him into existence through an interrupted becoming [*non seulement son temps toujours suspendu, mais ce qui le fait être par un devenir d'interruption*]" (AC 60/86).

No sooner has Blanchot situated the impossibility of retrospection in relation to the time, *toujours suspendu*, of writing than he recasts the crisis of self-recognition implied by it into terms that are more readily discernable. As if in response to a channeled request, he writes, "I have been asked—someone inside me has asked—to communicate with myself, as a way of introducing these two old stories, so old (nearly fifty years old) that . . . it is not possible for me to know who wrote them, how they were written, and to what unknown urgency they were responding" (*AC* 64). Indeed, retrospection is always made more difficult when called to a remote past. It was, simply, too long ago and the aging Blanchot (in his late seventies) complains of a failing memory. Though even as he reflects on how flawed his memory has become over the years, the greatest threat to understanding these old stories, he suggests, has little to do with the expanse of time separating him from their composition. Rather, throughout *Après coup* the act of retrospection will be persistently complicated, even impaired or blocked, by the future. "Nothing," writes Blanchot, "could have prepared me to write these innocent stories that resound with murderous signs of the future [*les présages meurtriers des temps futurs*]" (64/92).

The reflections in *Après coup* present the future in multiple ways but it certainly cannot be said that they ever culminate in a stable perspective. At once a prophetic tone internal to the stories in question and the force of a history *des temps futurs*, Blanchot reflects on the future as a dimension of time somehow in excess of itself. In his brief discussion of one of the stories, for instance, Blanchot suggests that perhaps it claims "to be a prophetic work, announcing to the past a future that is already there [*annonçant au passé un avenir déjà là*]" (*AC* 65/94). Against the totalizing gesture of the story, evinced by its temporal implosion of past and future, is set still another, far more deeply unretractable future: "Prophetic also," he writes, "but for me (today) in a way that is even more inexplicable, since I can only interpret it through events that took place and *were not known until much later*, in such a way that this later knowledge *does not illuminate but withdraws understanding from the narrative* [*de sorte que cette connaissance ultérieure n'éclaire pas, mais retire la compréhension au récit*]" (*AC* 65/94, emphasis added). That the historical future fails to offer a perspective from which Blanchot's early narratives can be comprehended is arguably as much a statement about the act of historical retrospection itself as it is about literature's relation to history. At one level, it is fairly obvious that any attempt to interpret the *récit* as "the reading of an already menacing future" (*AC* 67/96) is bound to end in an impasse. In this sense, Blanchot is resistant to its seeming convergence with history: "History," he writes, "does not control meaning [*L'histoire ne détient pas le sens*], any more than meaning, which is always ambiguous—plural—may be reduced to its historical realization, were this the most tragic and weightiest imaginable" (*AC* 67/96, translation modified).[36]

On the one hand, this statement is pointing more or less straightforwardly to the literary narratives' excess of meaning, one that cannot be reduced to whatever happens, before or after the fact, in history. On the other hand, however, given that the apparent task Blanchot has set himself is to consider these narratives in relation to history, could he not also be suggesting that there might be an excess of meaning right at the heart of history? As an instance of this excess, Blanchot's gesture of pointing to the violence done to meaning—"always ambiguous"—when it is reduced to its "historical realization" is itself an ambiguous statement: Is he referring solely to the meaning of the narratives in question or to meaning as such in relation to historical events? To rephrase the latter half of the question slightly: Might history not mean more than it realizes?

For try as he might, Blanchot seems nonetheless incapable of *not* thinking about it. "And yet," he writes in faltering prose, "difficult, after the fact, not to think about it [*Et pourtant, difficile, après coup, de n'y pas songer*]" (*AC* 66/95, translation modified). For Blanchot, it is both impossible to read the *récit* in terms of a history "to come" (it is ultimately "a story . . . which that death [in Auschwitz] cannot darken") and, it seems, impossible *not* to. In raising the issue of the problematic conflation of the two registers (that of literature with that of history), it seems unlikely that Blanchot is attempting to create a purely literary space cut off from history and immune to its effects (we will have more to say about this shortly). Rather, the impasse created by an attempt to resolve

the thoroughgoing uneasiness of their relation becomes the occasion
for a broader consideration of the difficulties involved in the task of
taking up history retrospectively.

In the lengthy passage cited above, the future imminent to the past,
described as "inexplicable," is of central importance to this questioning. Indeed, the passage abounds with time lapses as it multiplies the
moments at which the task of retrospection has failed to produce
understanding. From the perspective of 1983—that of "(today)"—
what does become clear is how preposterous it would be to grant the
young writer the powers of a clairvoyant. The literary narrative does
not constitute a prediction; it did not see the future coming. More
startling, though, is the contention made at a slight remove both from
the narratives themselves as well as from the aims of a straightforwardly retrospective understanding, that the future was not even
seen when it arrived; only later, "much later" Blanchot says, would
there be knowledge of these events. But even then—perhaps *especially*
then—the advantage of belatedness would still fail to generate a sense
of the past's necessary future.

Thus, all of these staggered moments of time-lapse—the "before"
of writing the narratives, the after of "what took place" whose knowledge would itself have to wait, and so on—prove insufficient to locate
the past's futurity, even that of "today." No amount of time, it seems,
will do. In the process of submitting his own literary production to
historical understanding, Blanchot remodels the *"après coup"* in such
a way that it bears little resemblance to the advantages of hindsight
that have come to be expected from such retrospective encounters.
The specificity of the future that Blanchot invokes—the singular
event that he refers to, simply, as "Auschwitz"—resides in its continual refusal to give itself to understanding.

Given the radical singularity of the text's articulation, one might
wonder what kinds of general insights it might afford. For the historical specificity of Blanchot's retrospective dilemma proves difficult to
generalize beyond his own example: Indeed, it hardly seems to have
any exemplary value at all. And yet it is precisely to its exemplarity
that Blanchot turns when, at the essay's conclusion and partially in
reference to his own narrative, he writes: "A narrative [*récit*] from
before Auschwitz. At whatever date it is written, every narrative [*tout
récit*] henceforth will be from before Auschwitz [*A quelque date qu'il
puisse être écrit, tout récit désormais sera d'avant Auschwitz*]" (*AC*
69, translation modified).

This last claim is strange and disconcerting, not least due to how its first phrase ("At whatever date") contends that time is of virtually no significance to it and then immediately supplements that contention with a seemingly clear temporal index, "from *before* Auschwitz." To this formulation (complex enough) is added *désormais*, a difficult word that means "in future," "henceforth" or "from now on" and that thus situates the claim as departing from today and stretching out into an indeterminate future, possibly into what Derrida has called a "permanent future."[37] With so many conflicting temporal and nontemporal registers intersecting in this statement, one feels as if the resources for sorting it out were lacking.

In a brief reading of these lines, Vivian Liska has argued that their aim is to shield or protect narrative from disaster. She writes: "In using the indefinite and shifting *désormais*, 'from now on,' he avoids actually inscribing the fissure caused by the event *into* literature, transporting it [that is, literature] instead 'backwards,' to the safe haven of the potentially 'idyllic' time 'before.'" In much the same vein, Geoffrey Hartman claims that in contrast to Adorno's statement about poetry after Auschwitz with which he seeks to "shield the Holocaust from profanation. . . ; Blanchot is concerned rather with defending art."[38] The suggestion shared by Hartman and Liska is that the *before* of Auschwitz constitutes an epoch or era untainted by disaster, a possibly innocent time into which the displacement of narrative will ensure its safeguarding. Equally clear is the extent to which, although Liska does note how Blanchot "disposes of chronological order," both of these readings reintroduce or presuppose for their analyses a conception of linear and objective chronological time, one wherein the *before* remains untainted and even untouched by the *after*.[39] However, is it not precisely this linear temporality that the passage is calling into question? Are the multiple temporal vectors of the passage not precisely that which is in need of explanation, constituting as they do its central enigma?

In the context of *Après coup*, "*d'avant Auschwitz*" signals something considerably other than, or considerably more than, the safe era of a historical "before." In addition to its straightforward understanding as a retrospective historical ascription, *d'avant Auschwitz* is also, at practically every level of Blanchot's text, bound to a sense of inexplicability, disquiet, and, indeed, danger: Although Blanchot can certainly be understood here as encouraging—to some extent— the notion that the Holocaust was "incomprehensible" it must, I think, also be read as the index of the nonexperience of *unfore-seeable imminence*. Would this not make the "idyllic past" even more uncanny and disturbing, not despite the fact that it is situated "before" but precisely because of it? For, the *before* is not so much configured as a past that is categorically and temporally distinct from that which will have come to pass as it is figured in danger-ous proximity to it. In other words, Blanchot does not seem to be suggesting that the *récits* are *not* touched by Auschwitz: They are, rather, *not yet* touched by it. From this perspective, might Blanchot's own tenacious theorizing the time of the *après coup* not itself be the enactment of a response to trauma?[40] For if, as Blanchot claims, all narratives will henceforth be "from before Auschwitz," what seems disconcertingly straightforward is that the "before Auschwitz"—the past, namely, that did not see the future coming—may lie in the future, in the unsettling and permanent possibility of its traumatic repetition.

§

Yet for all that, it is difficult to leave it there. Blanchot is explicitly involving himself here in a strangely damning assessment of the *récit*, strange not least because of how its impact is registered in a matter-of-fact tone solely as a function of time. An account, however pro-visional, is no doubt necessary. For, by making the *récit* a possible accomplice—without agent or act—to a certain kind of traumatic repetition, has he not resolved altogether too many of the tensions governing the relation between literature and history, playing rather too much the role of prophet?

In the essay "LIVING ON: Border Lines," Derrida has described the deeply ambivalent relation that Blanchot's oeuvre has to the genre of the *récit,* arguing that it is "a word that Blanchot has repeatedly insisted upon and contested, reclaimed and rejected, set down and (then) erased."[41] Lacoue-Labarthe has recently agreed with Derrida on this point, though he claims that Blanchot's relation to the genre is even more straightforward and categorical: "We know moreover," he writes, "that Blanchot explicitly, even solemnly denied or dismissed narrative as such."[42] Nonetheless, it remains difficult to know how to read the tenor of the claim in *Après coup*: Is it to be read as the final dismissal of the *récit* or its final blow (*coup*)? Is it a condemnation, a death sentence, a challenge, or an injunction?

There are doubtless other possibilities than the ones I have listed here. Though it is undoubtedly problematic that Blanchot himself declines to be more specific regarding any relevant differentiations at stake in his use of the term (*récit* designates virtually any kind of narrative), nonetheless an answer can be prepared by returning to the question of literature and in particular to its beginning, which for Blanchot consists in its own self-questioning. The forms of the *récit* to which he explicitly refers in *Après coup*—the *récit-fiction* for which *Sophie's Choice* is the referent (AC 98)[43]; the *récit* as *l'histoire* that, as we have seen, "does not control meaning"—all point toward a sense of the *récit* that is characterized by a marked resistance to self-questioning. They are, rather, *récits* that quite possibly embody the pretense of having, or indeed of being, the answer.

In this respect, could one not argue that *Après coup*, that is to say *this* text itself, puts back into play aspects of this questioning in order to bring it to bear on an impossible retrospective account of history? If it is possible to conceive Blanchot actively presenting the past as traumatic, it would thus be to expose a dimension of the future imminent in traumatic occurrence, one for which a narrative structure of recuperation, recovery or closure could never provide an account: its irrecuperable dimension of shock, surprise, or of a radical break in expectation. For Blanchot, there is no narrative or temporal logic—no logic at all—that can sustain the passage from the "before" of Auschwitz to its occurrence, much less to its relative position on an historical continuum.[44]

While Blanchot certainly shared in the political injunction of "Do not forget," he squarely rejected the notion that any mode of knowledge or representation could deliver a future severed from it. In the passages we have been reading, the sense is rather that narratives presenting themselves as a curative response to the ruptures and wounds of historical trauma are to some degree complicit with traumatic repetition if only because the latter's imminent futurity—its shock, discontinuity, rupture, and interruption—must, of necessity, disappear from those responses. That trauma may always interrupt claims made by narrative to have finally put it to rest, in the form of its own shocking reemergence: This, for Blanchot, constitutes the indiscernible condition of all political futures as well as it constitutes all modes of responsibility vis-à-vis the past, from now on.

In the extremity of these formulations, Blanchot contends not only that narrative does *not* do justice to the traumatic past but more specifically, that it fails at that task because narrative flattens out its time and ultimately effaces the dimension of futurity implicit to trauma that cannot possibly be squared with the punctuality of a narration. Geoffrey Hartman has recently described Blanchotian time in terms that emphasize its lack of punctuation: "Time loses its potentially redemptive aspect; it is not a present extended between meaningful beginning and meaningful end, or a history of disasters in whose aftermath we live, and which gives us importance by that fact. We glimpse a state without such forcible punctuation, and so without the possibility of a *récit*."[45] The indictment of narrative that we witness in *Après coup* is, I think, inseparable from the sense in which it tends to spare its readers from being exposed to the futurity of the threat permanently posed by trauma. For its retrospective structure must, of necessity, presuppose that the threat itself is passé, that it has been overcome.

For Blanchot this is no small matter, since it neutralizes the political dimension of the past. What Leslie Hill has pointed out, that for Blanchot "it is the future—a future without present or presence—that is the only properly political dimension,"[46] holds equally true for the past as it does for the present. Leveling down the time of traumatic occurrence to a historical moment, narrative would also substitute for the void or interval, which Blanchot is intent on keeping open, a teleological fiction that would subject to an occlusion the very opening of history to itself as an experience of the future. Or, to put it slightly differently, it would efface the dimension of shock, surprise, and blow (*coup*) by turning all accidents into chronological necessities, *après coup*. Even those narratives that, for the most well-intentioned reasons, seek to put an end to traumatic histories by relegating them to the past can only do so by effacing the very dimension of futurity that is most unique to traumatic historicity, and indeed, to the very possibility of historicity itself. If the *récit-fiction* bears the brunt of Blanchot's criticism here, it is because what is in question is a future that no narrative of its kind could ever represent, let alone see coming, but for which narratives "at whatever date they were written" will nonetheless bear some responsibility, *après coup*.

Admittedly the perspective, if we can even call it that, offered by *Après coup*—Blanchot calls it "this perspective (this non-perspective)" (69)—is a dim one, generated as it is on the grounds of a *retro-perspective* whose only continuity between past and present is inseparable from the gap or interval separating them. Nonetheless,

Blanchot's deep reservations about an ethos of narrative representation that seeks to efface this gap do not amount to a withdrawal from
political exigencies nor do they mean an abandonment of the obligation to bear historical witness. In fact, Blanchot's aporetic ethics of
memory are inseparable from his refusal of the impulse to seek closure. For what in *Après coup* is articulated as *disjunction* implies, at
other points, an *injunction*, an injunction to mourning as a mode of
vigilance that, because it neither produces knowledge nor relies upon
it, is incessant: "In the work of mourning, it is not grief that works:
grief keeps watch."[47]

On this point, Blanchot himself would become increasingly insistent. In "Do Not Forget," a letter written in 1988 to Salomon Malka,
Blanchot makes a claim as if in response to a voice incanted from
the outside: "Must it be repeated (yes, it must) that Auschwitz, an
event which endlessly interpellates us, imposes, through testimony,
the imprescriptable duty not to forget: remember, beware of forgetfulness and yet, in that faithful memory, *never will you know*."[48] This
injunction had appeared some years earlier in the following form:
"And how, in fact, can one accept not to know? We read books on
Auschwitz. The wish of all, in the camps the last wish: know what has
happened, do not forget, and at the same time never will you know."[49]
In underscoring that we "read books on Auschwitz," Blanchot suggests that documentation and historical reference are needed. But
at the same time, he also suggests that there is a limit to historical
knowledge. Attending to the limits of historical understanding does
not, however, mean putting a term to memory. Rather, for Blanchot,
those limits of what we can know constitute memory as an obligation
without limit: "Keep watch over absent meaning." In thus reciting the
oft-repeated formula of post-Holocaust ethics, "Do not forget," he
also translates it into an infinitely more difficult task.[50]

Après coup supplements the injunction to "know without knowing": With the suggestion that the futurity of the disaster's occurrence
irreducibly belongs to this nonknowledge, Blanchot also contends
that this futurity is one that will never answer to expectations, much
less conform to them, even after the fact. In this regard, the disquieting vacillation that takes place on the pages of *Après coup* can itself
be understood as a *ressassement éternel*, within which it is not just
the meaning of the words that is transmitted but a two-fold performance: that of a caesura within the retrospective subject and simultaneously, that of an enjoinder to displace the claims of historical

narrative to have safely recuperated the past, to bear witness—impossibly—to that which escapes historical presentation precisely because it lies in the interstices of history presented *as* linear narrative.

The ways in which Blanchot's postwar and post-*récit* writings attest to his vigilance over the "absent meaning" of disaster has been thoroughly attested, contested, and, at times, detested.[51] No doubt it will continue to be. All that needs to be stressed here is that Blanchot's notion of futurity does not involve a deferred present on the order of a "horizon of expectation," the contingency of which will always turn into a necessity as it passes into a meaningful past. Rather, Blanchot's understanding of the future is inseparable from its contingency in the past—namely, from the inability to have seen it coming. In this sense, his project in *Après coup* is aimed at interrupting the time of the assured orders of retrospective presentation, narrative, and history so that this aspect of the past's future remain, if not meaningful, then at least jarring to signification. To his readers who might see this project as pessimistic, despairing and groundless, there is perhaps no ultimate rejoinder except by pointing out that, for Blanchot, in no way was it to constitute an alibi for entrusting ourselves to failure (which would, in any case, involve a rigid set of expectations) or for abdicating on the need to make decisions. On the one hand, decision-making is itself dependent upon the ordeal of undecidability that is its condition of possibility. On the other hand, a nonredemptive account of memory open to—indeed grounded in—what it cannot possibly capture might be sufficient to open up the present or rather, to pose it as a question.

§

That the fact of the concentration camps, the extermination of the Jews and the death camps where death continued its work, are for history an absolute that interrupted history, this one *must* say, without, however, being able to say anything else.

—Maurice Blanchot

In quite a different sense, it is also worth pointing out that from somewhere beyond the end of *Après coup* (the text proper abruptly comes to a close with the word *Auschwitz*), without being able to say anything else, Blanchot nonetheless adds a further remark. Another step is taken, that is, a step (not) beyond.[52] The supplementary remark extends the text beyond the point of its having something to say. Just one more thing, Blanchot seems to be saying. Is this remark to be considered as a prolongation of the end or its interruption? Whatever the textual status of the remark that follows, in it Blanchot makes a complex invocation of hope, complicated not least because it is a hope that he nonetheless feels himself unjustified to possess: "I cannot hope for 'The Idyll' or 'The Last Word' to be read from this perspective (this non-perspective). And yet death without words [*la mort sans phrases*] remains something to be thought about—perhaps endlessly, to the very end. 'A voice comes from the other shore. A voice interrupts the saying of what has already been said' (Emmanuel Levinas)" (*AC* 100). If reading from this (non)perspective is ultimately a task that Blanchot cannot hope to ask of his readers, there is nonetheless an invocation made by a voice at the very periphery of this postscript, an other voice that is interruption itself. From within that very interruption of the text's end, then, interrupting Blanchot, interrupting the end's punctuality, a voice coming from "the other shore" is still audible, still within reach. A voice, in other words, interrupts "what has already been said" about *la mort sans phrases* of "Auschwitz" with an invitation to listen.

NOTES

INTRODUCTION

1. G. W. F. Hegel, preface to the 2nd ed., *Hegel's Science of Logic*, trans. A. V. Miller (Amherst: Humanity Books, 1969), 40.

2. G. W. F. Hegel, *Hegel's Phenomenology of Spirit*, trans. A. V. Miller (Oxford: Oxford University Press: 1977), 10.

3. On the growth, both in number and size, of testimonial archive projects since the 1980s, see Geoffrey Hartman, "The Ethics of Witness," in *Lost in the Archives*, ed. Rebecca Comay (Toronto: Alphabet City, 2002). Alongside the establishment of archives, the innumerable films that have appeared in recent years, as well as the literally thousands of works of fiction, philosophy, religious studies, critical theory, aesthetics, and neurobiology devoted to the topic of memory and the increased attendance at museum exhibits that openly engage the ethics and politics of memory, all bear witness to the unprecedented degree with which memory has entered public discourse (indeed so much so that a massive encyclopedic glossary of "memory terminology" has appeared in German. See Nicolas Pethes and Jean Ruchatz, eds., *Gedächtnis und Erinnerung: Ein interdisziplinäres Lexikon* [Hamburg: Rowohlts Taschenbuch, 2001]).

4. Jan Assmann, *Das kulturelle Gedächtnis* (Munich: Beck, 1999), 11, my translation.

5. For an early formulation of the role played by memories of defeat and suffering in the constitution of national unity, see Ernst Renan's lecture "Qu'est-ce qu'une nation?," delivered in 1882 at the Sorbonne; published in English as *What Is a Nation?*, trans. Wanda Romer Taylor (Toronto: Tapir Press, 1996).

6. Jean-Luc Nancy, *Being Singular Plural*, trans. Robert D. Richardson and Anne E. O'Byrne (Stanford, Calif.: Stanford University Press, 2000).

7. David Rieff, *Slaughterhouse: Bosnia and the Failure of the West* (New York: Simon & Schuster, 1995), 26ff.

8. Pierre Nora, "Between History and Memory: Les Lieux de Mémoire," in *Memory and Counter-Memory*, special issue of *Representations*, no. 26 (Spring 1989): 7–24.

1. NARRATIVE LIFE SPAN, IN THE WAKE

1. Jacques Derrida, *Mémoires for Paul de Man*, trans. Cecile Lindsay et al. (New York: Columbia University Press, 1989), 3. Further references will be given in the text as *MdM* followed by page number.

2. Plato, *Theaetetus*, in *The Collected Dialogues of Plato*, ed. Edith Hamilton and Huntington Cairns, trans. Hugh Tredennick (New York: Pantheon Books, 1961), 191d.

3. Plato, *Phaedo*, in *The Collected Dialogues of Plato*, ed. Edith Hamilton and Huntington Cairns (New York: Pantheon Books, 1966), 61b.Further references will be given in the text as *Ph* followed by page number.

4. Walter Benjamin, "The Storyteller," in *Illuminations*, ed. Hannah Arendt, trans. Harry Zohn (New York: Schocken Books, 1968), 83–110, here 97; in German: "Der Erzähler. Betrachtung zum Werk Nikolai Lesskows," in Benjamin, *Allegorien kultureller Erfahrung*, ed. Sebastian Kleinschmidt (Leipzig: Reclam, 1984), 380–406. Further references will be given in the text as ST followed by page number.

5. Walter Benjamin, "Theses on the Philosophy of History," in *Illuminations*, 257. Further references will be given in the text as TPH followed by page number. A newer translation of this essay ("Über den Begriff der Geschichte") as "Theses on the Concept of History" brings out the title's resonance with Arendt's "The Concept of History." See *Walter Benjamin: Selected Writings, Volume 4, 1938–1940*, ed. Howard Eiland and Michael W. Jennings (Cambridge, Mass.: Harvard University Press, 2003).

6. Hannah Arendt, "The Concept of History," in *Between Past and Future: Eight Exercises in Political Thought* (New York: Penguin, 1968), 41–90, here: 67–68. Further references will be given in the text as *BPF* followed by page number.

7. Jacques Le Goff, *History and Memory*, trans. Steven Rendall and Elizabeth Claman (New York: Columbia University Press, 1992), xii. Further references will be given in the text as *HM* followed by page number. Although it is certainly true that our own historical moment can hardly be said to be under the exclusive sway of historicist notions of progress and perfectibility, Dipesh Chakrabarty has recently warned against overly hasty pronouncements of the end of historicism. Chakrabarty points out that in fact, a great deal of contemporary historical writing remains deeply historicist and that even when historicism as such is rejected as an outdated mode of historiography, its notion of linear historical time continues to dominate historical writing, often to the point of foreclosing consideration of other temporal configurations. See Dipesh Chakrabarty, *Provincializing Europe: Postcolonial Thought and Historical Difference* (Princeton, N.J.: Princeton University Press, 2000), 22–23, 73.

8. Roland Barthes, "Le discours de l'histoire," cited in Le Goff, *History and Memory*, 119. Michel de Certeau makes a similar point in *The Writing of History* regarding the referential function of language—namely, that it has the ability to "introduce into the text an effect of reality." Michel de Certeau, *The Writing of History*, trans. Tom Conley (New York: Columbia University Press, 1988), 94.

9. For instance, when Le Goff addresses the account given by linguistics of the culturally determined modalities of past-present-future, he draws attention to how "language [expresses] temporal relations." This leads him to consider the insights of linguists who "insist on the construction of time in language, which goes far beyond the verb and concerns vocabulary, the sentence, and style. This leads some to refer to a 'chronogenesis.'" Le Goff, *History and Memory*, 4–5.

10. Le Goff, *History and Memory*, 108, 135ff.

11. Paul Ricoeur, *Time and Narrative*, vol. 1, trans. Kathleen McLaughlin and David Pellauer (Chicago: University of Chicago Press, 1984), 3. Further references will be given in the text as *TN* followed by page number.

12. The same point is made in *The Human Condition*, 44ff.

13. For a penetrating reflection on death as "border," see Derrida's *Aporias*, trans. Thomas Dutoit (Stanford, Calif.: Stanford University Press, 1993), especially the first section, "*Finis*," 1–42.

14. This point is also made by Julia Kristeva in *Hannah Arendt: Life Is a Narrative*, trans. Frank Collins (Toronto: University of Toronto Press, 2001), esp. Chapters 1 and 2.

15. Arendt, *Human Condition*, 10.

16. Aristotle, *Poetics*, ed. Frank L. Lucas (Oxford: Oxford University Press, 1968), 50b26. Further references will be given in the text as *P* followed by page number.

17. Although the explicit focus of *Time and Narrative* is not the theme of memory (as Ricoeur will later say in *La Mémoire, l'histoire, l'oubli*), it is nonetheless surprising that Ricoeur does not mention Arendt's work in the course of his treatment of historical discourse and narrative time, especially considering that he had written a preface to the reissue of the French translation of *The Human Condition* in 1983 (the same year in which *Time and Narrative* first appeared).

18. To be sure, there is more at stake for Arendt's political theory than a formal or structural analogy between politics, the memory of politics, and the condition of finitude. In both *The Human Condition* and *On Revolution*, she insists on birth and natality as the central categories of political thought, on the basis that political action would be unnecessary if humans were not born but were simply carbon copies of the same model. Biological natality, then, "the constant influx of newcomers" (a term she also fondly used in reference to her students), constitutes for Arendt the condition for the possibility of new beginnings, one implicit to all political action. The formulation remains squarely within a humanist paradigm: "The new beginning in birth can make itself felt in the world only because the newcomer possesses the capacity of beginning something anew, that is, of acting" (Arendt, *The Human Condition*, 11. See also *On Revolution* [London: Penguin Books, 1965], 42, 210–11).

19. In these sections, Arendt is more interested in the similarities between classical historiography and poetry than in their differences. In this respect, her analysis differs from Aristotle's—and is perhaps a kind of implicit quarrel with him over the claim that poetry has nothing to do with time—who

differentiated between the two on the basis that poetry teaches the universal and history is concerned with particulars. In drawing out the affinities between ancient Greek poetry and history, though, Arendt is making good on what is seldom recognized in readings of Aristotle's appraisal—namely, that history and poetry contend with each other precisely because each of them claims the transmission of the past as its own task.

20. This interpretation of Ulysses's weeping is informed by Rei Terada's work on emotion in *Feeling in Theory: Emotion after the "Death of the Subject"* (Cambridge, Mass.: Harvard University Press, 2001). Contrary to how emotion is conventionally understood to be the expression of a unified subject, Terada sees it as a kind of differential force, between subjective ideality and the external world, appearing in experience. Regarding the particular episode in *The Odyssey*, see Peter Bürger's brief but helpful essay, "Die Tränen des Odysseus," in *Die Tränen des Odysseus* (Frankfurt am Main: Suhrkamp, 1993), 7–11. See also Werner Hamacher's "History, Teary—Remarques on Valéry's *La Jeune Parque*," in *Phantom Proxies*, special issue of *Yale French Studies* 74 (1988): 67–94, for a penetrating analysis of the tears (*larmes*) in Valéry's *La Jeune Parque* as an unassimilable trace of self-division and as the tear in history between occurrence and object of cognition or knowledge (see esp. 81ff.)

21. Plato, *Symposium*, in *The Collected Dialogues of Plato*, ed. Edith Hamilton and Huntington Cairns (New York: Random House, 1961), 209b–c. Further references will be given in the text as S followed by page number.

22. Le Goff has commented on this "removal of Memory from the temporal realm" in terms of the radical separation that it inaugurates between history and memory: "When [memory] is put in the service of eschatology," he writes, "it also nourishes itself on a veritable hatred for history" (65).

23. Julia Kristeva has recently shown the degree to which Arendt's conception of human corporeality participates in this dualist legacy. Insofar as Arendt's thought locates what is properly human in *bios*, its "form of life," it is opposed to the undifferentiated *zoe* that humans share with animal and vegetative life and that concerns labor, biology, and the mute survival of the species. In her privileging of *bios* over *zoe*, Arendt expresses her denigration of the latter by bringing it into association with incommunicability, suffering, isolation, and the dumb repetitive labor of survival. As Kristeva argues, "the body presents itself as a major target of that tearing away from the *zoe*, if not as sworn enemy—the principal paradigm of alienation" (63). For an examination of how various artists of the post-Communist period challenge the Arendtian sense of unredeemable labor, see Charity Scribner's *Requiem for Communism* (Cambridge, Mass.: MIT Press, 2003). Coming to Arendt's (partial) defense, though, one could argue that her analysis offers some of the most compelling—if disputed—terms within which to articulate the political crises of modernity and that as such, her work opens up ways to situate some of the memorial dilemmas implicit to the crises to which modernity has given rise. Arendt's conceptions of memory and human life, beyond any particular bias on her part, are meticulous in how they clarify the problems associated with mourning Communism, in light of both the cynical brutality

with which labor was instrumentalized in the twentieth century and how the repetitive and monotonous structures that it put into place make it peculiarly resistant to memorial expression. A forceful examination of modernity's processes of de-humanization that takes Arendt's work as one of its points of departure is Giorgio Agamben's *Homo Sacer: Sovereign Power and Bare Life*, trans. Daniel Heller-Roazen (Stanford, Calif.: Stanford University Press, 1998).

24. Doubtless, it is this denigration that made Arendt resistant to the idea that her work be categorized as "political philosophy." In the 1964 Gaus-Arendt interview, for instance, she begins by taking issue with Gaus's characterization of her as a philosopher, on the grounds that philosophy has never been concerned with politics as such—see *The Portable Hannah Arendt*, ed. Peter Baehr (London: Penguin Books, 2004). For a theoretical development of this argument, see Arendt's posthumously published *Lectures on Kant's Political Philosophy*, ed. Ronald Beiner (Chicago: University of Chicago Press, 1982), in particular the "Fourth Session" (22ff.).

25. This substitution of loss for pure gain is consistent with the very means of Socrates's death: by poison (in the Greek, *pharmakon*). Given that the hemlock is presented to Socrates throughout the *Phaedo* as a *pharmakon*, the undecidability of its meaning as both "poison" and "remedy," to which Derrida has drawn attention, has important implications for the argument as a whole. Derrida writes that the poison "is transformed through the effects of the Socratic logos and of the philosophical demonstration in the *Phaedo* into a means of deliverance, a way toward salvation, a cathartic power. The hemlock has an ontological effect: it initiates one into the contemplation of the eidos and the immortality of the soul. *That is how Socrates takes it*" (Derrida, "Plato's Pharmakon," *Disseminations*, trans. Barbara Johnson [Chicago: University of Chicago Press, 1981], 126–27).

26. We will return to this issue of childhood amnesia in Chapter 2.

27. In *The Human Condition*, Arendt effects the contrast between these two competing forms of memory in her historical account of the relation between the *vita activa* and the *vita contemplativa*. For the Greeks, the *vita activa* was, first and foremost, political life, the life of action that owes its existence solely to the human condition of plurality. "Action, in so far as it engages in founding and preserving political bodies, creates the condition for remembrance, that is, for history," Arendt argues, a condition that allows men to obviate their own individual mortality. According to the hierarchy subsequently established by what Arendt calls the "philosophical *apolitia*" of late antiquity, the *vita contemplativa* began to be valued over all forms of human activity as the only truly free way of life, free not only from labor and work but also from political life (the Greek word for which—*skholē*—bears close ties to *askholia* or "unquiet"). The primacy of contemplation over activity rests on the conviction that no human activity, however lasting, can equal the unchanging eternity of the *kosmos*, itself unspeakable and unapproachable through human activity: "It is decisive," Arendt argues, "that the experience of the eternal has no correspondence with and cannot be transformed into any activity whatsoever" (Arendt, *Human Condition*, 20).

28. This description occurs in the context of Hegel's analysis of painting and in particular the question of how suitable painting is for the portrayal of Christ. *Hegel's Aesthetics: Lectures on Fine Art*, vol. 2, trans. T. M. Knox (Oxford: Oxford University Press, 1972), 822.

29. Catherine Malabou, *The Future of Hegel: Plasticity, Temporality and Dialectic*, trans. Lisabeth During (London: Routledge, 2005), 108. Further references will be given in the text as *FH* followed by page number.

30. In a journal entry from May 1954, Arendt articulates the Greek and Christian worldviews in terms of the relations each establishes between man and world: "Im Altertum ist der Mensch vergänglich; im Christentum ist die Welt, aber nicht der Mensch, vergänglich. Jeder christliche Tod ist eine Art Weltuntergang; jeder klassische Tod ist eine Art Gemordetwerden" (*Denktagebuch* [Munich: Piper, 2002], May 1954 (7): 482).

31. Werner Hamacher has addressed this issue of Christianity's withdrawal from politics and has pointed out that Christianity's claim to universality was the end result of the gradually widening distinction between the political community and the community of faith. He argues that Christianity's doctrinal *dis*interest in politics was the condition upon which its claim to universality could be made, a claim which would eventually lead to its expression in politics—what Hamacher calls "a particular kind of politicity"—as democracy's universal equality of individuals. See Werner Hamacher, "The Right to Have Rights (Four-and-a-Half Remarks)," in *And Justice for All? The Claims of Human Rights*, ed. Ian Balfour and Eduardo Cadava, special issue of *The South Atlantic Quarterly* 103, no. 2/3 (Spring/Summer 2004): 343–56. The insight that modern democracy is the structural heir to Christianity's universal equality of individuals has important consequences for how we understand memory today in relation to politics. In particular, it can help to clarify the often confusing assertion that an inherent affinity exists between them. From a certain perspective, of course, there is a degree of truth to the claim of an affinity if, by politics, we are referring to democracy's politicized version of the Christian claim to immortalization on the basis of the universal equality of individuals. While it is no doubt the case that democracy's claim to universal equality forms the basic condition of receptivity upon which memorial claims can be submitted to contestation and open scrutiny, the result is often that those claims to memory are read through the ciphers of individualism or subjectivism, both of which can sometimes work to de-politicize the intervention (especially since memory is so often structured by figures of collectivism that, by virtue of their attention to particularity, are often marginalized within a democracy, like those of ethnicity, nation, gender, linguistic belonging, etc.). That is not to say that memory is simply apolitical; rather, by accounting for the remnants of an apolitical Christian tenor in the ways that memory is made audible in a democracy, I am attempting to understand where memory's political potential might reside. In fact, recent developments of studies in collective memory—those taking place under the rubric of trauma theory, theories of witnessing, law and memory, and so on—are in the process of submitting the subjectivist or individualist notion of memory to rigorous questioning

in order to gauge other ways of thinking about its political and ethical potential. See, among others, Cathy Caruth, ed., *Trauma: Explorations in Memory* (Baltimore, Md.: Johns Hopkins University Press, 1995); Caruth, *Unclaimed Experience: Trauma, Narrative and History* (Baltimore, Md.: Johns Hopkins University Press, 1996); Dominick LaCapra, *Representing the Holocaust: History, Theory, Trauma* (Ithaca, N.Y.: Cornell University Press, 1996); LaCapra, *History and Memory after Auschwitz* (Ithaca, N.Y.: Cornell University Press, 1998), LaCapra, *Writing History, Writing Trauma* (Baltimore, Md.: Johns Hopkins University Press, 2000); and Kai Erikson, *A New Species of Trouble: The Human Experience of Modern Disasters* (New York: Norton, 1995).

32. In *The Hour of Our Death*, trans. Helen Weaver (Oxford: Oxford University Press, 1991), Philippe Ariès devotes the book's final section to "Death Denied," a phenomenon that he sees as unique in the history of death and specific to industrialized, urbanized, and politically secular areas of the West. Ariès articulates the central hypothesis of the section—that, blatantly, "society has banished death"—in terms that highlight its temporal implications: "There is no way of knowing that something has happened: the . . . hearse has become indistinguishable from the flow of traffic. Society no longer observes a pause; the disappearance of an individual no longer affects its continuity" (560). Despite the difficulties of Ariès's text in terms of its historicization and delimitation of the phenomenon of death—just how delineable can death be, asks Derrida, when it is delineation itself?—its suggestion that the temporality of mourning is disruptive of sequential continuous time is an interesting one. For Derrida's reading of Ariès's text, see *Aporias*, trans. Thomas Dutoit (Stanford, Cal.: Stanford University Press, 1993), 43ff.

33. Michel de Certeau, *The Writing of History*, trans. Tom Conley (New York: Columbia University Press, 1988), 4.

34. "The Storyteller" first appeared in German in 1936 and was translated into English in 1968 for the volume *Illuminations*, the first collection of Benjamin's work to appear in English, which Arendt both edited and introduced. Although Arendt worked on the *Illuminations* volume several years after writing *Between Past and Future* and *The Human Condition*, it is highly likely that she was familiar with the essay when she was developing her own formulations on memory, time, and narrative. Benjamin and Arendt were acquainted in Berlin and became friends during their exile years in Paris; Arendt was certainly in attendance when Benjamin lectured there. It is puzzling, to say the least, that Benjamin's essay is never explicitly mentioned by Arendt, either in her introductory essay to *Illuminations* or, to my knowledge, in any of her other works (including "The Concept of History," where its relevance is most evident). The most one can say, then, is that whatever influence it had on her own thinking about narrative and memory was indirect or of a deeply complex nature. For an account of their friendship, as well as of the publishing endeavors she undertook in the United States to honor it, see Elizabeth Young-Bruehl, *Hannah Arendt: For Love of the World*, 2nd ed. (New Haven, Conn.: Yale University Press, 2004), esp. 157–68. See also

Shoshana Felman's *The Juridical Unconscious: Trials and Traumas in the Twentieth Century* (Cambridge, Mass.: Harvard University Press, 2002), 131–66, for an examination of Arendt's *Eichmann in Jerusalem* (London: Penguin Books, 1994), both in terms of how it defends legal testimony as a narrative means by which to contain historical trauma as well as how its stylistic aspects are governed by insistent and complex references to "The Storyteller": ones which constitute a subtext of unmourned loss—a story, in short, that Arendt cannot tell.

35. To be sure, the threshold or rupture here is historical (Benjamin does implicitly "date" it at 1918) but not in the sense that would allow it to be taken up on a temporal continuum. In fact, the essay's first indication of a more complex perspective on history is its resistance to the conventional understanding of dating as part of the process by which history becomes recuperated in narrative. See Shoshana Felman's reading of this passage and its strategy of dating in *The Juridical Unconscious,* 26ff. See too Giorgio Agamben's brief description of this passage in terms of how it marks out the difficult—because constantly shifting—historical threshold of modernity in *Infancy and History: An Essay on the Destruction of Experience*, trans. Liz Heron (London: Verso Books, 1993), 13.

36. Benjamin, "On Some Motifs in Baudelaire," in Benjamin, *Illuminations*, 155–200, here 157.

37. Ibid.,163. Not only does *Erlebnis* resist narration; it also resists translation. Zohn prudently avoids translating both *Erlebnis* and *Erfahrung* as "experience" (or translating *Erlebnis* as "lived experience," which simply obscures the difference between them) and instead emphasizes how an *Erlebnis* remains fixed to the moment in which it was lived.

38. Benjamin's early essay on language, "On Language as Such and the Language of Man," denounces as "bourgeois" the notion that language is primarily communication. As Ian Balfour notes, however, the category of bourgeois is not at all circumscribed within the historical, social, or political conditions of modernity; in fact, Benjamin locates the provenance of this conception of language in the Garden of Eden, where the seducing serpent promises Adam and Eve the knowledge of good and evil. See Walter Benjamin, "On Language as Such and the Language of Man," in *Reflections*, ed. Peter Demetz, trans. Edmund Jephcott (New York: Schocken Books, 1978), 314–32 and Ian Balfour, *The Rhetoric of Romantic Prophecy* (Stanford, Calif.: Stanford University Press, 2003), 6–12.

39. Benjamin's use of *Augenblick* in this context is far from Heidegger's deployment of the term. Here, the term is being used to generate a sense of how the hegemony of information's mode of language stands to normalize temporal fracture: when information dominates, time is constituted as a conglomeration of unrelated, random, and disconnected moments, the time in which the event or occurrence happens in "real time," instantly passing into oblivion. Not only does the time of information preclude the possibility of narrated experience (*Erfahrung*), the normalization of its temporal fracture also stands to neutralize the disruptive force of any singular instant. This latter brings us closer to Heidegger's interpretation of

Augenblick, which possesses an epiphanic quality: it is the force of a singular moment that suspends linear time. See Heidegger, *Being and Time*, trans. Joan Stambaugh (Albany: State University of New York Press, 1996), especially Section 6.

40. For a reading of Hegel's sign and how it functions in relation to symbolic art, see the analysis in Chapter 3.

41. G. W. F. Hegel, *Enzyklopädie der philosophischen Wissenschaften 3*, vol. 10 of *G. W. F. Hegel Werke in 20 Bänden mit Registerband* (Frankfurt am Main: Suhrkamp Verlag, 1986), §458. See Derrida's powerful reading of Hegel's semiology in "The Pit and the Pyramid," in *Margins of Philosophy*, trans. Alan Bass (Chicago: University of Chicago, 1982), 69–108.

42. One of the very few stories that Benjamin actually cites in the essay (and the only other one to be singled out as "exemplary" or *exemplarisch*) strengthens the suggestion that the essay metonymically links its own critique of language to Hegel's semiotics of memory. Invoking virtually the same complement to the pyramid as Hegel had done, Benjamin cites a story, "Unexpected Reunion" ("Unverhofftes Wiedersehen"), in which a miner dies in a mining accident. The miner's body remains interred in the mining shaft where, inadvertently, it is embalmed in industrial chemicals. Since his body has been spared the processes of decay and decomposition, his bride is easily able to recognize him many, many decades later. Both the story proper and Benjamin's citation of it are incredibly rich; we will not go into detail here, except to remark on one feature that is of special interest for us. A central point of both the story and of Benjamin's evocation of it is that the past is not purely or simply past (as it would be, say, for the practitioner of historicism, who thinks of the past in terms of "how it really was"), but is rather marked as an unexpected and surprise moment of recognition that occurs between the present and the past. I will subsequently develop this idea that Benjamin sees a "memory of the present" in this coupling of history with the kind of futurity implied by surprise.

43. "Preface," *Between Past and Future: Eight Exercises in Political Thought* (New York: Penguin, 1968), 6.

44. For an exploration of narrative teleology that bears comparison with the one being developed here, see Sartre's *Nausea* for Roquentin's landmark analysis (*Nausea*, trans. Lloyd Alexander [New York: New Directions, 1964], 39–40).

45. On the relation between "to come" (*à venir*) and futurity (*avenir*) see, among other of his writings, the *Passages* interview with Jacques Derrida ("The Deconstruction of Actuality," reprinted in *Negotiations: Interventions and Interviews, 1971–2001*, ed. and trans. Elizabeth Rottenberg [Stanford, Calif.: Stanford University Press, 2002], 85–117).

2. MEMORY IN THEORY

1. John Locke, *The Second Treatise of Government*, ed. C. B. Macpherson (Indianapolis, Ind.: Hackett, 1980), §14. Further references will be given in the text as *STG*, followed by paragraph number.

2. Jean-Jacques Rousseau, "Discourse on the Origin of Inequality," in *The Basic Political Writings*, trans. Donald A. Cress, introduction by Peter Gay (Indianapolis, Ind.: Hackett, 1987), 38–39.

3. Neal Wood, *The Politics of Locke's Philosophy* (Berkeley: University of California Press, 1983), 1.

4. Nicholas Jolley, *Leibniz and Locke: A Study of the New Essays on Human Understanding* (Oxford: Oxford University Press, 1984), 125, 128. Charles Taylor's discussion of what he calls "Locke's Punctual Self" in *The Sources of the Self* also draws attention to the continuing influence that Locke has on understandings of the self: "Locke's tremendous influence, not only in the eighteenth century, but right through to today . . . helps to understand why we think of ourselves as 'selves' today" (*Sources of the Self* [Cambridge, Mass.: Harvard University Press, 1989], 174ff). To which I would add: Locke not only helps us to understand *why* we think of ourselves as "selves," but he could also help us understand *how* we derive the construct of the self in the first place.

5. Hans Aarsleff, *From Locke to Saussure: Essays on the Study of Language and Intellectual History* (Minneapolis: University of Minnesota Press, 1982), 43

6. John Locke, *An Essay Concerning Human Understanding*, ed. John W. Yolton (London: Everyman's Library, 1961), Book 2, Chapter 27, Section 9. All further references to the text will be cited as *Essay*, and given by book number, chapter, and section following the citation. In using this version of Locke's text, I am following Hans Aarsleff, who points out that it is based on the 1706 edition, the last to receive Locke's own revisions (Aarsleff, *From Locke to Saussure* 69).

7. In attending more to the dynamics internal to the argument and less explicitly to the historical context in which Locke composed his treatise, my intention is not to deny the importance of the historical context in which it was written. Exhaustive analysis of these conditions has been undertaken, for example, in Wood, *Politics of Locke's Philosophy*. Rather, what I am attempting to recognize is a more complex sense of its historicity, one which moves beyond the contextual significance that Locke's text had in and for its own time, by reading the text both through the propositions it makes and through the ways those propositions might be internally disarticulated and recuperated by the development—or more aptly perhaps, by the movement—of the text itself. In Derrida's sense of "memory work," I contend that memory is not simply something that we read about in texts on memory—not just an object of study—but that the work of reading is itself memory work. About this relation of reading to the work of memory, Derrida writes,

> The very condition of deconstruction may be at work, in the work, *within* the system to be deconstructed; it may *already* be there, already at work . . . participating in the construction of what it at the same time threatens to deconstruct. One might then be inclined to reach this conclusion: deconstruction is not an operation that supervenes *afterwards*, from the outside, one fine day; it is always already at work in the work. . . . Since the disruptive force of deconstruction is always already

contained within the architecture of the work, all one would finally have to do to be able to deconstruct, given this *always already*, is to do memory work. (Derrida, *MdM* 73)

8. John Yolton has convincingly argued that in the seventeenth century, innate ideas and principles were widely held as being necessary for the stability of religion, morality, and natural law and that, in attacking the naive accounts given of innate ideas and innate principles, Locke was in fact attacking the powerful positions of the conservative ecclesiastic and Royalist classes, ones whose tremendous authority continued until well after the publication of the *Essay*. See John W. Yolton, *John Locke and the Way of Ideas* (Oxford: Oxford University Press, 1956). See also Wood, *Politics of Locke's Philosophy*, which relates Locke's criticism of innate ideas and principles to the development of a politics of individualism and social environmentalism (see esp. the text's introduction, and 151ff.). For a general overview of what is philosophically at stake in Locke's critique of innate knowledge, see Margaret Atherton, "Locke and the Issue over Innateness," in *Locke*, ed. Vere Chappell (Oxford: Oxford University Press, 1998), 48–59.

9. I. G. W. Leibniz, "Preface," in *New Essays on Human Understanding*, trans. Peter Remnant and Jonathan Bennett (Cambridge: Cambridge University Press, 1981), 48.

10. Aristotle, "On Memory" in *The Complete Works of Aristotle*, vol. 1, ed. Jonathan Barnes (Princeton, N.J.: Princeton University Press, 1984), 449b, 9–16.

11. Ibid., 450a, 25–450b, 10.

12. Ibid., 451a, 19–24.

13. In the treatise, Aristotle uses a description of the imagination (the faculty of making pictures) to explain memory images. That is, in place of a separate analysis of the faculty of memory, Aristotle uses the imagination's ability to produce images as a means by which to elaborate on what memory does. Thus in his account, the temporal dimension of "before" and "after" is what differentiates memory from the imagination (450a). However, this distinction is so fragile and, in some ways, so unconvincing, as to produce a certain anxiety in the text regarding the slippage between the two. After having discussed the "mnemonic token" as a "picture and a likeness," he writes, "We can now understand why it is that sometimes, when we have such processes . . . we do not know whether this really implies our having had perceptions corresponding to them, and we doubt whether the case is or is not one of memory" (451a, 5). The implication of this slippage between memory and the imagination will be examined in greater detail in relation to its narrative dramatization in Locke.

14. Jeffrey Andrew Barash, "The Sources of Memory," *Journal of the History of Ideas* 58, no. 4: 707–17, here 712–13.

15. Aristotle, "On the Soul," in *The Complete Works of Aristotle*, vol. 1, 430a, 17–26.

16. Barash. "The Sources of Memory," 713.

17. On Locke's relation to Aristotelian philosophy, see Wood, *Politics of Locke's Philosophy*, 82, 87–88. While Locke repeatedly commended

Aristotle's writings, he also felt that his philosophy had not gone far enough and so was in some measure responsible for the scholastic nature of much of the dogmatic Aristotelianism of Locke's own time. In his polemic with Stillingfleet, for example, Locke makes the following comment: "that acute and judicious philosopher, if he had gone farther in that matter, would have done as I have done" (quoted in Wood 211). In another respect, Wood argues that Locke's treatise was, mostly by association with Bacon and the Royal Society, made the object of attack by his contemporary Aristotelians who represented the "kind of hairsplitting intellectual specialist he so detested" (82).

18. Several commentaries have argued that many of the philosophical criticisms launched against Locke's essay are misplaced, on the basis that his orientation was not philosophical at all but was, rather, based on a set of practical reflections concerning what humans could and could not know. Aarsleff has even suggested that the root of the misunderstanding could be a semantic one: the "word 'understanding' in the title is to be taken in its active sense as meaning something like 'ways of getting to know something'—'mind' is no synonym for it. . . . . The aim of the *Essay* was much more limited than Leibniz saw" (*From Locke to Saussure* 55). See also Jolley's account in *Leibniz and Locke* of the project's modest and practical aims regarding the question of personal identity (and how, on the basis of the *Essay*'s practical orientation, Leibniz was forced to concede more to Locke than could be coherently sustained by his metaphysical orientation). While many disputes with Locke's philosophy have often revolved around issues and concerns that were not necessarily Locke's own, Aarsleff's contention that "mind" is no synonym for "understanding" does not seem entirely accurate. In fact, Locke himself sometimes seems to use the term "mind" as a synonym for "understanding," and he most often uses the word "understanding" as a substantive noun, indicating an entity with attributes and not simply a general process of knowledge acquisition. On this question, I tend to agree with Cathy Caruth, who argues that Locke's "humble" project is at times governed by an almost inebriated sense of the capacity of human reason. In *Empirical Truths and Critical Fictions: Locke, Wordsworth, Kant, Freud* (Baltimore, Md.: Johns Hopkins University Press, 1991), she writes of Locke's *Essay* that "its apparent subject, the limitation of reason, really tells of a new and unbounded power of reason. . . . Locke's project is to establish the certainty of this self-knowledge, which is represented as a kind of self-reflection in an enclosed and lighted realm" (5).

19. Joseph Butler, "Of Personal Identity," in *Analogy of Religion* (1736); reprinted in John Perry, ed., *Personal Identity* (Berkeley: University of California Press, 1975), 99–105, here 100.

20. According to Kenneth Winkler, Butler fails to realize that for Locke, consciousness of a past act is something more than the knowledge of a preexisting fact and that it involves an appropriation of it as one's own—that is, the act or experience must be represented as one's own. See "Locke on Personal Identity," *Journal of the History of Philosophy* 29 (1991): 201–26, here 206.

21. Thomas Reid, "Of Identity," *Essays on the Intellectual Powers of Man*, 1785; reprinted in Perry, ed., *Personal Identity*, 107–12. David Hume will also launch an attack against "the nature of *personal identity,* which has become so great a question in philosophy, especially of late years in *England*" that brings Butler and Reid's criticisms together. Hume's invective circles around the obvious problem that it is impossible to remember every single event and thought that one has over the course of one's life. It is only half in jest that Hume asks the question: "Who can tell me, for instance, what were his thoughts and actions on the first of *January* 1715, the 11th of *March* 1719, and the 3rd of *August* 1733?" For Hume, the obvious absurdity of the question is apt, for it reveals the absurdity of the theory: That if one cannot remember what happened on certain days of one's life, then one is forced to concede that "the present self is not the same person with the self of that time" (309). He concludes the passage with the following challenge: "'Twill be incumbent on those, who affirm that memory produces entirely our personal identity, to give a reason why we can thus extend our identity beyond our memory" (*A Treatise of Human Nature* [1739–40] [London: Penguin Books, 1985], 310–11). What needs to be underscored is the rhetorical use to which Hume puts the calendar as the sole expression of Lockean time (an interpretation that, it should be added, Locke's own discussion of temporal succession in Book 2 as "the train of ideas which constantly succeed on another in his understanding" does little to dispel). As I will attempt to show in the final pages of this chapter, though, the trajectory of Locke's argument as he attempts to construe personal identity evokes a temporal dimension that is at odds with that of succession.

22. In fact, one of Locke's most prominent supporters, Edmund Law, recalls the Latin *persona* in his 1769 defense of Locke (his "A Defence of Mr. Locke's Opinion Concerning Human Identity" was published separately, and then included in the 1777 edition of Locke's *Works*, and in three subsequent editions), when he writes, "The word person, then, according to the received sense in all classical authors, standing for a certain guise, character, or quality *i.e.* being in fact a mixed mode, or relation, and not a substance" (cited in Kenneth P. Winkler "Locke on Personal Identity," 212).

23. See Aarsleff, *From Locke to Saussure* (Minneapolis: University of Minnesota Press, 1982) 66.

24. *Oxford English Dictionary*, 2nd. ed. (Compact edition) s.v. "person."

25. On this point, see Joshua Foa Dienstag, *Dancing in Chains: Narrative and Memory in Political Theory* (Stanford, Calif.: Stanford University Press, 1997), who suggests that, although the presence of God is vital to certain elements of Locke's political theory, the project of the *Essay* is to separate the mind of man from the mind of God. Such a separation does not deny the existence of God or the certitude of divine wisdom; what it does do, however, is question a certain way of knowing God and hence, our access to a certain kind of divine wisdom (27ff.).

26. Locke's passion for travel literature is well documented. See D. Carey, "Locke, Travel Literature, and the Natural History of Man," *Seventeenth*

Century 11 (1996): 259–80. See also Aarsleff, *From Locke to Saussure*, 45, 71n9, and Wood, *Politics of Locke's Philosophy*, 31, 81, 153, 191n24.

27. In fact, the strangeness of the story probably accounts for why it has been omitted from most abridged editions of the *Essay*. It has, however, been reincluded in the 1999 abridged edition brought out by Penguin Classics.

28. The source of the story is Sir William Temple (1628–99) and his *Memoirs of what came to pass in Christendom, from the War begun 1672 to the peace concluded 1679*. I have consulted the second edition, which is held in the collections of the Thomas Fisher Rare Book Library, University of Toronto.

29. Locke concludes the episode as follows: "The Prince, it is plain, who vouches this story, and our author who relates it from him, both of them call this talker a *parrot*; and I ask any one else, who thinks such a story fit to be told, whether if this *parrot* and all of its kind had always talked, as we have a prince's word for it, as this one did, whether, I say, they would not have passed for a race of rational animals; but yet another for all that, they would have been allowed to be men, and not *parrots*?"

30. Disguising an incredible narrative as an historical one is the basis for Hegel's primary objection to the use of the fable as an instructional moral lesson. In the *Aesthetics*, he writes: "We have after all become accustomed in fables as such so to represent the lesson as the first thing that the occurrence related is itself merely a cloak and therefore an event purely fabricated for the purpose of the lesson. But such cloaks, especially when the incident described cannot possibly have occurred in the life of real animals, i.e. in accordance with their natural character, are extremely wearisome inventions, meaning less than nothing" (vol. 1, 388).

31. Paul de Man, "The Epistemology of Metaphor," in *Aesthetic Ideology*, ed. Andrzej Warminski (Minneapolis: University of Minnesota Press, 1996), 34–50, here 41n. Further references will be given in the text as EM followed by page number. De Man's essay examines the ways in which the attempt to control and contain the effects of literary figure in philosophical discourse not only results in the disturbing proliferation of such figures, but also accounts for our dismissal of them as merely decorative, or frivolous adjuncts to an otherwise logically sound argument.

32. For an analysis of Locke's presentation of the arbitrary or conventional nature of language and its implicit critique of the Adamic doctrine of language that was widespread in his time, see Aarsleff, *From Locke to Saussure*. Of particular interest in Aarsleff's analysis is how it relates Locke's treatment of language to the critique of innatist principles.

33. The example Locke uses to illustrate this point is the word *life*: "There are few names of complex ideas which any two men use for the same just precise collection. It is hard to name a word which will not be a clear instance of this. *Life* is a term, none more familiar. Anyone almost would take it for an affront to be asked what he meant by it. And yet if it comes in question whether a plant that lies ready formed in the seed have life, whether the

embryo in an egg before . . . it is easy to perceive that a clear, distinct, settled idea does not always accompany the use of so known a word as that of *life* is" (*Essay* 3.10.22).

34. Neal Wood argues that Locke's critique of innate ideas was not a purely academic exercise but also shows his deep political convictions. In particular, the critique of innatism was to serve as a means to undermine the kinds of unquestioned authorities—clerical, monarchal, feudal—prevalent in Locke's time (and whose faltering would culminate, momentarily, in The Glorious Revolution of 1688) that attained and retained their authority solely by virtue of birthrights or unquestioning obedience (see Wood, *Politics of Locke's Philosophy*). As Wood makes clear, although Locke was far from being a democrat or a radical in the current sense of those words, his treatise did become the handbook for the emergent middle class.

35. Some of the concerns Locke raises with respect to pedagogy and language acquisition in *Some Thoughts Concerning Education*, ed. Ruth Grant and Nathan Tarcov (Indianapolis, Ind.: Hackett, 1996), published three years after the *Essay*, reflect the *Essay*'s anxieties about the relation of language to consciousness. Witness, for instance, his vehement opposition to the acquisition of language through the exercise of committing passages of text to memory: "Languages," he writes, "are to be learned only by reading and talking and not by scraps of authors got by heart," a method which, Locke argues, fills the heads of children with "a train of other people's words" (132–34). Although Locke's appeal here is clearly for a pedagogy that makes learning relevant to the lives of modern children, when read in the context of the *Essay*, the emphasis placed in his description on the dead and deadeningly foreign quality of language learned and recited by rote reads more like a displaced version of the more generalized threat to consciousness that language's foreignness poses. As an aside: given Locke's attention to a child's linguistic development, why does he make so little of his observation, in the *Essay*, that children acquire language as parrots do? Moreover, if it is indeed true that adults have a much more difficult time learning languages than children do, could it not be argued that self-consciousness poses a hindrance to language acquisition? The most striking implication of this is that if young children were fully self-conscious, they would never learn to speak. The question, of course, then becomes whether the differential between self-consciousness and language is limited to the event of childhood language acquisition. Through the force of his own "observations," Locke would have to answer in the negative.

36. Caruth, *Empirical Truths and Critical Fictions*, 12, 14.

37. Caruth suggests that the narrative of overcoming that informs the transition from sensation to reflection is not isolated to its instance in Locke's text but is also one that also informs the analyses of some of Locke's modern commentators. This tendency highlights the allure of thinking about "sensation" as a purely physiological mechanism, one which is overcome by "reflection" as a means more suited to understanding what is proper to the mind (Caruth, *Empirical Truths and Critical Fictions*, 9ff.)

38. For this insight, I am again indebted to Cathy Caruth, who contends that "the physiological loss of childhood is used to 'explain' the mental forgetting of childhood experience; and the empirical basis of the former 'history' gives to the latter 'explanation' the appearance of descriptive truth" (Ibid. 29).

39. *Oxford English Dictionary*, 2nd ed. (Compact edition), s.v. "infant."

40. Derrida addresses the notion of "before" in terms of how it invokes a certain indiscernibility between past and future in *Specters of Marx: The State of the Debt, the Work of Mourning, and the New International*, trans. Peggy Kamuf (London: Routledge, 1994), xix, 17.

41. See Annette Wieviorka, *L'Ère du témoin* (Paris: Plon, 1998), esp. the book's final chapter.

3. MOURNING MEMORY

1. Charles Taylor, *Sources of the Self: The Making of Modern Identity* (Cambridge, Mass.: Harvard University Press, 1992), 174. Further references will be given in the text as *Sources* followed by page number.

2. G. W. F. Hegel, *Lectures on the History of Philosophy*, vol. 3, trans. E. S. Haldane and Frances H. Simson (London: Routledge, 1968), 310, translation modified; in German: *Vorlesungen über die Geschichte der Philosophie*, vol. 3, ed. Gerd Irrlitz (Leipzig: Reclam, 1971), 362. Further references will be given by page number in the text—the English translation will be given first, followed by the German.

3. This citation comes from a brief paragraph that seems to have been deleted from the English translations: "The life of the individual is becoming more and more a matter of indifference." It is found on page 346 of the German and it is in the context of Hegel's argument that extensive biographical details about a philosopher are superfluous to an understanding of their work.

4. Martin Heidegger, *Hegel's Phenomenology of Spirit*, trans. Parvis Emad and Kenneth Maly (Bloomington: Indiana University Press, 1994), 82.

5. Ibid., 142. Kojève, who by all accounts was committed to Hegel's thought as a means with which to think the future, nonetheless also defines Absolute Knowledge as "the end of time." According to his influential account, Hegel's "human or historical Time—that is, Time in which the Future . . . takes primacy" is overcome in absolute Knowledge that, being "the *last* moment of Time—that is, a moment without a *Future*—is no longer a temporal moment" (*An Introduction to the Reading of Hegel*, ed. A. Bloom, trans. J. H. Nichols Jr. (Ithaca, N.Y.: Cornell University Press, 1969), 140, 149). Joshua Foa Dienstag has also argued that Hegel's philosophy of memory has little or no contemporary relevance in that it yields no thinking of futurity. See his *Dancing in Chains: Narrative and Memory in Political Theory* (Stanford, Calif.: Stanford University Press, 1997), where he repeatedly puts the stress on Hegel's "absence of a future," "the lack of a future" (144), the troubling nature of "Hegel's silence on the future" (145).

6. Hegel, *Phenomenology of Spirit*, 487. Further references will appear in the text as *Phen* followed by page number.

7. Donald Verene, *Hegel's Recollection: A Study of Images in the Phenomenology of Spirit* (Albany: State University of New York Press, 1985), 108.

8. Jacques Derrida, *Glas*, trans. John P. Leavey Jr. and Richard Rand (Lincoln: University of Nebraska Press, 1986), 226. Further references will be given in the text as *Glas* followed by page number.

9. Heidegger makes this claim in *Being and Time*, 392.

10. Werner Hamacher has also alluded to the difficulty this circularity entails for reading: "And thus every new reading of Hegel's writings finds itself confronted by the dilemma of inevitably figuring at a place already appointed for it within the text it seeks critically to locate, of already being grasped by what it struggles to grasp, of already belonging in advance to what it would appropriate understandingly for itself. It finds itself already read by what it seeks to read" (*Pleroma—Reading in Hegel*, trans. Nicolas Walker and Simon Jarvis [Stanford, Calif.: Stanford University Press, 1998], 1).

11. Derrida posits the stakes of thinking the temporal remain(s) of Hegel in terms of the problematic that they—the remain(s)—"fall outside the circle" of Absolute Knowing, though without being its negative. As such, even the lexicon of "falling outside" does not do justice to the problem: "The remain(s), it must be added, would not fall from it at all" (*Glas* 226), but rather would remain within it as "a suspended remain(s)." A remain(s) that is neither a persistent permanence, nor the cast-off residue of an operation, Derrida suggests that any remain(s) of time in Hegel must remain suspended in the circle of Absolute Knowing itself. Insofar as Derrida poses the question of how to read what remain(s) of time in the future-oriented mode of suspension and suspense, my reading of Hegel is an attempt to follow his important gesture.

12. In a brilliant analysis in her *The Future of Hegel*, Catherine Malabou has demonstrated the disservice done to the analysis of time in Hegel's work when it is limited by reference to the places and the times of its treatment within the system (largely in the *Philosophy of Nature* of the Jena writings and in the *Encyclopedia*). In particular, she suggests that those treatments themselves demand that we renounce the well-known and familiar notions of time; by the same token, Malabou argues that they require an "opening-out of the meaning of time" (*FH* 3). Malabou's notion of "opening-out" implies a nonrigidity or nonfixity to Hegel's time, one that both has the power to give form *and* to be subject to formation, a double temporality that Malabou names "plasticity."

13. There are, of course, important exceptions. See Paul de Man, "Sign and Symbol in Hegel's *Aesthetics*," in *Aesthetic Ideology*, ed. Andrzej Warminski (Minneapolis: University of Minnesota Press, 1996); Gregg M. Horowitz, *Sustaining Loss: Art and Mournful Life* (Stanford, Calif.: Stanford University Press, 2001), 56–90; and Jean-Luc Nancy, *The Muses*, trans. Peggy Kamuf (Stanford, Calif.: Stanford University Press, 1996), esp. "The Girl

Who Succeeds the Muses," 41–56. And interestingly, if Donald Verene does not explicitly address the question of art or aesthetics in his treatment of memory in the *Phenomenology*, it is to attribute a general aesthetic structure—the play of images, the role of metaphor and rhetorical expression, the imagination, etc.—to the whole of the text's speculative force, which he describes as a "colossus of memory" (3). Working from Lauer's contention of the affinity between poetic imagination and speculative reason, Verene notes that "the language of memory" in the *Phenomenology* "is the image" (109) without, though, taking up the issue of translation between language and image raised by this statement.

14. Martin Donougho, "Hegel's Art of Memory," in *Endings: Questions of Memory in Hegel and Heidegger*, ed. Rebecca Comay and John McCumber (Evanston. Ill.: Northwestern University Press, 1999), 139–59, here 139.

15. For a theoretically meticulous assessment of Hegel's "end of art" in terms of its status as intellectual rumor, see Eva Geulen. *The End of Art: Readings in a Rumor after Hegel*, trans. James McFarland (Stanford, Calif.: Stanford University Press, 2006), 1–18; in German: *Das Ende der Kunst: Lesarten eines Gerüchts nach Hegel* (Frankfurt am Main: Suhrkamp, 2002), 9–35. In due course, we will return to Geulen's analysis of Hegel's pronouncement of the "end of art."

16. G. W. F. Hegel. *Hegel's Aesthetics: Lectures on Fine Art*, vol. 1, trans. T. M. Knox (Oxford: Oxford University Press, 1975); in German: *Vorlesungen über die Ästhetik*, vols. 13 and 14, ed. Eva Moldenhauer and Karl Marcus Michel (Frankfurt am Main: Suhrkamp, 1986). Further references will be given in the text as *Aesth* followed by page number. In cases where there are slight discrepancies in the translation or where the original phrasing is important, the page numbers of the German edition will follow the English.

17. Peter Szondi has pointed to the geographical and historical specificity of what, for Hegel, is at an end—that is, the art of ancient Greece: "Die höchste Bestimmung, das ist eben der unmittelbare Zusammenhang mit der göttlichen Wahrheit. Dieser Zusammenhang ist für Hegel ein für allemal an der griechischen Kunst in exemplarischer Weise sichtbar geworden" ("Hegels Lehre von der Dichtung," in *Poetik und Geschichtsphilosophie 1*, ed. Senta Metz and Hans-Hagen Hildebrandt. [Frankfurt am Main: Suhrkamp, 1974], 303).

18. Berel Lang, *Holocaust Representation: Art within the Limits of History and Ethics* (Baltimore, Md.: Johns Hopkins University Press), 165ff. Lang's formulation is pretty much an exact inversion of Aristotle's privileging of the universal mandate of art over the attention that history pays to particulars: Lang suggests that exactitude about particulars ties history to truth more in our day than an artistic residue of attachment to universals could.

19. Ibid., 163. It is not within the scope of this argument to adjudicate Lang's claim (or Danto's, for that matter) that art has become idolatrous in our day; nor is this the place to discuss the understanding of artistic immortality as a species of idolatry. Suffice it to say, though, that despite the assurance with which Danto's position is advocated here, his is not an entirely

uncontested reading; indeed, his rather conventional "Hegelian" interpretation—one in which the end of art signals the end of art's material embodiment of human truths and becomes wholly a matter of rational reflection
on art—has recently become the subject of pertinent critical discussion—
namely, in J. M. Bernstein's recent "The End of Art (Again)" (2003), and
Gregg M. Horowitz's *Sustaining Loss: Art and Mournful Life* (Stanford,
Calif.: Stanford University Press. 2001). The core of Danto's argument—that
art after the "end of art" defines itself solely through the stance it adopts
toward its own history—certainly generates the sense of art's hermetical
relation to itself or to its own development; however, one could also suggest
that the arts, precisely in getting involved with their various historical developments as part of their own artistic practices, are cultural forms within
which "historical development" as such and the ethos of representing those
developments in terms of an immediate relation to the past need not be taken
at face value. As such, modern art could just as easily be understood as an
arena within which the pressure of various notions of historicity, of materiality, and of the various traditions of art are brought to bear not only on
conventional discourses of history but also on the cultural production of art
itself. In other words, one does not have to disagree with the general direction of Danto's argument in order to underscore the complexity of what it
might mean for art to adopt a stance toward its own history, something his
analyses takes to be self-evident. There is thus plenty of room within Danto's
theory of "the end of art" to suggest implications which are quite different
from his own.

20. Stephen Houlgate, "Hegel and the 'End' of Art," *Owl of Minerva*
29, no. 1 (Fall 1997): 1–19. Further references will be given in the text as
HEA followed by page number. What is limiting about Houlgate's interpretive strategy, as laudable as it is for him to nuance the "end" of art away
from its rather more apocalyptic overtones, is the extent to which he goes
on to assess the state of contemporary art in terms of the "definitive end"
of art that "up until his own death, Hegel had hoped to prevent" (19). In
other words, Houlgate's nuancing of the reception of Hegel's formulation is
compromised by the introduction of his own apocalyptic tone, which comes
complete with the wholesale end of humanism and "man" that he finds in
abstract expressionist art.

21. Geulen, *The End of Art*. Further references will be given in the text as
EA followed by page number.

22. The basis of the distinction between art and nature corresponds to
the difference between products of art and those of nature: artistic objects
belong to a higher spiritual realm than do objects in nature. The example
Hegel uses to illustrate his point is the freedom that appears in even the most
useless of thoughts in comparison to the sun that, however necessary (and
beautiful), is by no means free.

23. For a consideration of art's loss of autonomy in relation to philosophy, see Jere Surber's "Art as a Mode of Thought: Hegel's Aesthetics and
the Origins of Modernism," in *Hegel and Aesthetics*, ed. William Maker
(Albany: State University of New York Press, 2000), 45–59. Surber contests

the orthodoxy that Hegel's theory of art serves as an antidote to the modernist abandonment of wholeness or the "aesthetic ideal," and instead suggests that Hegel's aesthetic theory is a central participant in the modernist development whereby art is no longer autonomous from thinking. Indeed, in Surber's estimation, the practices of modern art making are virtually inseparable from their own theoretical impulses, and it is this, he claims, that modern art has inherited from Hegel.

24. Terry Pinkard's recent *German Philosophy 1760–1860: The Legacy of Idealism* (Cambridge: Cambridge University Press, 2002) does not engage Hegel's aesthetic writings but is nonetheless relevant to the current argument insofar as Pinkard locates the enduring relevance of German idealism to the contemporary world largely in the critical stance that the former developed toward inherited (ecclesiastic or aristocratic) traditions, a stance out of which critical reflectivity as such arose. One of the central ironies of Pinkard's text lies in the very notion of a "legacy" within the context of a philosophical and social movement that called into question the notion of legacy as such. More seriously, though, what Pinkard does not seem to detect is the extent to which, for our own age, the question is not so much about the traditional allegiances that we continue to bear but rather, that the past seems to offer us almost no bearings at all.

25. This modern dilemma of the relation between art and the discursive rationality of art theory (or, more pointedly, their inseparability) often meets with resistance or hostility on the part of artists and art departments toward overly intellectual art theory. Take, for instance, Barnett Newman's famous put-down of Suzanne Langer: "Aesthetics is to art what ornithology is to the birds." Contrasting what is living (art, birds) to what is dead and deadening (aesthetics, ornithology), Newman's claim that thought kills what would otherwise be a living object also informs critiques taking place under the auspices of museum studies departments regarding the disenchantment or "musealization" of culture. In both cases, modern reflection on art is understood to be a means of deadening what would otherwise be a relation to a living object.

26. Paul de Man, "Sign and Symbol in Hegel's *Aesthetics*," in *Aesthetic Ideology*, ed Andrzej Warminski (Minneapolis: University of Minnesota Press, 1996), 100–101.

27. On the significance of digestion and eating for Hegel's early writings on Christianity, see Werner Hamacher, *Pleroma—Reading in Hegel*.

28. Hegel evokes this double function of memory frequently, as in the early sections of the *Aesthetics* when he describes the various artworks of a culture as a kind of vessel in which its key aspects are preserved. He most probably has the art of ancient Greece in mind when he suggests that "in works of art the nations have deposited their richest inner intuitions and ideas, and art is often the key, and in many nations the sole key, to understanding their religion and philosophy" (*Aesth* 7). Precisely because artworks have memory as their source, they themselves can, in certain cultural instances, serve *as* sources of memory, and as forces of continuity over vast stretches of time. This suggestion—that the significance of ancient Greek artistic practices in

particular be understood as both determined *by* and *as* memory—remains basically unchallenged up to our own time. To cite one recent instance, Egyptologist Jan Assmann formulates the importance of memory for the ancient Greeks in terms very similar to Hegel's: "Since Mnemosyne was the mother of the nine Muses, her name came to stand for the totality of cultural activities as they were personified by the different Muses. By subsuming these cultural activities under the personification of memory, the Greeks were viewing culture not only as based on memory but as a form of memory in itself" (*Moses the Egyptian: The Memory of Egypt in Western Monotheism* [Cambridge, Mass: Harvard University Press, 1997], 15).

29. See Peter Fuss and John Dobbins, "Spirit as Recollection: Hegel's Theory of the Internalizing of Experience," *Idealistic Studies* 11, no. 2 (May 1981): 142–50, for an articulation of this position in terms of the recollection of individuals. For Fuss and Dobbins, recollection in Hegel's work operates as a force of reconciliation, wherein fundamental differences of experience are internally resolved. It is through this force of internalization, they suggest, that the individual is capable of consciously integrating and internalizing discrepancies in its own experience. Moreover, it is as a function of this ability that the individual is also able to forge a nontransient, timeless sense of itself and its world: The discrepancy between one's experience of the world and one's conceptualization of it represents the beginning of "the intellective activity through which one's experience is . . . literally re-collected, into one's ultimate statement concerning one's self and world, one's timeless identity and reality" (146).

30. This sense of giving voice to another mode of temporality, rather than simply affirming the universal quality of memory over all that is transient, is also evoked by Hegel's suggestion that "memory" is already a "picture [*in dem Bilde der Erinnerung*]." The description of memory that already has it figured as an image or picture implies that it is already functioning in terms of an aesthetic relation to sensuousness, and thus, to temporality.

31. In the discussion of the historical variants of clothing and their adequacy for expressing spirit, Hegel again invokes what is fundamentally a historical distinction between the ancient mode of dress and that of his own day. Unsurprisingly, the Greek practice of dressing in formless "drapes"— toga-like, one might surmise—is singled out as the form of dress most worthy of praise. It is signified by the same word, *Gewand*, that Hegel uses in the formulation regarding the role of memory, and is praised over and above the form of modern *Anzügen*—Knox translates it as "clothing," but it would be more accurate as "suits," a word which still today brings to mind all the connotations of strangulation and constraint that Hegel means to evoke in his discussion of them (*Aesth* 165/216). See Philippe Lacoue-Labarthe's analysis of the figures of veiling as they pertain to the clothing of Greek statuary in the essay "The Unpresentable," in *The Subject of Philosophy*, ed. Thomas Trezise, trans. Hugh Silverman et al. (Minneapolis: University of Minnesota Press, 1993), 116–47, esp. 141ff.

32. Timothy Bahti, *Allegories of History: Literary Historiography after Hegel* (Baltimore, Md.: Johns Hopkins University Press, 1992), 108–9.

Further references will be given in the text as *AH* followed by page number. Bahti's reading of the *Aesthetics* is exemplary for the detail and rigor of its argument; however, some of the contradictions that he locates in Hegel's presentation of the Greek "exemplary individual" can be attributed to the fact that he does not take the teleological circularity of the relation between body and spirit into account—one which is, of course, incompatible with the modern notion of a body-soul duality. In short, Bahti's reading keeps to the time of Hegel's modern interpretation, without seeing that there is another kind of time—circular—also in play here. Furthermore, much of the complexity of Hegel's argument arises out of the non-unity of the time being articulated in it. By exploiting the resources of both the historical and teleological-circular modes of argumentation and temporality, Hegel is in some way attesting to the *untimeliness* of his own exposition. I hope to make the force of this untimeliness more explicit toward the end of the chapter.

33. The three main stages of art history recognized by Hegel in the *Aesthetics* are symbolic, classical, and romantic art, each of which is defined by the specific relationship expressed in it between idea and form. In the first or symbolic stage, a powerful idea is expressed in a variety of forms that are inadequate to its expression. Hence, Hegel's emphasis on the "stricter sense of the word" here refers to *symbolon* as two halves that are distinct from each other, or have been broken away from each other. The result of this internal breaking, or difference of form and idea, is that the form must be distorted in an attempt to accommodate the transcendent power of the idea. Hegel took ancient Egyptian and Indian art as examples of this, with their animal-headed gods and monstrous demons and heroes.

34. G. W. F. Hegel, *Lectures on the Philosophy of Religion*, vol. 3, 169–70. Quoted in Malabou, *Future of Hegel*, 115.

35. See "Sense-Certainty" in the "Consciousness" chapter of the *Phenomenology of Spirit*, particularly 9 58–62.

36. See Beat Wyss's "Klassizismus und Geschichtsphilosophie im Konflikt: Aloys Hirt und Hegel" for a discussion of the role played by the newly emerging ethos of the museum in the development of Hegel's *Aesthetics*. According to Wyss, it was the play of de- and recontextualization that made thinking about art in modernity both possible and necessary. The removal of the art object from its edifying context within aristocratic/feudal and ecclesiastical structures of power made it possible for art to win its new context within the modern museum (117), giving art a spiritual value in excess of that given to it by its narrowly religious or monarchical contexts. As such, the task of thinking art in terms of this excess fell to aesthetic theory: "The transfer of the artwork from the palace to the museum had its philosophical counterpart in the aesthetic" (*Kunsterfahrung und Kulturpolitik im Berlin Hegels*, ed. Otto Pöggeler and Annemarie Gethmann-Siefert, *Hegel-Studien/Beiheft* 22 [1983], 115–30, here 118, my translation).

37. Such a claim is made by Donald Verene, who has formulated Hegelian memory in terms of different registers of language: "The first language of infinity is the image; infinity can later be formed as a concept" (Verene, *Hegel's Recollection* 7). My interest here is the status of that image that

makes its first appearance as "language" and, moreover, what is implied and contained by the "later" in which infinity can be formed as a concept—i.e., the implications of that temporal distance or gap through which the image as "first language" comes to be constituted as the language of philosophical knowledge.

38. Knox translates this line as "the breath and air of affliction," which, for two reasons, seems misleading. Firstly, the translation of *Trauer* by "affliction" is not a great translation in that it obscures the parallel that Hegel's argument is in the process of developing with scholarly "mourning" (*Trauer*). Secondly, his translation of *Hauch und Duft* as "breath and air" renders the experience of mourning potentially more lofty and disembodied than does Hegel's appeal to breathing and smelling.

39. On the relations among destiny (*Geschick*), sending (*schicken*), and historicity (*Geschichtlichkeit*), and their properly futural dimension, see Heidegger's *Being and Time*, 352–53.

40. Immanuel Kant, "Comparison of the Aesthetic Value of the Various Fine Arts" (Part 1, §53 of "Critique of Aesthetic Judgment"), in *Critique of Judgment*, trans. Werner S. Pluhar (Indianapolis, Ind.: Hackett, 1987): 326ff.

4. SPECULATING ON THE PAST, THE IMPACT OF THE PRESENT

1. Heidegger, *Being and Time*, 394.

2. G. W. F. Hegel, "Actuality," §3, in *Hegel's Science of Logic*, 529; in German: "Die Wirklichkeit," in *Wissenschaft der Logik* 2, vol. 6 of *G. W. F. Hegel Werke*, ed. Eva Moldenhauer and Karl Markus Michel (Frankfurt am Main: Suhrkamp, 1986), 186.

3. Hegel, *Introduction to the Philosophy of History*, trans. Leo Rauch (Indianapolis, Ind.: Hackett, 1988), 64, translation modified; in German: *Vorlesungen über die Philosophie der Geschichte*, vol. 12 of *G. W. F. Hegel Werke*, 83. Further references will be given in the text as *IPH* followed by page number. Due to discrepancies between the authoritative German edition (edited by Karl Hegel and published in 1840) and existing English translations (those of Robert Hartmann, J. Sibree, and Leo Rauch, the latter of which I will be using throughout the chapter), I will include the German page reference for citations where the meaning or the focus of the original passage has been altered.

4. On this point, see Ian Balfour's "Reversal, Quotation (Benjamin's History)" *Modern Language Notes*, 106 (1991): 622–47, here 622–23.

5. G. W. F. Hegel, *The Philosophy of History*, trans. J. Sibree (New York: Dover, 1956), 442; in German: 524. Further references will be included in the text as *PhH* followed by page number. Under the "end of history," Hegel places the period that extends from the Reformation to today. The "formally absolute principle" that marks that end of history is the triumph of subjective freedom, the liberty of all individuals.

6. In the English edition of the complete lectures, Sibree translates the phrase *historische Rüstkammer* as "historic lumber-room." Although

224 Notes

consistent with a sense of boredom instilled by the overaccumulation of history, it is not what Hegel says. Leo Rauch's translation of the phrase as "historic arsenal" is more accurate, restoring the sense of history's explosive potential, even or perhaps especially in the context of its accumulation.

7. In the course of his remarkable analysis of the figures of veiling and unveiling in Hegel's *Aesthetics*, Philippe Lacoue-Labarthe observes that the "worst case" of misreading would interpret the *Phenomenology of Spirit* as a "narrative tragedy," a "novelistic epos" or "Odyssey of Consciousness," and points to Hegel's own claim that the concept needs to pass through a "partly narrative exposition" as an "anticipatory assurance" of its proper presentation (*Subject of Philosophy* 135). A similar thinking should, I think, be "tested" for its relevance to Hegel's concept of history (or what he calls *die Prosa der Geschichte*, indicating its resolute investment in the narrative form); in other words, Lacoue-Labarthe's contention opens up the possibility that Hegel's narrative of history can be understood in terms that are not wholly narrative or, what amounts to the same thing, in terms that mark the dénouement of linear representation in general.

8. In German the modern period is known as *Neuzeit*, literally "new time." According to the Grimm brothers' *Deutsches Wörterbuch* (1889), it first appeared in Freiligrath in 1870. Reinhart Koselleck states that prior to the term's formalization as a concept, the expression *die neue Zeit* had been used in eighteenth-century historiography; see Koselleck, *Vergangene Zukunft: Zur Semantik geschichtlicher Zeiten* (Frankfurt am Main: Suhrkamp, 1988), 302ff. This convention is followed in *The Philosophy of History*.

9. Kojève, *Introduction to the Reading of Hegel*, 164.

10. Dienstag, *Dancing in Chains*, 154.

11. Friedrich Nietzsche, "The Utility and Liability of History for Life," in *Unfashionable Observations*, trans. Richard T. Gray (Stanford, Calif.: Stanford University Press, 1995), 143.

12. Heinrich Heine, "Zur Geschichte der Religion und Philosophie in Deutschland," in *Die Romantische Schule und andere Schriften über Deutschland* (Cologne: Könemann, 1995), 175.

13. G. W. F. Hegel, *Aphorisms from the Wastebook*, ed. Jon Stewart (Evanston, Ind.: Northwestern University Press), 247.

14. *Aphorismen aus Hegels Wastebook*, ed. Eva Moldenhauer and Karl Michel Marcus, vol. 2 of *G. W. F. Hegel. Werke*, 557. This aphorism does not appear in the English edition, which is an abridgement.

15. Hegel, *IPH*, 54/72: "No one is left behind by his time, even less does he leap over it" (*noch weniger überspringt er dieselbe*).

16. Nietzsche, "The Utility and Liability of History for Life," 86–87: "It is only to the extent that I am a student of more ancient times—above all that of ancient Greece—that I, as a child of our time, have had such unfashionable (*unzeitgemäße*) experiences. But I have to concede this much to myself as someone who by occupation is a classical philologist, for I have no idea what the significance of classical philology would be in our age, if not to have an unfashionable effect—that is to work against the time and thereby have an effect upon it, hopefully for the benefit of a future time."

17. Hegel, *The Encyclopedia of the Philosophical Sciences* §82, addition. Quoted by Jean-Luc Nancy in *The Speculative Remark (One of Hegel's Bons Mots)*, trans. Céline Surprenant (Stanford, Calif.: Stanford University Press, 2001), 188n22.

18. In these passages, Hegel probably has Kant's writings on history in mind: principally, the "Perpetual Peace" essay with its list of imperatives for institutions that would bring about lasting peace, one that hesitates on the question of their future realization; see Kant, "Perpetual Peace," in *On History*, trans. Lewis White Beck (New York: Macmillan, 1963), 114ff. See also Kant's "Idea for a Universal History According to a Cosmopolitan Perspective" wherein the "single theme" of world history—"the hidden plan of nature" that men act rationally—is admitted to be a regulative but unknown (hence the "hidden") principle. Regarding Hegel's anti-idealism, his use of the expression *absoluter Idealismus* can be misleading, especially when it becomes conflated with what is ordinarily called "idealism." Kojève makes this point in the Twelfth Lecture (1938–39) of his *Introduction to the Reading of Hegel*, 150ff.

19. Nietzsche, "On the Utility and Liability of History for Life," 156.

20. Dienstag, *Dancing in Chains*, 197.

21. Hegel places great historical importance on oratory and speeches in this section. Against those that see speeches as mere talk, for instance, he charges that "*that* talk is itself mere babble" (*lediglich Geschwätz*), 4–5.

22. This is no mere speculation on Hegel's part. In fact, Hegel's formulation is taken practically verbatim from Book 1 of Thucydides's *The Peloponnesian War*, where the method and the aims of the work are explicated: "Insofar as these facts involve what the various participants said both before and during the conflict," Thucydides writes, "recalling the exact words was difficult for me regarding the speeches I heard myself and for my informants about speeches made elsewhere; in the way I thought each would have said what was especially required in the given situation, I have stated accordingly, with the closest fidelity on my part to the overall sense of what was actually said" (Thucydides, *The Peloponnesian War*, Book 1, trans. Steven Lattimore [Indianapolis, Ind.: Hackett, 1998], 13).

23. On the semantic history of *historia magistra vitae*, see Reinhardt Koselleck's *Vergangene Zukunft: Zur Semantik geschichtlicher Zeiten*, 38–65; in English: *Futures Past: On the Semantics of Historical Time*, trans. Keith Tribe (New York: Columbia University Press, 2004). See also Timothy Bahti's *Allegories of History* for a discussion of exemplary history in the contexts of jurisprudence and rhetoric (10–18), and, for a discussion of its role in moral instruction, see Engel, "Die deutsche Universitäten und die Geschichtswissenschaft," *Historische Zeitschrift* 189 (1959): 223–378, specifically 238ff. On Greek historiography more generally and its relation to conceptions of modern history, in addition to Arendt's *Between Past and Future* and *The Human Condition*, see also Jacques Le Goff's *History and Memory*, trans. Steven Rendall and Elizabeth Claman (New York: Columbia University Press, 1992), which questions the understanding that modern history is the successor to Greek historiography on the grounds of their radically incommensurable roles (154, 161ff, 184).

24. For instance, the prognostic function of history is still articulated—albeit qualified by unmistakable tones of irony or resignation—in Frederick the Great's famous assessment that the scenes of history repeat themselves, so it is only necessary to change the names (*Histoire de mon temps*, 1746, quoted in Koselleck, *Vergangene Zukunft*, 30). The ubiquitous *appel* for memory as an antidote to historical repetition—"Never Again"—is evidence of its continued survival in the political rhetoric of our own time.

25. See Joachim Ritter's *Hegel und die Französische Revolution* (Frankfurt am Main: Suhrkamp, 1965) for a general assessment of the relation of Hegel's philosophy to the French Revolution as well as a summary of Hegel's opposition to the notion that even a political restoration involved some kind of "return" to the past (34–39). On the point of Hegel's practical aversion to "restoration" and the theoretic place this aversion holds within his understanding of time, see Jacques D'Hondt's *Hegel in His Time*, trans. John Burbidge, foreword H. S. Harris (Peterborough, Ontario: Broadview Press, 1988).

26. The revolutionary tenor of Hegel's formulations resonates with a remark made by Jean-Luc Nancy in the course of an analysis that attempts to open up historic time to a thinking of "time opened up"—namely, that "'historic' time is always the time of the changing of the world, which is to say, in a certain sense, of a *revolution*" (*The Birth to Presence*, trans. Brian Holmes et al. [Stanford, Calif.: Stanford University Press, 1993], 165).

27. Hannah Arendt, *On Revolution* (London: Penguin Books, 1990), 42. Further references will be given in the text as *Rev* followed by page number.

28. "Awe and wonder" is a close match to Kant's characterization of the reaction to the aesthetic sublime as "amazement bordering on terror" (*Critique of Judgment*, trans. Werner Pluhar [Indianapolis, Ind.: Hackett, 1987], 129). For his part, Hegel too will characterize the prevailing mood of the revolutionary period as one of *erhabene Rührung*, or "sublime emotion" (*PhH* 447/529).

29. While Arendt's assessment of the post-Kantian turn to history is indisputable, it is not altogether accurate in relation to Hegel's reaction to the French Revolution, which is in many ways more complex than her description suggests. In fact, many of her own insights into what ultimately brought about its failure—its terrifying surfeit of pity and the confrontation with an absolutist monarchy, to name only two—are also issues that Hegel addresses. As Rebecca Comay has recently argued, Hegel's unflinching analysis of the French Revolution in the *Phenomenology of Spirit* contains penetrating insights into the aporias and continuously repeated violence of political modernity; see Comay, "Dead Right: Hegel and the Terror" in *And Justice for All? The Claims of Human* Rights, ed. Ian Balfour and Eduardo Cadava, special issue of *South Atlantic Quarterly* 103, no. 2/3 (Spring/Summer 2004): 375–96.

30. On Arendt's criticism of Marx for having given the Hegelian world-historical view a prophetic function, see the April 1951 entry in her *Denktagebuch*; in English: *The Promise of Politics*, ed. Jerome Kohn (New York: Schocken Books, 2005), 70.

31. That the revolutionary demand for freedom and liberty would ultimately be understood as the fruit of necessity is, according to Arendt, "perhaps the most terrible and, humanly speaking, least bearable paradox in the whole body of modern thought" (*Rev* 54).

32. This is the view held by Reinhart Koselleck, whose analysis of this passage from Hegel considers it in terms of a conception of historical time whose emphasis would come to be placed on the unforeseeability of the future (*Vergangene Zukunft* 58–59). Koselleck is right to place emphasis on the temporal implications of the passage, but I would resist identifying it with an epochal preoccupation with the future's open-endedness, for reasons that I hope to make clear in what follows.

33. I am unsure as to whether or not he ever makes use of the term. We should, however, note that the term *Zeitgeist* was very much in the air, having been coined by Herder in 1769 as a translation of Christian Adolph Klotz's use of the term *genius saeculi* (which, despite its being in Latin, is also a modern term). *Der Zeitgeist* is the title of a poem written by Friedrich Hölderlin sometime between 1797 and 1799.

34. Again, Thucydides: "The absence of romance in my history will, I fear, detract somewhat from its interest; but if it be judged useful by those inquirers who desire an exact knowledge of the past as an aid to the interpretation of the future, which in the course of human things must resemble if it does not reflect it, I shall be content" (*The Peloponnesian War* 13).

35. Hegel, *Phen* §29.

36. Ibid.

37. On the difference between Hegel's Absolute Idea and the traditional notion of idea or ideal (one opposed to "the real"), see Stanley Rosen's careful analysis in *G. W. F. Hegel: An Introduction to the Science of Wisdom* (New Haven, Conn.: Yale University Press, 1974), 237 ff.

38. For this and the following passage, I have modified Rauch's translation of *Trauer* as "sorrow" to "grief" or alternatively "mourning" in order to maintain the sense that history's loss involves a kind of death.

39. Not least due to Benjamin's famous reading of the Paul Klee painting *Angelus Novus* in his "Theses on the Concept of History," which could be read, in many of its aspects, as a reversal of the Hegelian theme: "Where we perceive a chain of events, he sees one single catastrophe which keeps piling up wreckage upon wreckage [*Trümmer auf Trümmer*] and hurls it in front of his feet" (TPH 253–64).

40. We should, though, pause to take note of the poetic structure of this second-to-last phrase, "although life leads to death, death also leads to life." It has the structure of a chiasm, one that, by virtue of German grammar (where the verb is deferred or postponed until the end of the sentence) is more forceful in the original, where the two terms are exactly symmetrical: *Leben Tod . . . Tod Leben*. The reversal (or more precisely, the reversibility) of the order of the terms provides a resource for the destabilization of the binary opposition between them: more precisely, the chiasm maintains a difference within sameness, not as a function of the terms' identity or simultaneity—they are neither identical nor simultaneous—but as a function of the

spacing of language. Also interesting in this regard is that the deferral of the verb in German—generally thought to suspend meaning, make one wait for it—intensifies the effect of the chiasmus, allowing it to produce an uncanny sense (if not precisely a meaning) of its own: that is, that the relation between life and death neither subsumes one into the other nor is it one of radical opposition; rather, it is one of cohabitation and spacing. In other words, the chiasmatic relation of "life" to "death" is the translation into language of the structure of ruins.

41. In an earlier section of the text, Hegel contrasts the restlessness of youth to old age, which is associated with ripeness of judgment and disinterestedness (*IPH* 39); likewise, as is well known, the East is characterized as the "childhood of history" (*IPH* 105) and the Germanic world, "history's old age" (*IPH* 97).

42. "We cannot ever give up thinking; that is how we differ from the animals" (*IPH* 10); "Man is not free, when he is not thinking" (*IPH* 439).

43. The English translation of the last sentence reads as follows: "It is (at one and the same time) a preservation and a transfiguration." The translation of *Verklären* by "transfiguration" does not quite seem to measure up to the thought here but since there is no ready alternative, a brief explanation follows above. The English translation gives the impression that while these operations are occurring simultaneously, *Erhalten* and *Verklären* remain distinct from one another, a sense no doubt augmented by the exclusively religious connotation of the substantive-form "transfiguration" (*die Verklärung*).

44. G. W. F. Hegel, *Hegel's Science of Logic*, trans. A. V. Miller, foreword by J. N. Findlay (New York: Humanity Books, 1969), 106; in German: *Wissenschaft der Logik*, vol. 5 of *G. W. F. Hegel Werke*, 113–14.

45. Ibid., 107.

46. Recalling Paul de Man's quip that he had never felt so at risk of a car accident as he did after hearing a report on the average number of mental decisions unconsciously made while driving, one could make the argument that a certain level of abstraction is required for a (safe) experience of particularity itself.

47. Ibid., 107.

48. In the early Jena essay, "Wer denkt abstrakt?" (1807), Hegel ferociously parodies this kind of reduction and relegates it to the worst form of abstract thinking, by virtue of which a single fact about a person (the fact of a market-woman selling rotten eggs, for instance) is adduced to explain everything else about them. See *Jenaer Schriften*, vol. 2 of *G. W. F. Hegel Werke*, 575–81.

49. Hegel uses the word *reduction* in this positive sense to characterize what is lacking in Spinoza's determination of *Unendlichkeit* (endlessness): The problem with Spinoza's formulation, Hegel contends, is that he failed to show how "die unendliche Vielheit sich notwendig . . . reduziert" (unlimited variety necessarily reduces itself) to the determinations of thought and extension (*Wissenschaft der Logik* 2, vol. 2 of *G. W. F. Hegel Werke*, 196).

50. I owe parts of this formulation to Catherine Malabou's treatment of the blunting or sharpening mechanism of spirit in *The Future of Hegel*, 148ff.

51. Hegel, *Phen* §28.

52. Ibid., §13.

53. Walter Kaufmann, *Hegel: Texts and Commentary*, trans. and ed. Walter Kaufmann (New York: Anchor, 1966), 23.

54. On the German preposition *an*, see Jean-Luc Nancy, *The Speculative Remark*, 88ff., where he lists its multiple meanings of "next to, by, very close to, nearby, along, to the brim or to the edge of." Strictly speaking, none of these meanings signify the ipseity of the *an sich* (a term also used by Hegel), or the meaning of "intrinsic" as self-identical (see also footnote 10 of "The Speculative Proposition").

55. This is, in fact, the reason Hegel gives for the tenor of the conclusion. Right before the onset of the historical narrative—beginning with "The Oriental World"—he admits to having only traced the "long road" of spirit "in summary" or as an overview (*übersichtlich*). Yet, he is quick to qualify his description by suggesting that perhaps the logical articulation of history is something in excess of a mere introduction after all: "length of time [*Länge der Zeit*] is something entirely relative, and the element of Spirit is eternity. A proper duration [*eine eigentliche Länge*] cannot be said to belong to it" (*Phen* 110/141).

56. Donald Phillip Verene, *Hegel's Recollection: A Study of Images in the Phenomenology of Spirit* (Albany: State University of New York Press, 1985), 5; Timothy Bahti, *Allegories of History*, 80. Although not dealing specifically with Hegel, Joshua Wilner's *Feeding on Infinity* (Baltimore, Md.: Johns Hopkins University Press, 2000) contains insightful analyses of the rhetoric of internalization in the Romantic period.

57. As is well known, Hegel praises rote memory (*Gedächtnis*) in the *Encyclopedia of the Philosophical Sciences* for being the form of memory closest to thinking (*denken*). This has been taken up most notably by Jacques Derrida in "The Pit and the Pyramid" and Paul de Man's "Sign and Symbol in Hegel's *Aesthetics*," but also in Nancy's *The Speculative Remark*.

58. Kaufmann, *Hegel: Texts and Commentary*, 53.

59. Ibid.

60. Jean-Luc Nancy, "The Surprise of the Event," in *Being Singular Plural*, trans. Robert D. Richardson and Anne E. O'Byrne (Stanford, Calif.: Stanford University Press, 2000), 159–76.

61. Charles Taylor, *Hegel and Modern Society* (Cambridge: Cambridge University Press, 1979), 97.

62. Hegel, preface to *Phenomenology of Spirit* §15.

63. Hegel, *Hegel's Science of Logic*, 553/217.

64. Stanley Rosen, *G. W. F. Hegel: An Introduction to the Science of Wisdom* (New Haven, Conn.: Yale University Press, 1974), 32.

65. Charles Taylor, *Hegel and Modern Society*, 97.

66. Hegel, *Hegel's Science of Logic*, 570/239: "Die Notwendigkeit ist das Sein, *weil* es ist—die Einheit des Seins mit sich selbst, das sich zum *Grunde* hat; aber umgekehrt, weil es einen Grund hat, ist es nicht Sein, ist es schlechthin nur *Schein*, *Beziehung* oder *Vermittlung*" (emphasis in original).

67. Ibid., 551/216.

68. John Burbidge, "The Necessity of Contingency," in Burbidge, *Hegel on Logic and Reason* (Albany, State University of New York Press, 1992), 49.

69. Hegel, *Hegel's Science of Logic*, 551/240.

70. The German *Zufall* means a chance occurrence or a coincidence (*Zufälligkeit* is the substantive form of contingency); *zufallen* means "to befall," or "to happen."

71. Burbidge, "Necessity of Contingency," 50.

72. In "Ousia and Grammē," Derrida invokes Heidegger's demand to think that which could not have been otherwise—the philosophical "tradition"—in order to suggest that the thought of the *not otherwise* is itself the site of discernment, difference, even a sort of contingency: "There is produced in the thought of the impossibility of the otherwise, in this *not otherwise*, a certain difference, a certain trembling, a certain decentering that is not the position of an other center" (*Margins of Philosophy*, trans. Alan Bass [Chicago: University of Chicago Press, 1982], 38).

73. See Sylviane Agacinski's *Time Passing: Modernity and Nostalgia*, 16–28, for a discussion of how the absence of transcendent eternal models contributes to this sense of lost necessity.

5. IN LIEU OF A LAST WORD

1. These sorts of demands that Blanchot's writing makes on its readers are summarized by Paul de Man in "Impersonality in the Criticism of Maurice Blanchot," in *Blindness and Insight: Essays in the Rhetoric of Contemporary Criticism*, introduction by Wlad Godzich (Minneapolis: University of Minnesota Press), 62ff.

2. Marc Redfield, entry on "Maurice Blanchot," *Johns Hopkins Guide to Literary Theory and Criticism*. 2nd ed., ed. M. Groden, M. Kreiswirth, and I. Szeman (Baltimore, Md.: Johns Hopkins University Press, 2005).

3. Ann Smock, "Infinite Conversation: Maurice Blanchot, 1907–2003," *Radical Philosophy*, no. 120 (July/August 2003): 58–60, here 58.

4. Maurice Blanchot, "Orpheus's Gaze," *The Space of Literature*, trans. and introduction by Ann Smock (Lincoln: University of Nebraska Press, 1982), 173.

5. On the affinities, some familiar and some not, between Freudian psychoanalysis and the speculative dialectic of Hegel in relation to the teleology of successful mourning, see Rebecca Comay's "Mourning Work and Play," in *Research in Phenomenology* 23: 105–30.

6. Nietzsche, "The Utility and Liability of History for Life," 89 (emphasis in original).

7. Sigmund Freud, "Mourning and Melancholia," in *On Metapsychology: The Theory of Psychoanalysis*, vol. 11 of the Penguin Freud Library, trans. James Strachey (London: Penguin, 1984), 253; in German: "Trauer und Melancholie," in vol. 10 of *Gesammelte Werke*, ed. Anna Freud et al. (Frankfurt am Main: S. Fischer, 1946), 430. Further references will be given in the text as MM followed by page number.

8. Gillian Rose, *Mourning Becomes the Law: Philosophy and Representation* (Cambridge: Cambridge University Press, 1996). Further references will be given in the text as *ML* followed by page number.

9. Gillian Rose, "Potter's Field," in *Mourning Becomes the Law* (Cambridge: Cambridge University Press, 1996). The chapter is also collected in *Maurice Blanchot: The Demand of Writing*, ed. Carolyn Bailey Gill (London: Routledge, 1996), 190–209.

10. Maurice Blanchot, "Literature and the Right to Death," trans. Lydia Davis, in *The Work of Fire* (Stanford, Calif.: Stanford University Press, 1995); in French: "La Littérature et le droit à la mort," in *La Part du feu* (Paris: Gallimard, 1949). Further references will be given in the text as LRD followed by page number; numbers for the original follow those for the translation. For specific details regarding the essay's publication, see note 13 below.

11. In suggesting that Blanchot develops a "philosophy of language" in "Literature and the Right to Death," I am following the contention of Andreas Gelhard in *Das Denken des Unmöglichen: Sprache, Tod und Inspiration in den Schriften Maurice Blanchots* (Munich: Wilhelm Fink, 2005); he argues that although Blanchot is writing about the differences between literary language and that of philosophy (or ordinary language), what is ultimately at stake in the essay is language *as such*. However, it seems important to point out that Blanchot is not a philosopher in any conventional sense, and his is not an attempt to pose the question of language in terms of its strict conceptuality. This is also a point made by James Phillips in his analysis of the essay in "Dying Is Not Death: The Difference between Blanchot's Fiction and Hegel's Concept," in *Colloquy: text theory critique* 19 (2005): 57–68. The stakes of Blanchot's refusal of strict conceptuality will, I think, become clearer as we go.

12. Blanchot's essay should be read as an explicit critical response to Sartre's *Qu'est-ce que la littérature?* (Paris: Gallimard, 1985; orig. published in *Les temps modernes* in 1947).

13. The essay first appeared in two parts in the journal *Critique* (in November 1947 and January 1948). In 1949, Blanchot included it as the final essay in the collection *La Part du feu* (*The Work of Fire*, 1982). Unfortunately, the demarcation between the two parts was lost in transition, owing in all probability to a misunderstanding on the part of the typesetter. In any case, the second half of the essay—which deals exclusively with the question of language—begins with a sentence which is now, confusingly, in the middle of a paragraph: "Literature is bound to language" (322/311 in *La Part du feu*) For these details as well as for a meticulous reading of the essay, see Gelhard's *Das Denken des Unmöglichen*, 13, 79ff.

14. In light of the remarkable overlap between Blanchot's work and Levinas's during this period, one might situate these formulations in relation to Levinas's non-self-identity of being that is worked out in the course of a distinction he makes between the image and the represented object in the 1948 essay "La réalité et son ombre," published in *Les temps modernes* in 1948, about a year after *Qu'est-ce que la littérature?* The same cross-pollination is, I think, evident in the two thinkers' explorations of temporality: The après

coup in Blanchot bears comparison to the immemorial past in Levinas's work and, even more to the point historically, to what Levinas suggestively calls *entretemps* in "La réalité et son ombre."

15. Christopher Fynsk, "Crossing the Threshold: On 'Literature and the Right to Death,'" in *Maurice Blanchot: The Demand of Writing*, 70–90, here 73 (emphasis in the original).

16. As is perhaps already clear, Blanchot is *not* engaging in a critique of Hegel on the grounds of an injustice done to immediate sensuous being. Neither this critique nor its concomitant resuscitation of sensuous being are among Blanchot's concerns; as I hope to make clear, the feverish task of literature's language for Blanchot has nothing to do with rescuing sensuous being or of reestablishing sense-certainty; rather, the concern has to do with a relation to the "annihilated," to the survival of the dead *as such*. This point is made by Gelhard in *Das Denken des Unmöglichen*, 87.

17. In a nuanced reading of the differences between this conception of negativity in language and Hegel's, Rodolphe Gasché argues that the "essential bond" of this passage names the condition for the possibility of communication and address. Gasché argues it is not as a fullness or certitude that the "I" approaches the thing in its essential separation from itself but that mortality is also the condition for the "I" to speak. Hence between the "I" (which takes place only in speech) and its referent, there is a "space between" and not, as is arguably the case for Hegel, a moment of speculative reflection of the Self in the other, or the other as other-of-self. See Rodolphe Gasché, "The Felicities of Paradox: Blanchot on the Null-Space of Literature," in *Maurice Blanchot: The Demand of Writing*, 52.

18. Notwithstanding Gelhard's persuasive argument that no penchant for the "real thing" governs these references; rather, Blanchot has borrowed virtually every one of them from various interlocutors, from Sartre's *Qu'est-ce que la littérature?*, from Hegel and from Kojéve's reading of him and, as mentioned earlier, from Mallarmé (see Gelhard, *Das Denken des Unmöglichen*, 8off.).

19. "Afterwardsness" is the English translation that Jean Laplanche has proposed for Freud's term *Nachträglichkeit*. See his "Notes on Afterwardsness," in *Essays on Otherness*, trans. John Fletcher (London: Routledge, 1999), 260–65, and Cathy Caruth, "An Interview with Jean Laplanche," accessed May 7, 2013. http://muse.jhu.edu/journals/postmodern_culture/uo11/11.2caruth.html. My reasons for using the term in this context will become clearer in the second half of the chapter.

20. For a discussion of the literary materialism of this essay in the context of its comparison with that developed in the work of Paul de Man, see Hector Kollias, "A Matter of Life and Death: Reading Materiality in Blanchot and de Man," in *After Blanchot: Literature, Criticism, Philosophy*, ed. Leslie Hill, Brian Nelson, and Dimitris Vardoulakis (Newark: University of Delaware Press, 2005), 123–36.

21. Of this same passage, Christopher Fynsk writes that literature "may well have succeeded in abandoning a signified meaning but it cannot avoid signifying this abandonment: its language continues to show its own intention and expose its pretense" ("Crossing the Threshold" 77).

22. James Phillips has articulated this "tarrying" in terms of the failure language experiences when it tries to consummate its own movement in the achievement of sense: "The essentialising movement of language is never consummated, since the materiality of the word is as much the vehicle of ideality as its obstacle. The word can never realize itself as non-existence and hence can never properly claim to be the non-material essence of what it names, because it at the same time has to maintain a foothold in materiality through its own thingliness as a written, spoken or neurologically encrypted word" ("Dying Is Not Death" 65).

23. On the question of the disavowal of language in philosophy, read in the context of literature's metaphysical infamy, see again Phillips, "Dying Is Not Death, 65. Phillips argues that at one level, Blanchot's essay aims at the deceitful practices inherent to an attentiveness to language, deceptions that literature—in contrast to philosophy—plays at honestly.

24. Jacques Lacan, *Ecrits: A Selection*, trans. Alan Sheridan (New York: Norton, 1977), 48.

25. Blanchot, *Writing of the Disaster*, trans. Ann Smock (Lincoln: University of Nebraska Press, 1986), 1. Originally published as *L'écriture du désastre* (Paris: Gallimard, 1980)

26. Andrzej Warminski, "Dreadful Reading: Blanchot on Hegel," *Yale French Studies* 69 (1985): 267–75, here 269, 272, 274.

27. Three exceptions to this general trend are Gary D. Mole, "Blanchot, *L'Idylle*, and the Play of Ambiguity," in *Lévinas, Blanchot, Jabès: Figures of Estrangement* (Gainesville: University Press of Florida, 1997); Michael Holland, "An Idyll?," in *After Blanchot*, ed. Hill, Nelson, and Vardoulakis, 80–99; and Michael Rothberg's *Traumatic Realism: The Demands of Holocaust Representation* (Minneapolis: University of Minnesota Press, 2000).

28. Vivian Liska, "Two Sirens Singing: Literature as Contestation in Maurice Blanchot and Theodor W. Adorno," in *The Power of Contestation: Perspectives on Maurice Blanchot*, ed. Kevin Hart and Geoffrey H. Hartman (Baltimore, Md.: Johns Hopkins University Press, 2004), 80–100, here 97; Steven Ungar, *Scandal and Aftereffect: Blanchot and France since 1930* (Minneapolis: University of Minnesota Press, 1995), 68.

29. The English translation of the volume's title is *Vicious Circles: Two Fictions and "After the Fact,"* trans. Paul Auster (Barrytown, N.Y.: Station Hill Press, 1985). I will come back to the particular effacements in the title's translation in due course. Further references to "After the Fact" will be given in the text as *AC* (for *Après coup*) followed by page number. Due to other errors and inconsistencies in the translation, major changes will be made wherever necessary. Significant divergences and amendments will be explained in footnotes.

30. Holland, "An Idyll?," 82. I am also indebted to Holland's piece for its navigation of the complex history of these stories, carried out with impressive bibliographic assiduity.

31. *Ressassement* is a now-rare substantive form of the verb *ressasser*, meaning to "rehash," "to ruminate," "to go over," "to revisit," "to examine in detail," etc. According to *Trésor de la langue française*, it is known

in linguistics as "the frequent repetition of the same words" (the example it gives is the lamentation of David over the death of Absalom in Samuel II.19.1: "O my son Absalom, O Absalom, my son, my son"). The English translation as *Vicious Circles* is, in any case, a gross misapproximation.

32. Ibid., 83.

33. The English translation removes all sense of a disjunction between the sequence of the text's title and the ordering of the texts: *"Après coup" précédé par "Le Ressassement éternel"* is translated as *Vicious Circles: Two Fictions and "After the Fact."* Holland also draws attention to the inversions played out in the text's title.

34. In a brief mention of the text in a note to his "Lapsus Absolu," Hent de Vries characterizes it not as an addition to the two *récits*, but as a kind of super-imposition; see "Lapsus Absolu: Notes on Maurice Blanchot's *The Instant of My Death*" in *The Place of Maurice Blanchot*, ed. Thomas Pepper, special issue of *Yale French Studies* 93 (1998): 30–59, specifically footnote 21. In another vein, Philippe Lacoue-Labarthe lists *Après coup* among Blanchot's *attestations* ("The Contestation of Death," in *The Power of Contestation*, 141–55).

35. From the perspective of this reading, it is difficult not to mention that, in addition to these aspects internal to the text's makeup, "après-coup" is Lacan's translation for the Freudian concept of *Nachträglichkeit* ("belated-ness" or "afterwardsness"). Blanchot has replaced the hyphen between the two words with a space, which indicates that it is being used as an adverb and not a substantive. Nonetheless, the resonances with and displacements of the psychoanalytic concept are striking.

36. The English translation has "History does not *withhold* meaning" for the first part of this phrase, turning it into practically the opposite of what Blanchot wrote.

37. In *Demeure*, Derrida devotes his final remarks to the word, for him "one of the most beautiful, and one of the most untranslatable" (102). For Rothberg, who reads *Après coup* more or less as a displaced *prise de con-science* regarding Blanchot's right-wing political writings of the 1930s, this "henceforth" (*désormais*) seems to pose significant interpretive problems: on the one hand, he describes its significance in terms of "the importance of the noncontemporaneity of all events, of their tendency to be understood only retrospectively" (*Traumatic Realism* 82) and on the other hand, at the close of the same paragraph, he writes, "The 'from now on' of Blanchot's 'Après Coup' signifies that at some point (or series of points) we have become con-temporaries of the Holocaust" (83).

38. Liska, "Two Sirens Singing," 98; Geoffrey Hartman, "Blanchot's Silence" (unpublished manuscript), cited in Liska.

39. In another context, Hartman has proposed translating the statement in question as "whatever the date it was written, every story henceforth will be *as if* written before Auschwitz" ("Maurice Blanchot: The Spirit of Lan-guage after the Holocaust," in *The Power of Contestation*, 46–64, here foot-note 25). While the interpretation Hartman proposes works to soften some-what the disquiet of the French original, one must admit that it does so at the expense of fidelity to it.

40. To a large extent, the strangely abstract quality of traumatic repetition emerges in Blanchot's writing as a resistance to direct historical reference. Though as a consequence his work has proven exasperatingly evasive about the Holocaust (as even his admirers are likely to concur), I am interested in how this resistance to direct reference might paradoxically assist our efforts at capturing a certain historical or epochal concreteness vis-à-vis the Holocaust, beyond the consolations of much of its artistic representation on the one hand and historical closure on the other.

41. Jacques Derrida, "LIVING ON: Border Lines," in *Deconstruction and Criticism*, ed. Harold Bloom (London: Routledge, 1979), 94. The essay originally appeared in English and was later published in French in *Parages* (Paris: Galilée, 1986). The citation in question is found on page 140 of the French version.

42. Philipe Lacoue-Labarthe, "The Contestation of Death," in *Power of Contestation*, 149.

43. Blanchot alludes to *Sophie's Choice*, the 1979 Holocaust novel by William Styron (a film version of which was made in 1982). In the context of that reference, it is worth pointing out (as Blanchot himself does in the course of his reading) that the 1936 narrative "The Idyll" ends on a deeply redemptive note, affirming the death of one character by having it open onto "the superb and victorious sky" that "still bound her under the mirror of spring" (*Vicious Circles* 36). Strikingly, *Sophie's Choice* ends with the similar affirmation "that it is morning, excellent and fair." One could, I think, suggest that Blanchot's chief objection to *Sophie's Choice* is to the deceit performed in this final line: Its investment in closure and in the redemptive effects of morning is inseparable from the advent of a present apparently untainted by the disastrous past, and this, putatively *in its wake*. Regarding other aspects of the "(today)" in which Blanchot is writing, one could also mention the American series, *Holocaust*, which was aired on French state television in 1979, and which inaugurated a new level of commodification of Holocaust narratives (for details, see Annette Wieviorka's *L'Ère du témoin* [Paris: Plon, 1998], esp. Chapter 3). One can doubtless also sense a degree of calculation involved in the writing of this piece, given the interest in Blanchot's right-wing journalism of the 1930s that had been mounting in the late 1970s and early 1980s.

44. Of course, Blanchot is not alone in this assertion (though, as far as I am aware, he is the first to have grounded the problem of narrating Auschwitz in terms of the "before" as opposed to the "after"). Of relevance here is Arendt's contention of the unprecedented nature of totalitarianism— i.e., its radical departure from any preexisting form of governance—as well as her claim that the experience of the concentration camps would never form the basis of a political community; see *Origins of Totalitarianism* (New York: Meridian Books, 1960), 441ff. Historian Christian Meier has recently made the rather more moral claim that attempts to make Auschwitz meaningful "can seem like an after-the-fact insult" (*From Athens to Auschwitz: The Uses of History*, trans. Deborah Lucas Schneider [Cambridge, Mass.: Harvard University Press, 2005], 137). In a different register, see also Cathy

Caruth's "Trauma and Experience: Introduction," in *Trauma: Explorations in Memory* (Baltimore, Md.: Johns Hopkins University Press, 1995) for a consideration of how the impact of trauma consists in its belatedness, "in its refusal to be simply located, in its insistent appearance outside the boundaries of any single place or time" (9).

45. Geoffrey Hartman, "Maurice Blanchot: The Spirit of Language," 63.

46. Leslie Hill, *Maurice Blanchot: Extreme Contemporary* (London: Routledge, 1997), 9.

47. Blanchot, *Writing of the Disaster*, 51.

48. Maurice Blanchot, "Do Not Forget," (1988) in *The Blanchot Reader*, ed. Michael Holland (Cambridge: Blackwell, 1996), 244–49. The phrase "Do not forget" is also used as a title for a piece, "N'Oubliez pas!," published in *La Quinzaine littéraire*, no. 459 (March 1986): 11–12.

49. Blanchot, *Writing of the Disaster*, 82.

50. See Sarah Guyer's recent essay "The Pardon of the Disaster" for a discussion of the particular characteristics of Blanchot's "Do Not Forget." Calling it a "fragmentary imperative that leaves one obliged to remember what she never could have known" (95), Guyer draws attention to how it is always set in quotation marks, indicating that the phrase is both voiced and cited, and that it has no object that would answer who or what must not be forgotten ("The Pardon of the Disaster," *SubStance* 35, no. 1 [2006]: 85–105).

51. For a thorough and probing exploration of that writing and its reception, see Hartman, "Maurice Blanchot: The Spirit of Language."

52. The epigram of this section comes from a text entitled *Le Pas au-delà*. Its translation into English as *The Step Not Beyond*, trans. Lycette Nelson (Albany: State University of New York Press, 1992) attempts to capture the ambiguity of the word *pas*: as well as signifying "step," it is also a sign of the negative.

BIBLIOGRAPHY

Aarsleff, Hans. *From Locke to Saussure: Essays on the Study of Language and Intellectual History.* Minneapolis: University of Minnesota Press, 1982.

Agacinski, Sylviane. *Time Passing: Modernity and Nostalgia.* Trans. Jody Gladding. New York: Columbia University Press, 2003.

Agamben, Giorgio. *Homo Sacer: Sovereign Power and Bare Life.* Trans. Daniel Heller-Roazen. Stanford, Calif.: Stanford University Press, 1998.

———. Infancy and History: An Essay on the Destruction of Experience. Trans. Liz Heron. London: Verso Books, 1993.

———. *Language and Death.* Trans. Karen E. Pinkus with Michael Hardt. Minnesota: The University of Minnesota Press, 2006.

Arendt, Hannah. *Between Past and Future: Eight Exercises in Political Thought.* New York: Penguin, 1961.

———. "The Concept of History." *Between Past and Future: Eight Exercises in Political Thought.* New York: Penguin, 1961.

———. *Denktagebuch.* 2 Vols. Edited by U. Ludz and I. Nordmann. Munich: Piper, 2002.

———. *The Human Condition.* New York: Doubleday Anchor, 1958. 23ff.

———. *Lectures on Kant's Political Philosophy.* Edited by Ronald Beiner. Chicago: University of Chicago Press, 1982.

———. *On Revolution.* London: Penguin Books, 1990.

———. *The Origins of Totalitarianism.* New York: Meridian Books, 1960.

———. *The Portable Hannah Arendt.* Edited by Peter Baehr. London: Penguin Books, 2004.

———. *The Promise of Politics.* Edited by Jerome Kohn. New York: Schocken Books, 2005.

Ariès, Philippe. *The Hour of Our Death.* Second Edition. Trans. Helen Weaver. Oxford: Oxford University Press, 1991.

Aristotle. *On Memory. The Complete Works of Aristotle.* Vol. 1. Edited by Jonathan Barnes. Princeton, N.J.: Princeton University Press, 1984.

———. *On the Soul. The Complete Works of Aristotle.* Vol. 1. Edited by Jonathan Barnes. Princeton, N.J.: Princeton University Press, 1984.

———. *Poetics.* Edited by Frank L. Lucas. Oxford: Oxford University Press, 1968.

Assmann, Aleida. *Der lange Schatten der Vergangenheit. Erinnerungskultur und Geschichtspolitik.* Munich: C. H. Beck, 2006 [English translation forthcoming with Fordham University Press].

———. *Erinnerungsräume: Formen und Wandlungen des kulturellen Gedächtnisses.* Munich: C. H. Beck, 1999 [*Cultural Memory and Western Civilization: Functions, Media, Archives.* Cambridge: Cambridge University Press, 2012].

———. *Zeit und Tradition. Kulturelle Strategien der Dauer.* Cologne: Böhlau, 1999.

Assmann, Jan. *Das kulturelle Gedächtnis.* Munich: Beck, 1999.

———. *Moses the Egyptian: The Memory of Egypt in Western Monotheism.* Cambridge, Mass.: Harvard University Press, 1997.

Atherton, Margaret. "Locke and the Issue over Innateness," in *Locke.* Edited by Vere Chappell. Oxford University Press, 1998.

Bahti, Timothy. *Allegories of History: Literary Historiography after Hegel.* Baltimore, Md.: Johns Hopkins University Press, 1992.

Balfour, Ian. "Reversal, Quotation (Benjamin's History)." *Modern Language Notes,* 106 (1991), 622–47.

———. *The Rhetoric of Romantic Prophecy.* Stanford, Calif.: Stanford University Press, 2002.

Balfour, Ian and Eduardo Cadava, eds. *And Justice for All? The Claims of Human Rights.* Special issue of *The South Atlantic Quarterly* 103, nos. 2/3 (Spring/Summer 2004).

Barash, Jeffrey Andrew. "The Sources of Memory," *Journal of the History of Ideas.* Vol. 58, No. 4, 707–17.

Benjamin, Walter. "Der Erzähler. Betrachtung zum Werk Nikolai Lesskows," in Benjamin, *Allegorien kultureller Erfahrung.* Edited by Sebastian Kleinschmidt. Leipzig: Reclam, 1984: 380–406.

———. "On Some Motifs in Baudelaire," in Benjamin, *Illuminations.* Edited by Hannah Arendt. Trans. Harry Zohn. New York: Schocken Books, 1936.

———. "The Storyteller," in Benjamin, *Illuminations.* Edited by Hannah Arendt. Trans. Harry Zohn. New York: Schocken Books, 1936.

———. "Theses on the Philosophy of History," in Benjamin, *Illuminations.* Edited by Hannah Arendt. Trans. Harry Zohn. New York: Schocken Books, 1936.

Bernstein, J. M. "The End of Art (Again)." Complete version of a paper presented at the *Arts in Question* conference (2003) (http://www.bampfa. berkeley.edu/bca/forms/bernstein.pdf).

Bident, Christophe. *Maurice Blanchot: Partenaire Invisible.* Seyssel: Champ Vallon, 1998.

Blanchot, Maurice. *"Après coup" précédé par "Le Ressassement éternel."* Paris: Les Éditions de Minuit, 1983.

———. "Do Not Forget," in *The Blanchot Reader.* Edited by Michael Holland. Oxford: Blackwell, 1995: 245–52.

———. "Literature and the Right to Death." Trans. Lydia Davis. *The Work of Fire.* Trans. Charlotte Mandell. Stanford University Press, 1995.

———. *The Space of Literature.* Trans. Ann Smock. Lincoln: University of Nebraska Press, 1982.

———. *Vicious Circles: Two Fictions and "After the Fact"* Trans. Paul Auster. Barrytown, N.Y.: Station Hill Press, 1985.

———. *The Writing of the Disaster.* Trans. Ann Smock. Lincoln: University of Nebraska Press, 1986.

Bohrer, Karl Heinz. "Historische Trauer und Poetische Trauer," in *Merkur* 12, no. 53 (December 1999): 1127–41.

Burbidge, John W. "The Necessity of Contingency" in *Hegel on Logic and Religion.* Albany: State University of New York Press, 1992.

Bürger, Peter. "Die Tränen des Odysseus." *Die Tränen des Odysseus.* Frankfurt am Main: Suhrkamp, 1993.

Butler, Joseph. "Of Personal Identity" (1736), in *Personal Identity.* Edited by John Perry. Berkeley: University of California Press, 1975: 99–105.

Carey, D. "Locke, Travel Literature and the Natural History of Man," *Seventeenth Century* 11 (1996): 259–80.

Caruth, Cathy. "An Interview with Jean Laplanche," in *Postmodern Culture* 11, no. 2 (January 2001).

———. *Empirical Truths and Critical Fictions: Locke, Wordsworth, Kant, Freud.* Baltimore, Md.: Johns Hopkins University Press, 1991.

———. "Trauma and Experience: An Introduction," in Caruth, ed. *Trauma: Explorations in Memory.* Baltimore, Md.: Johns Hopkins University Press, 1995.

Chappell, Vere, ed. *Locke.* Oxford: Oxford University Press, 1998.

Comay, Rebecca. "Dead Right: Hegel and the Terror," in *And Justice for All? The Claims of Human Rights.* Edited by Ian Balfour and Eduardo Cadava. Special issue of *The South Atlantic Quarterly* 103, no. 2/3 (Spring/Summer 2004): 375–96.

———. "Mourning Work and Play," *Research in Phenomenology* 23: 105–30.

De Certeau, Michel. *The Writing of History.* Trans. Tom Conley. New York: Columbia University Press, 1988.

De Man, Paul. "The Epistemology of Metaphor," in *Aesthetic Ideology.* Edited by Andrzej Warminski. Minneapolis: University of Minnesota Press, 1996.

————. "Impersonality in the Criticism of Maurice Blanchot," in *Blindness and Insight: Essays in the Rhetoric of Contemporary Criticism*. Intro. Wlad Godzich. Minneapolis: University of Minnesota Press, 1983: 60–78.

————. "Sign and Symbol in Hegel's *Aesthetics*," in *Aesthetic Ideology*. Edited by AndrzejWarminski. Minneapolis: University of Minnesota Press, 1996.

Derrida, Jacques. *Aporias*. Trans. Thomas Dutoit. Stanford, Calif.: Stanford University Press, 1993.

————. "The Deconstruction of Actuality." *Negotiations: Interventions and Interviews, 1971–2001*. Ed and trans. Elizabeth Rottenberg. Stanford, Calif.: Stanford University Press, 2002.

————. *Demeure: Fiction and Testimony*. Trans. Elizabeth Rottenberg. Stanford, Calif.: Stanford University Press, 2000.

————. *Glas*. Trans. John P. Leavey Jr. and Richard Rand. Lincoln: University of Nebraska Press, 1986.

————. "Living On: *Border lines*." In *Deconstruction and Criticism*. Edited by Geoffrey Hartman. London: Routledge Press, 1979: 74–176 (French: "Survivre" in *Parages*. Paris: Galilée, 1986: 119–218.)

————. *Mémoires for Paul de Man*. Trans. Cecile Lindsay et al. New York: Columbia University Press, 1989.

————. *Margins of Philosophy*. Trans. Alan Bass. Chicago: University of Chicago Press, 1982.

————. "Plato's Pharmakon." *Disseminations*. Trans. Barbara Johnson. Chicago: University of Chicago Press, 1981.

————. "The Pit and the Pyramid." *Margins of Philosophy*. Trans. Alan Bass. Chicago: University of Chicago Press, 1982.

————. *Specters of Marx: the State of the Debt, the Work of Mourning, and the New International*. Trans. Peggy Kamuf. London: Routledge, 1994.

D'Hondt, Jacques. *Hegel in His Time*. Trans. John Burbidge. Foreword H. S. Harris. Peterborough, Ontario: Broadview Press, 1988.

Didi-Huberman, Georges. *Devant le Temps: Histoire de l'Art et Anachronisme des Images*. Paris: Les Éditions du Minuit, 2000.

Donougho, Martin. "Hegel's Art of Memory." *Endings: Questions of Memory in Hegel and Heidegger*. Edited by Rebecca Comay and John McCumber. Evanston, Ill.: Northwestern University Press, 1999.

Einstein, Paul. *Traumatic Encounters: Holocaust Representation and the Hegelian Subject*. Albany: State University of New York Press, 2003.

Esch, Deborah. *In the Event: Reading Journalism, Reading Theory*. Stanford, Calif.: Stanford University Press, 1999.

Felman, Shoshana. *The Juridicial Unconscious: Trials and Traumas in the Twentieth Century*. Cambridge, Mass.: Harvard University Press, 2002.

Foa Dienstag, Joshua. *Dancing in Chains: Narrative and Memory in Political Thought*. Stanford, Calif.: Stanford University Press, 1997.

Freud, Sigmund. "Mourning and Melancholia," *On Metapsychology: The Theory of Psychoanalysis*. Trans. James Strachey. London: Penguin, 1984: 245–68.

———. "Trauer und Melancholie," *Gesammelte Werke*. Vol. 10. Edited by Anna Freud et al. Frankfurt am Main: S. Fischer, 1946.

Fuss, Peter, and John Dobbins. "Spirit as Recollection: Hegel's Theory of the Internalizing of Experience." *Idealistic Studies*. 11, 1981: 142–50.

Fynsk, Christopher. "Crossing the Threshold: On 'Literature and the Right to Death,'" in *Maurice Blanchot: The Demand of Writing* Edited by Carolyn Bailey Gill. London: Routledge, 1996: 70–91.

Gasché, Rodolphe. "The Felicities of Paradox: Blanchot on the Null-Space of Literature," in *Maurice Blanchot: The Demand of Writing*. Edited by Carolyn Bailey Gill. London: Routledge, 1996: 34–69.

Gelhard, Andreas. *Das Denken des Unmöglichen: Sprache, Tod und Inspiration in den Schriften Maurice Blanchots*. Munich: Wilhelm Fink, 2005.

Geulen, Eva. *Das Ende der Kunst: Lesarten eines Gerüchts nach Hegel*. Frankfurt am Main: Suhrkamp, 2002.

———. *The End of Art: Readings in a Rumor after Hegel*. Trans. James McFarland. Stanford, Calif.: Stanford University Press, 2006.

Gill, Carolyn Bailey, ed. *Maurice Blanchot: The Demand of Writing*. London: Routledge, 1996.

Guyer, Sarah. "The Pardon of the Disaster," in *SubStance* 35, no.1 (2006): 85–105.

Hamacher, Werner. "History, Teary—Remarques on Valéry's *La Jeune Parque*" in *Phantom Proxies*. Special issue of *Yale French Studies* 74 (1988): 67–94.

———. *Pleroma—Reading in Hegel*. Trans. Nicolas Walker and Simon Jarvis. Stanford, Calif.: Stanford University Press, 1998.

———. "The Right to Have Rights (Four-and-a-Half Remarks)" in *And Justice for All? The Claims of Human Rights*. Edited by Ian Balfour and Eduardo Cadava. Special issue of *The South Atlantic Quarterly* 103, no. 2/3 (Spring/Summer 2004): 343–56.

Hart, Kevin, and Geoffrey H. Hartman, eds. *The Power of Contestation: Perspectives on Maurice Blanchot*. Baltimore, Md.: Johns Hopkins University Press, 2004.

Hartman, Geoffrey H. "Maurice Blanchot: The Spirit of Language after the Holocaust." in *The Power of Contestation: Perspectives on Maurice Blanchot*. Edited by Kevin Hart and Geoffrey H. Hartman. Baltimore, Md.: Johns Hopkins University Press, 2004: 46–64.

Hegel, Georg Wilhelm Friedrich. "Aphorisms from the Wastebook." Trans. Susanne Klein et al. in *Miscellaneous Writings of G. W. F. Hegel. Edited by* Jon Stewart. Evanston: Northwestern University Press, 2002.

———. *Aphorismen aus Hegels Wastebook*. Volume 2 of *Jenaer Schriften 1801–1807. Werke*. Edited by Eva Moldenhauer and Karl Markus Michel. Frankfurt am Main: Suhrkamp, 1986.

———. *Hegel's Aesthetics: Lectures on Fine Art*, 2 Vols. Trans. T. M. Knox. Oxford: Oxford University Press, 1998.

———. *Hegel's Science of Logic*. Trans. A. V. Miller. Forward by J. N. Findlay. New York, Humanity Books, 1969.

———. *Introduction to the Philosophy of History*. Trans. Leo Rauch. Indianapolis, Ind.: Hackett, 1988.

———. *Lectures on the History of Philosophy*. Volume 3. Trans. E. S. Haldane and Frances H. Simson. London: Routledge, 1968.

———. *The Philosophy of History*. Trans. J. Sibree. New York: Dover, 1956.

———. *Hegel's Phenomenology of Spirit*. Trans. A. V. Miller. Oxford: Oxford University Press, 1977.

———. *Vorlesungen über die Ästhetik. Werke*. Edited by Eva Moldenhauer and Karl Markus Michel. Frankfurt am Main: Suhrkamp, 1986.

———. *Vorlesungen über die Geschichte der Philosophie*. Volume 3. Edited by Gerd Irrlitz Leipzig: Reclam, 1971.

———. *Vorlesungen über die Philosophie der Geschichte*. Volume 12 of *Werke*. Edited by Eva Moldenhauer and Karl Markus Michel. Frankfurt am Main: Suhrkamp, 1986.

———. *Wissenschaft der Logik*. Volume 6 of *Werke*. Edited by Eva Moldenhauer and Karl Marcus Michel. Frankfurt am Main: Suhrkamp, 1986.

Heidegger, Martin. *Being and Time*. Trans. Joan Stambaugh. Albany: State University of New York Press, 1996.

———. *Hegel's Phenomenology of Spirit*. Trans. Parvis Emad and Kenneth Maly. Bloomington: Indiana University Press, 1994.

Heine, Heinrich. "Zur Geschichte der Religion und Philosophie in Deutschland." *Die Romantische Schule und andere Schriften über Deutschland*. Cologne: Könemann, 1995.

Hill, L., B. Nelson and D. Vardoulakis, eds. *After Blanchot: Literature, Criticism, Philosophy*. Newark: University of Delaware Press, 2005.

Hill, Leslie. *Blanchot: Extreme Contemporary*. London: Routledge Press, 1997.

Holland, Michael. "An Idyll?" in *After Blanchot: Literature, Criticism, Philosophy*. Edited by Leslie Hill, Brian Nelson and Dimitris Vardoulakis. Newark: University of Delaware Press, 2005: 80–99.

Holland, Michael, ed. *The Blanchot Reader*. Cambridge: Blackwell Publishers, 1995.

Horowitz, Gregg M. *Sustaining Loss: Art and Mournful Life*. Stanford, Calif.: Stanford University Press, 2001.

Houlgate, Stephen. "Hegel and the 'End' of Art." *Owl of Minerva*. 29, no. 1 (Fall 1997).

Hume, David. *A Treatise of Human Nature*. London: Penguin Books, 1985.

Jolley, Nicholas. *Leibniz and Locke: A Study of the New Essays on Human Understanding*. Oxford: Oxford University Press, 1984.

Kant, Immanuel. *Anthropology from a Pragmatic Perspective*. Trans. Victor Lyle Dowdell. Carbondale: Southern Illinois University Pres, 1978.

———. *Critique of Judgment*. Trans. Werner Pluhar. Indianapolis, Ind.: Hackett, 1987.

———. "Perpetual Peace." *On History*. Edited by and Trans. Lewis White Beck. New York: Macmillan, 1963.

Kaufmann, Walter. *Hegel: Texts and Commentary*. Trans. and Edited by Walter Kaufmann. New York: Anchor Books, 1966.

Kojève, Alexandre. *Introduction to the Reading of Hegel: Lectures on the Phenomenology of Spirit*. Edited by Allan Bloom. Trans. James H. Nichols Jr. Ithaca, N.Y.: Cornell University Press, 1969.

Kollias, Hector. "A Matter of Life and Death: Reading Materiality in Blanchot and de Man." In *After Blanchot: Literature, Criticism, Philosophy*. Edited by Leslie Hill, Brian Nelson and Dimitris Vardoulakis. Newark: University of Delaware Press, 2005: 123–36.

Koselleck, Reinhart. *Futures Past: On the Semantics of Historical Time*. Trans. Keith Tribe. New York: Columbia University Press, 2004.

———. *Vergangene Zukunft. Zur Semantik geschichtlicher Zeiten*. Frankfurt am Main: Suhrkamp, 1989.

Kristeva, Julia. *Hannah Arendt: Life Is a Narrative*. Toronto: University of Toronto Press, 2001.

Lacan, Jacques. *Écrits: A Selection*. Trans. Alan Sheridan. London: W. W. Norton, 1977.

Lang, Berel. *Holocaust Representation: Art within the Limits of History and Ethics*. Baltimore, Md.: Johns Hopkins University Press, 2000.

Lacoue-Labarthe, Philippe. "The Contestation of Death," in *The Power of Contestation: Perspectives on Maurice Blanchot*. Edited by Kevin Hart and Geoffrey H. Hartman. Baltimore, Md.: Johns Hopkins University Press, 2004: 141–55.

———. *The Subject of Philosophy*. Edited by Thomas Trezise. Trans. High Silverman et al. Minneapolis: University of Minnesota Press, 1993.

Laplanche, Jean. "Notes on Afterwardsness," in *Essays on Otherness*. Trans. John Fletcher. London: Routledge, 1999: 260–65.

Le Goff, Jacques. *History and Memory*. Trans. Steven Rendall and Elizabeth Claman. New York: Columbia University Press, 1992.

Leibniz, I. G. W. *New Essays on Human Understanding*. Trans. Peter Remnant and Jonathan Bennett. Cambridge : Cambridge University Press, 1981.

Levinas, Emmanuel. "Réalité et son ombre," *Les temps modernes* no. 38 (1948): 771–78.

Liska, Vivian. "Two Sirens Singing: Literature as Contestation in Maurice Blanchot and Theodor W. Adorno" in *The Power of Contestation: Perspectives on Maurice Blanchot*. Edited by Kevin Hart and Geoffrey H. Hartman. Baltimore, Md.: Johns Hopkins University Press, 2004: 80–101.

Locke, John. *An Essay Concerning Human Understanding*. Edited by John W. Yolton. London: Everyman's Library, 1961.

———. *Second Treatise of Government*. Edited by C. B. Macpherson. Indianapolis, Ind.: Hackett, 1980.

———. *Some Thoughts Concerning Education*. Edited by Ruth Grant and Nathan Tarcov. Indianapolis, Ind.: Hackett, 1996.

Loraux, Nicole. "Eloge de l'anachronisme en histoire." *Le Genre humain* 27, 1993: 23–39.

Malabou, Catherine. *The Future of Hegel: Plasticity, Temporality and Dialectic*. Trans. Lisabeth During. London: Routledge, 2005.

Meier, Christian. *From Athens to Auschwitz: The Uses of History*. Trans. Deborah Lucas Schneider. Cambridge, Mass.: Harvard University Press, 2005.

Mole, Gary D. *Lévinas, Blanchot, Jabès: Figures of Estrangement*. Gainesville: University Press of Florida, 1997.

Nancy, Jean-Luc. *Being Singular Plural*. Trans. Robert D. Richardson and Anne E. O'Byrne. Stanford, Calif.: Stanford University Press, 2000.

———. *The Birth to Presence*. Trans. Brian Holmes et al. Stanford, Calif.: Stanford University Press, 1993.

———. *The Muses*. Trans. Peggy Kamuf. Stanford, Calif.: Stanford University Press, 1996.

———. *The Speculative Remark (One of Hegel's Bons Mots)*. Trans. Celine Surprenant. Stanford, Calif.: Stanford University Press, 2001.

Nietzsche, Friedrich. "The Utility and Liability of History for Life" in *Unfashionable Observations*. Trans. Richard T. Gray. Stanford, Calif.: Stanford University Press, 1995.

Nora, Pierre. "Between History and Memory: Les Lieux de Mémoire." In

Memory and Counter-Memory. Special issue of *Representations*, no. 26 (Spring, 1989), 7–24.

Perry, John, ed. *Personal Identity*. Berkeley: University of California Press, 1975.

Phillips, James. "Dying Is Not Death: The Difference between Blanchot's Fiction and Hegel's Concept" in *Colloquy: text theory critique* (10) 2005: 57–68.

Plato. *Phaedo. The Collected Dialogues of Plato*. Edited by Edith Hamilton and Huntington Cairns. New York: Pantheon Books, 1966.

Pinkard, Terry. *German Philosophy 1760–1860: The Legacy of Idealism* Cambridge: Cambridge University Press, 2002.

Redfield, Marc. "Maurice Blanchot," in *Johns Hopkins Guide to Literary Theory and Criticism*. 2nd edition. Edited by M. Groden, M. Kreisworth, and I. Szeman. Baltimore, Md.: Johns Hopkins University Press, 2005.

Renan, Ernst. *What Is a Nation?* [*Qu'est ce qu'une nation?*]. Trans. Wanda Romer Taylor. Toronto: Tapir Press, 1996.

Reid, Thomas. "Of Identity" (1785) in *Personal Identity*. Berkeley: University of California Press, 1975: 107–12.

Ricoeur, Paul. *Time and Narrative*. Volume 1. Trans. Kathleen McLaughlin and David Pellauer. Chicago: University of Chicago Press, 1984.

Rieff, David. *Slaughterhouse: Bosnia and the Failure of the West*. New York: Simon & Schuster, 1995.

Ritter, Joachim. *Hegel und die Französische Revolution*. Frankfurt am Main: Edition Suhrkamp, 1965.

Rose, Gillian. *Mourning Becomes the Law: Philosophy and Representation*. Cambridge: Cambridge University Press, 1996.

———. "Potter's Field: Death Worked and Unworked." *Maurice Blanchot: The Demand of Writing*. Edited by Carolyn Bailey Gill. London: Routledge, 1996: 190–208.

Rosen, Stanley. *G. W. F. Hegel: An Introduction to the Science of Wisdom*. New Haven: Yale University Press, 1974.

Rothberg, Michael. *Traumatic Realism: The Demands of Holocaust Representation*. Minneapolis: University of Minnesota Press, 2000.

Rousseau, Jean-Jacques. "Discourse on the Origin of Inequality." *The Basic Political Writings*. Trans. Donald A. Cress. Intro. Peter Gay. Indianapolis, Ind.: Hackett, 1987.

Sartre, Jean-Paul. *Nausea*. Trans. Lloyd Alexander. New York: New Directions, 1964.

———. *Qu'est-ce que la littérature?* Paris: Gallimard, 1985. English translation: *"What Is Literature?" and Other Essays.* Trans. Jeffrey Mehlman and Bernard Frechtman. Cambridge, Mass.: Harvard University Press, 1988.

Scribner, Charity. *Requiem for Communism.* Cambridge, Mass.: MIT Press, 2003.

Szondi, Peter. "Hegels Lehre von der Dichtung." *Poetik und Geschichtsphilosophie I.* Edited by Senta Metz and Hans-Hagen Hildebradt. Frankfurt am Main: Suhrkamp, 1974.

Surber, Jere. "Art as a Mode of Thought: Hegel's Aesthetics and the Origins of Modernism." *Hegel and Aesthetics.* Edited by William Maker. Albany: State University of New York Press, 2000.

Taylor, Charles. *Hegel and Modern Society.* Cambridge: Cambridge University Press, 1979.

———. *Sources of the Self: The Making of Modern Identity.* Cambridge, Mass.: Harvard University Press, 1989.

Terada, Rei. *Feeling in Theory: Emotion after the "Death of the Subject."* Cambridge, Mass.: Harvard University Press, 2001.

Terdiman, Richard. *Present Past: Modernity and the Memory Crisis.* Ithaca Cornell University Press, 1993.

Thucydides, *The Peloponnesian War.* Book 1. Trans. Steven Lattimore. Indianapolis, Ind.: Hackett, 1998.

Ungar, Steven. *Scandal and Aftereffect: Blanchot and France since 1930.* Minneapolis: University of Minnesota Press, 1995.

Verene, Donald Phillip. *Hegel's Recollection: A Study of Images in the Phenomenology of Spirit.* Albany: State University of New York Press, 1985.

Wieviorka, Annette. *L'Ère du témoin.* Paris: Plon, 1998.

Winkler, Kenneth P. "Locke on Personal Identity," *Journal of the History of Philosophy* 29 (1991): 201–26. Reprinted in *Locke.* Edited by Vere Chappell. Oxford: Oxford University Press, 1998: 149–74.

Wood, Neal. *The Politics of Locke's Philosophy.* Berkeley: University of California Press, 1983.

Wyss, Beat. "Klassizismus und Geschichtsphilosophie im Konflikt: Aloys Hirt und Hegel." *Kunsterfahrung und Kulturpolitik im Berlin Hegels.* Edited by Otto Pöggeler and Annemarie Gethmann-Siefert. *Hegel-Studien/Beiheft* 22. 1983.

Yolton, John W. *John Locke and the Way of Ideas.* Oxford: Oxford University Press, 1956.

Young-Bruehl, Elizabeth. *Hannah Arendt: For Love of the World.* 2nd edition. New Haven: Yale University Press, 2004.

INDEX